Casualties of Care

Casualties of Care

IMMIGRATION AND THE POLITICS OF HUMANITARIANISM IN FRANCE

MIRIAM TICKTIN

UNIVERSITY OF CALIFORNIA PRESS
Berkeley   Los Angeles   London

University of California Press, one of the most distinguished university presses in the United States, enriches lives around the world by advancing scholarship in the humanities, social sciences, and natural sciences. Its activities are supported by the UC Press Foundation and by philanthropic contributions from individuals and institutions. For more information, visit www.ucpress.edu.

University of California Press
Berkeley and Los Angeles, California

University of California Press, Ltd.
London, England

Library of Congress Cataloging-in-Publication Data

Ticktin, Miriam Iris.
    Casualties of care : immigration and the politics of humanitarianism in France / Miriam Ticktin.
        p.   cm.
    Includes bibliographical references and index.
    ISBN 978-0-520-26904-0 (alk. cloth) — ISBN 978-0-520-26905-7 (pbk. : alk. paper)
    1. Emigration and immigration—Government policy—France.
2. Humanitarianism—France.   I. Title.
    JV7925.2.T53 2011
    325.44—dc22

                                            2011008975

Manufactured in the United States of America

20 19 18 17 16 15 14 13 12 11
10 9 8 7 6 5 4 3 2 1

In keeping with a commitment to support environmentally responsible and sustainable printing practices, UC Press has printed this book on 50-pound Enterprise, a 30% post-consumer-waste, recycled, deinked fiber that is processed chlorine-free. It is acid-free and meets all ANSI/NISO (Z 39.48) requirements.

For my parents, Marlene and Saul

Illness is—as you say—the only way (Form) of life in capitalism.

Jean-Paul Sartre, letter to *Socialist Patients' Collective, 1972*

Contents

Illustrations

FIGURES

TABLES

Acknowledgments

This book is about the political struggle for equality. My thanks go first, then, to the political actors so central to this book: the *sans-papiers* and the *sans-papières*. I thank them for letting me get to know them as people and for sharing their stories and travails with me. I also thank the many people working for social justice who generously allowed me to join in their struggles: in particular, I thank Claudie Lesslier, Clara Domingues, and Catherine Quentier at Rajfire; and Anne-Marie and Florence for their exceptionally warm reception and for sharing their commitment to care and justice.

The seeds for this project began a long time ago, when I was an undergraduate at Princeton University. I thank Jorge Klor de Alva, Natalie Zemon Davis, and Moshe Sluhovsky for helping to shape the first inklings of this as a research interest, in their teachings about French history, universalism and multiculturalism, and the politics of immigration. Robert Young, at Oxford, taught me about larger postcolonial contexts, which had a profound impact on my thinking. At Stanford University, where I began this project in its dissertation form, I owe the greatest debt to my doctoral committee: Jane Collier, Sylvia Yanagisako, Akhil Gupta, and Purnima Mankekar. They played a principal role in shaping this scholarship, and they did so in part by showing me the meanings of feminist community and exchange. I would love to give my students all that they gave to me. I especially thank Jane and George Collier for being model mentors; the intellectual engagement, generosity, and kindness they showed me were unparalleled, and I do not think I will ever be able to match the high standards they set as both mentors and human beings in the world. I also want to thank Paulla Ebron and Mary Lou Roberts for their good-humored and yet essential guidance. I was particularly fortunate to meet Ann Stoler at that time, who was on leave and based at Stanford and who helped me shape the questions that still guide my work. I am now even more fortunate to have her as my colleague. Of course, I could not have survived the experience without those who were at once intellectual interlocutors, friends, and often roommates and carpool mates: Falu Bakrania, Carole Blackburn, Robert Blecher, Bakirathi Mani, Michael Montoya, Sameer Pandya, Rashmi Sadana, Doug Smith, Nancy Stalker, Rebecca Stein, and Gillian Weiss.

It was after I began my research in Paris that I met Didier Fassin, who became my advisor and mentor on the French side. As both anthropologist and medical doctor, he opened the doors to so many ideas, field sites, and communities. I can truly say this book would not be recognizable without his guidance. I thank him for his invaluable mentorship and for his unfailingly brilliant insights. He suggested that I do a *co-tutelle* between the EHESS and Stanford, to create links between the various intellectual communities, and I thank him for that wonderful opportunity as well. In Paris, I also benefited greatly from the advice and support of Catherine Wihtol de Wenden, Smaïn Laacher, and later, Michel Agier, Nacira Guénif-Souilamas, and Sylvie Tissot. My life in Paris was enriched immeasurably by the friendship of Idir Amara and Nora Meziani, Sarah Gensburger and Renaud Thominette, Yvonne Sebon, and Dave and Josette Spector; I thank them for their generosity in opening their homes and communities to me.

As a Mellon postdoctoral fellow at Columbia University's Society of Fellows, in addition to learning how to teach, I deepened my understanding of the political, social, and philosophical foundations of rights, humanitarianism, and politics by teaching the intensive Contemporary Civilization course. I feel particularly grateful to have met Bashir Abu-Manneh, Sandrine Bertaux, and Ilana Feldman at the Heyman Center; the collaborations we began together there have deeply influenced this book and continue to shape my thinking in profound ways. The process of writing, teaching, and editing with Ilana has taught me more than I can express.

At the University of Michigan, which Ilana Feldman quite rightly described to me as the "ur-institution," I really began to rethink and reshape this project. I benefited enormously from my colleagues in women's studies, who helped me to develop the gendered lens of the project, among many other things: Amal Fadlalla, Dena Goodman, Anna Kirkland, Peggy McCracken, Jonathan Metzl, Nadine Naber, Andrea Smith, Carroll Smith-Rosenberg, and Elizabeth Wingrove. Other colleagues and friends around the university also offered much-needed direction, accompanied by deep ties of friendship: Thomas Abowd, Arun Agrawal, Sunita Bose-Partridge, Joshua Cole, Fernando Coronil, Anna Curzan, Shafei Dafalla Mohamed, Deirdre Delacruz, Mamadou Diouf, Frieda Ekotto, Geoff Eley, Hussein Fancy, William Glover, Daniel Herwitz, Paul Johnson, Farina Mir, Gina Morantz-Sanchez, Jennifer Robertson, Loren Ryter, Julie Skurski, Peggy Somers, Neil Safier, Atef Said, Garry Venable, and Geneviève Zubrzycki. Most of all, I thank my junior faculty writing group for being the most supportive and intellectually stimulating community one could ever hope for: Rebecca Hardin, Eduardo Kohn, Nadine Naber, Julia Paley, Damani Partridge, Gayle Rubin, and Elizabeth Roberts.

Drawn by the mix of people and uneven conditions of life in the big cities at the heart of the book, I was very lucky to land at the New School for Social Research in New York City. I am grateful to be a part of such a vibrant anthropology department, full of innovative and energetic colleagues, and I thank them for their support and intellectual engagement throughout this process: Larry Hirschfeld, Nicolas Langlitz, Hugh Raffles, Vyjayanthi Rao, Janet Roitman, Ann Stoler, Sharika Thiranagama, and Charles Whitcroft, our quietly essential department manager. Hugh gets extra credit for coming up with the book's title! I have also been lucky to have productive and supportive interactions with other colleagues at the New School, including those at my (until recently) other home in the Graduate Program in International Affairs: Nehal Bhuta, Michael Cohen, Stephen Collier, Sakiko Fukuda-Parr, Rachel Heiman, Nina Krushcheva, Gustav Peebles, and Rachel Sherman.

There are so many other colleagues and friends dispersed across institutions and countries whose thoughtful engagements have really pushed me to think through the arguments of the book, but I only have space to mention a few of them here: Arash Abizadeh, Nadia Abu El-Haj, Lila Abu-Lughod, Talal Asad, Lawrence Cohen, Deborah Cowen, Jennifer Culbert, Allen Feldman, Eric Klinenberg, Andrew Lakoff, Saba Mahmood, Samuel Moyn, Davide Panagia, Sherene Razack, Todd Shepard, Paul Silverstein, Neferti Tadiar, and Ananya Vajpeyi. A special thanks to those who have become my community in New York and have nurtured me through the last gasps of this project: Linda Gaal, Rebecca Jordan-Young and Sally Cooper, Fabienne Hara, Natasha Iskander, Jeff Dolven, Nnenna Lynch and Jonathon Kahn, Bakirathi Mani and Mario Ruiz, Kate Zuckerman and Simon Lipskar, Aurore Deuss and Karim Bouabdelli.

I owe a particularly important debt to those who have read all or parts of the manuscript in great detail. I will never be able to express how grateful I am for all the time and care they put into reading, editing, and then often rereading and reediting: Ilana Feldman, Dasa Francikova, Lochlann Jain, Tobias Rees, Rachel Sherman, Joseph Slaughter, Sharika Thiranagama, and Carole Vance. In particular, I want to express my gratitude to Rashmi Sadana, who has read this material over and over again since its inception at Stanford and somehow still manages to muster enthusiasm and offer new insights and unyielding solidarity; and to Nadine Naber, who read every word of this manuscript and has been a sister to me throughout the process. Thanks also goes to the wonderful working group Oxidate, whose members have read many parts of this manuscript and have offered invaluable critical insight into its framing and content: Lochlann Jain and Jake Kosek (our treasured organizers), and Joseph Dumit, Cori Hayden, Joseph Masco, Jonathan Metzl, Michelle Murphy, Diane Nelson, Jackie Orr, and Elizabeth Roberts.

I received generous support to conduct the research that informs this book. The dissertation research was funded by the Social Science and

Humanities Research Council of Canada, a Phi Beta Kappa Scholarship Award, an O'Bie Shultz Dissertation Fellowship from the Institute for International Studies at Stanford, and a Graduate Research Opportunity Grant from the Dean of Humanities and Sciences at Stanford. The writing process was funded by a Mellon Foundation grant from the Stanford Institute for Women and Gender, a Giles Whiting Fellowship in the Humanities, and a fellowship from the Research Institute of Comparative Studies in Race and Ethnicity at Stanford. Follow-up research trips to Paris were made possible by research funds at the University of Michigan. The International Center for Advanced Study at NYU—directed by Thomas Bender and run by Timothy Mitchell (2006–7)—offered me an invaluable year away from teaching to actually sit down and make this into a book, and I found the theme "rethinking the social" particularly generative.

I could never have put this together without the adept and assiduous research assistance of Carol Wang, and I would not have been able to wade through the complexities of the French legal system without the guidance of Rachid Bendacha. Patrick Dodd did the thankless job of getting permissions for all my images and of tracking down French sources. I am thrilled to have been pushed by so many of my students to give answers to what it means to "do good" in the world. I cannot thank John Bowen, Sally Engle Merry, Peter Redfield, and Richard Wilson enough for their immensely thoughtful, generous, and thorough reviews of the book, and Ken Wissoker for supporting this project from the start. I am indebted to Reed Malcolm at University of California Press for seeing the potential in this book and then seeing it through with such calm commitment, to Julie Van Pelt for such a careful and painstaking job of copyediting, and to Emily Park and Kalicia Pivirotto at University of California Press for their expert handling of the manuscript.

Finally, I would like to thank my family for helping me through the extended and often painful labor of this book. I write in memory of Adina Back, with whom I shared the trials and tribulations of writing books that never seemed to finish. Peter Gager shaped this project in a profound way from the earliest moments at Princeton: intellectually, emotionally, and by teaching me how to write. How lucky I am to have three sisters as best friends and coconspirators in life, who sustain me in a way no one else could! I thank them—Leah, Tamara, and Jessica—as well as my brothers-in-law, Gustavo de la Peña and Adam Rubin, and my four little nieces (Dahlia, Lola, Kaya and Ylang) who bring hope with them into the world. To my parents, Marlene and Saul, whose own courageous paths from India and South Africa have intimately shaped the preoccupations of this book—justice, compassion, discrimination, and inequality—I do not have words to thank them enough. And to Patrick Dodd: like his painting on the cover of this book, his sensitivity to people and to the colors in the world has taught me to see differently and has inspired me to live more fully. He has enriched my life beyond measure. The unspoken process we shared in the wee hours of the night as I wrote and he painted can be felt on each page of this book.

Introduction

In January 2000, newspapers reported that fifty-eight undocumented Chinese immigrants were found dead in the cold-storage container of a Dutch truck. The large number of deaths drew particular attention to the issue of migrants crossing borders under extremely dangerous conditions, given the ever more stringent border controls in the new "Fortress Europe." But this was far from the first story of its kind. Deaths had been reported around ports of entry into Europe at least since the mid-1990s—asylum seekers attempting to cross through the Channel Tunnel from France into the United Kingdom, holding on to Eurostar trains from above and below, others drowning en route from North Africa to Spain's Canary Islands. The overwhelming response to these life and death crossings, however, was the increasing popularity of right-wing, anti-immigrant politicians, from Pim Fortuyn in the Netherlands, to Jörg

Haider in Austria, to ultra-right-wing Front National leader Jean-Marie Le Pen in France. They set the terms of debate about immigration across Europe, pulling their views into the mainstream.

In this climate of anti-immigrant sentiment, a number of seemingly innocuous, exceptional, humanitarian measures were put in place for undocumented immigrants in France. These were framed by the state as protecting basic human dignity in the face of acute suffering. They were not considered part of regular state policies on immigration; in fact, they were explicit exceptions to the contentious politics of immigration, grounded instead in the moral imperative to relieve suffering. They were enacted in the name of care and compassion, in clear opposition to the exclusionary rhetoric that accompanied discussions of immigration. These exceptions included the "illness clause," a humanitarian exception embedded in the 1998 immigration law, which gives legal residency papers to those already in France who have pathologies of life-threatening consequence, if they are declared unable to receive proper treatment in their home countries. The exceptions also included humanitarian measures granting papers to exceptional victims of violence against women, as in the case of forced marriages and repudiations, which were later extended to victims of human trafficking. These clauses—while enacted only as exceptions to otherwise strict immigration laws—seemed to offer a glimpse of solidarity with the immigrant's plight in an increasingly repressive political environment.

This book argues that, in a climate of closed-door immigration policies, these exceptional "apolitical" humanitarian clauses—and the transnational institutions, discourses, and practices that give them shape—have come to play a critical role in the governing of immigrants in France, but with often unintended consequences. In medical clinics for the disenfranchised, where social workers and doctors worked hand in hand, my ethnographic research revealed that one of the first questions they asked their undocumented clients was, "Are you sick?" And if the patient answered yes, they would ask, almost too eagerly, "*How* sick?" I gradually understood that they answer they hoped for was "Very sick" because this provided the one clear means by which to apply for papers. Similarly, activists fighting for immigrant women's rights found themselves in the uncomfortable position of searching for evidence of gendered forms

of violence, like rape or forced marriage, as these became the most significant factors by which one could prove one's "humanity," worthy of
humanitarian exception.

These humanitarian exceptions play a role in what I think of as a politics
based on care and protection, produced as a moral imperative to relieve
suffering. By invoking a politics of care, I mean to address the central
place of benevolence and compassion in contemporary political life, especially when enacted under the threat of emergency or crisis, as solutions
to global problems of inequality, exploitation, and discrimination. Here,
what I think of as "regimes of care"—which include humanitarianism,
certain movements for human rights, and the network against violence
against women—are a set of regulated discourses and practices grounded
on this moral imperative to relieve suffering. They come together through
a diverse set of actors such as NGOs, international institutions, legal
regimes, corporations, the military, and states. And yet, as I will argue,
these regimes of care ultimately work to displace possibilities for larger
forms of collective change, particularly for those most disenfranchised.

The first aim of this book, then, is to reveal how immigration, a political issue of the highest order, has come to be managed in significant ways
by sentiments and practices of care and compassion. The second aim is
to explore what this actually means—what does it mean to have care
do the work of government? Differently phrased, in the context of large
movements of people and goods that mark our era, what does it mean
to allow sick and sexually violated bodies to cross borders while impoverished ones cannot? To this end, the book focuses on the constitution of
the primary subject of care: the morally legitimate suffering body. Here, I
make two related arguments. First, I suggest that embedded in this politics of care and compassion is a belief in the universality of suffering; this
means that suffering can be recognized wherever it is found, that it can
be measured and understood, and that—crucially—a response to it is
morally mandated. In practice, as we will see, suffering is recognized
and responded to by looking to the biological body and is apprehended
through medical and scientific techniques and rationales, which are considered universal and objective. Indeed, I will demonstrate that there are
two intersecting movements that bring medical and scientific techniques

to bear in the desire to ease suffering: medical humanitarianism and the movement against violence against women. These two "languages of the good" are not usually thought of in the same frame, but I view them as two ways by which to name and enact a politics based on protecting the imagined universal suffering body.

The second part of this argument proposes that, while taken as a universal, what physical injury entails is actually far from clear: the meaning of suffering and of bodily integrity is mediated by social, political, cultural, and economic contexts and histories and, in particular, by these transnational regimes of care. The affective component of humanity— that which creates a category with morally resonant force—does not map directly onto a biological humanity or onto that which is supposedly revealed by medico-scientific techniques. That is, biological measures do not always compel moral action in the name of humanity.[1] Instead, the suffering body must be recognized as *morally legitimate,* a qualification that turns out to be both exceptional and deeply contextual. This unacknowledged mediation has important consequences when politics happens in the name of care and protection and when the object of care and protection is bodily integrity. For instance, why is the universal suffering body best exemplified by the sick body, or by the racialized, sexually violated body? A politics of immigration based on this type of care and compassion gives papers to an HIV+ Malian woman, an Algerian child with cancer, and a gay Moroccan man gang-raped by Moroccan policemen and closes doors to most others, making these strangely desirable conditions for immigrants. Noticeably absent are the laboring bodies, the exploited bodies: these are not the exception, but the rule, and hence are disqualified as morally legitimate. In this sense, unusual pathologies turn political—they become means to papers; sexual violence becomes something to remember and recount, not to forget and forbear.

The third aim of the book is to explore the effects and consequences— intended or not—of this politics of care. Sick bodies are given recognition by the state over laboring bodies, but only as long as they remain sick; this gives immigrants rights, not as equal citizens, but only insofar as they are—and remain—disabled. Both NGOs and the French state give attention to women who are subject to exceptionally violent or exoticized practices, such as excision or modern slavery, but this renders them visible as victims of cultural pathologies and hence in need of help, rescue—not equal rights. This population of second-class, disabled citizens—more mobile than other so-called able-bodied migrants—is the "new humanity," produced and protected by regimes of care that focus on morally legitimate suffering bodies.

As a part of the production of this new humanity, each set of humanitarian exceptions I trace is accompanied by a form of policing or surveillance—harsher security measures were pushed through under humanitarian pretexts, and victims moved all too easily from endangered to dangerous, innocent to delinquent. Rather than furthering solidarity or equality in the face of discriminatory policies and laws, then, my third argument is that these clauses, based on care and compassion, enable a form of "armed love" in which the moral imperative to act is accompanied, explicitly or implicitly, by practices of violence and containment. I mean by this that brutal measures may accompany actions in the name of care and rescue—measures that ultimately work to reinforce an oppressive order. As such, these regimes of care end up reproducing inequalities and racial, gendered, and geopolitical hierarchies: I suggest that this politics of care is a form of *antipolitics.*

In what follows, I introduce each of these three primary aims and their related arguments; developing them further, of course, is the work of the rest of the book.

I. WHY CARE, WHY NOW?

How and why did regimes of care come to be an important means of enacting politics, in this specific case, the politics of immigration? As I will demonstrate, the power and reach of regimes of care goes well beyond France, but much of my ethnographic evidence comes from the French context, where I conducted two and a half years of fieldwork in Paris and its *banlieues* (urban peripheries, or "outer cities" as opposed to inner cities) between 1999 and 2008. My initial period of research took place between 1999 and 2001, but I returned each year after that for several weeks, drawn by the unending shifts in law, policy, and activism and by my own political engagement with the struggles of undocumented immigrants, or the *sans-papiers*. In a context of heightened anti-immigrant sentiment, where one might say that immigrants are "today's proletarians" (Balibar 2004:50), the movement by and for the sans-papiers offered a key ethnographic site by which to think about what "politics" means in our world—where its borders lie and what constitutes political action.

Of course, the issue of immigration is by no means new in France; what is now termed "the immigrant question," which puts immigration at the center of political debate, is grounded in post–World War II migrations from the French colonial empire. The first big mobilizations of undocumented immigrants in France occurred not long after, in 1972, and struggles have been ongoing ever since (Siméant 1998). While the majority of sans-papiers come from former colonies, and while France's relationship to its immigrants is shaped in large part by the tension between its republican ideas of universal equality and inclusion, and the bitter legacy of French colonialism, their contemporary predicament is also the result of a changing global context. The increasing disparities in wealth between the global North and South have led to ever greater movements of people; and yet there is simultaneously an increasing tension between regimes of circulation for capital and people—capital circulates relatively freely, whereas people cannot—a consequence of the changed relationship between states and capital. The European Union has signed various accords to coordinate the circulation of capital with security concerns about people, starting with the Schengen Agreement of 1985, but this has played out at the expense of an ever more policed and surveilled Fortress Europe. In the French context, this has meant that while the demand for workers in certain sectors has grown, increasingly restrictive legislation has forced borders closed. Many undocumented immigrants came into France legally in the 1990s and fell out of status because of changing French legislation (Fassin and Morice 2000). Without having done anything different, they were suddenly categorized as "illegal."

This context—a fluctuating global political economy, French colonial history, and the changing contours of the European Union—helped to shape the way in which regimes of care became important players in the governing of immigrants in France. The sans-papiers came into full public view in the early 1990s, reacting to a center–right-wing government whose mandate included policies of zero immigration and harsh policing tactics.[2] Their movement rejected any association with criminality embedded in terms like "clandestine," and refused to let others speak on their behalf. This was very much a political movement *by* sans-papiers, *for* sans-papiers. Their struggle against what they argued were violations of basic human rights—such as arbitrary detention, police harassment, regular identity checks, and practices such as deporting parents away from children—was instrumental in getting the Socialists elected in 1997. Despite this, anti-immigrant sentiment continued to rise. Fed by fear about border control, internal security, and cultural integration, the leader of the ultra-right-wing xenophobic Front National, Jean-Marie Le Pen, advanced to the second round of the 2002 election ahead of outgoing Prime Minister Jospin, leading to a feeling of crisis in French politics. In this climate, the political buzz words "law and order" and "security" were linked to "immigration," rendering the politics of immigration almost too hot to touch. This meant that only in exceptional cases, with a moral imperative to relieve suffering, were immigrants given legal entry; the tendency otherwise was to close the doors as much as possible to all other forms of immigration.[3] In this context, the sans-papiers' requests for papers were increasingly treated on a case-by-case basis, adjudicated primarily by morally driven sentiments of benevolence and compassion, in circumstances of emergency.

Before I discuss this emphasis on benevolence and compassion, I want to be clear that those who work in the business of care—be it with humanitarian organizations, human rights groups, or against gender-based violence—have not necessarily asked to play a role in the politics of immigration in France, or in any politics for that matter. In fact, as I was often told, many eschew political mandates. The state nurses who received sick sans-papiers in their quest for papers did not see themselves as political actors. They were there to help in cases of urgent need. So why turn to practices of care and compassion? The context of this shift certainly includes the retreat of forms of government like the welfare state and the growth of what James Ferguson and Akhil Gupta (2002) call "transnational governmentality," which describes the way that NGOs, activists, international organizations, as well as corporations come to govern in zones the state has ceded or abandoned.[4] However, I want to suggest that, in the context of this form of governmentality, there is nevertheless an emphasis on care: those who intervene in the name of compassion are looked to as morally and ethically untainted, the only allowable, legitimate response to injustice and suffering. In this sense, "humanitarian government" is considered a force for the greatest good in international relations, and humanitarian NGOs have become privileged, autonomous interlocutors (see Agier 2008; Calhoun 2008; de Waal 2007; D. Fassin 2007b; and Pandolfi 2008). This is not simply the case in international relations; as former Médecins sans Frontières (MSF) president Rony Brauman relates, in both France and Belgium, polls have highlighted what he calls the "overvalorization of the political abilities of humanitarianism" (2004:414). In the first poll, more than two-thirds of Belgians felt that MSF was the best organization to grapple with ethnic-political violence in Burundi, a former Belgian colony; in the second poll in France, people voted that humanitarian organizations were the best suited to resolve conflicts in Europe, ahead of NATO, the European Union, and the French government (Brauman 2004).

That said, these regimes of care have particular resonance in France; clearly, care and compassion are not guiding principles everywhere or in all circumstances. For instance, up until January 4, 2010, in the United States, HIV+ immigrants were excluded or deported rather than cared for. The French have much invested in their identity as global moral leaders: France is the originator of both the NGO Médecins sans Frontières, or Doctors without Borders (winner of the 1999 Nobel Peace Prize and now nearly synonymous with humanitarianism in the contemporary world), and the 1789 Declaration of the Rights of Man and Citizen, on which the 1948 Universal Declaration of Human Rights is largely based, and the French claim these forms of transnational government as national achievements. Indeed, it was the lobbying of the now transnational medical humanitarian organizations like Médecins sans Frontières and Médecins du Monde (MDM, or Doctors of the World), along with other health-based NGOs, that helped write the illness clause into French law.

While this context helps to explain how regimes of care have come to play a role in the politics of immigration in France, two different field-work sites and methods of ethnographic research nevertheless pushed me to actually identify this connection, which took place at the microlevel; this emphasis on care was certainly not written into the policy directives. In fact, quite the opposite, since these regimes of care explicitly facilitate exceptional means of entry for cases deemed apolitical; ethnographic methods were one of the few means by which to understand what was happening on the ground. I think of the first set of field sites as "activist," where, using a feminist methodology of solidarity, that is, based on mutuality and coresponsibility, I worked with many activist associations on the issue of the sans-papiers, immigration, human rights, and social justice more broadly.[5] While this included working with many different types of activists and immigrants, Rajfire (in English, the Network for the Liberty of Immigrant and Refugee Women) was the primary activist group I engaged with.[6] Rajfire's goal was to change the laws and fundamental conditions that instituted women as dependent on husbands and fathers for their papers and rights, and hence unable to get out of violent or exploitative situations. The women who came for help with papers and/or to be active in the network had almost all experienced some form of violence, from domestic violence, rape, exploitation, and forced prostitution, to "modern slavery," but this was understood and approached by Rajfire as the effect of intersecting legal, political, economic, and historical inequalities and the effect of the laws and policies of the French state. Through this set of field sites, I got involved with the political action by and for sans-papiers.

My second set of field sites engaged the French state and those involved in producing "expert" knowledge. I interviewed and did participant observation with state representatives who managed immigrants and refugees as well as with medical experts who treated them. Here I include state officials, from immigration officers to state doctors to legal experts, as well as hospital clinics, social workers, nurses, and doctors. In my work with both activists and state representatives, I noticed that sans-papiers had to foreground their stories of suffering in order to be heard. This focus on suffering turned into a closer look at the medical realm when I decided to focus on the illness clause, the exceptional humanitarian clause that provides legal papers to sans-papiers who are "seriously ill" and unable to get treatment in their home countries, so that they can receive treatment in France.[7] I attended sessions several times a week with state medical officials who received requests for papers by sans-papiers who were ill. I was present with the doctors and nurses when the sans-papiers came to present their pathologies. This in turn led me to conduct research with humanitarian organizations and other doctors, nurses, and hospital clinics who worked with sans-papiers. I saw care and compassion come to play a leading role, but not just in the medical realm, in the name of the sick body; eventually, as this book relates, this occurred also in the activist realm, in the name of violence against women.

The situation I describe in this book, then, is one in which other actors—such as the sans-papiers movement—are out there, imagining or enacting the larger project of collective change, yet they end up competing with these regimes of care to shape the future. Just as humanitarians intervene in war-torn zones, working to ease the immediacy of suffering, so too are they now called on to intervene to ease the suffering when larger societal and political structures of the global North let increasingly large portions of the population fall through the cracks. Regimes of care like humanitarianism govern the less desirable portions of the population when the state turns a blind eye to their presence. In this sense, regimes of care are part of the transnational circulation of capital and labor, linking the political economy of immigration to the political economy of humanitarian emergencies. In other words, these morally driven institutions and practices end up "doing" politics despite not having a political mandate, unable to extract themselves from the mix of contemporary transnational regimes of labor, capital, and governance.

II. THE PROTAGONIST: THE MORALLY LEGITIMATE SUFFERING BODY

This book is foremost concerned with those who fall outside the ambit of care by nation-states, a group whose numbers are increasing as social welfare programs crumble but that is still perhaps best exemplified by

undocumented immigrants. It argues that the imagined universal suffering body is the primary subject of care for those on the margins of nation-
states, the central figure of a politics grounded in the moral imperative.
Everything revolves around it: care, compassion, and protection are
enacted in its name. This is a body imagined outside time and place,
outside history and politics, one that can (therefore) be universally recognized (Malkki 1996; D. Fassin 2001a). It is distinctly counterposed to
previous political protagonists of the 1960s and 1970s, such as the worker
and the colonial militant,[8] in that these are both highly situated—geographically, historically, racially, and of course, politically. The key to its
power and its appeal is its unquestioned universality: that is, the underlying assumption is that we can recognize suffering wherever we see
it, because there is a common denominator to being human, located in
our bodies, particularly in our bodies in pain (Scarry 1985). Yet, while
institutions and social movements take action in order to protect it, this
imagined universal suffering body appears rarely, if ever—it is glimpsed
only in moments of crisis, such as during war, famine, floods, and violence that immediately threaten its integrity. So actions and interventions
in the name of the moral imperative—even when grounded by a belief
in a universal humanity—take place as exceptions, performed in situations of crisis or with the rhetoric of emergency, when there is no other
recourse. The imagined suffering body is a victim without a perpetra-
tor—a sufferer, pure and simple, caught in a moment of urgent need. No
one is responsible for her suffering; those who act to save her do so from
the goodness of their hearts, out of moral obligation.

While tracing the appearance of and work done by this central figure,
this book inquires into the nature of the suffering body on the ground.
It argues that the suffering body must actually be configured as *morally legitimate* in order to be recognized as "universal." In this sense, I
am interested both in the embodied forms of suffering that are considered legitimate as well as what exceeds this legitimacy; my research paid
attention to the complex forms of personhood and performance that ultimately get channeled into the figure of the morally legitimate suffering
body. Who gets to embody this paradoxically privileged position as the
most disenfranchised, the most wretched of the earth, the most worthy

of care? And what political realities are reproduced or dependent on this figure? This book identifies and describes the subjects and populations that are actually produced *as* this figure.

Let me back up for a moment to explain how moral legitimacy comes to play such a critical role in rendering the universal body recognizable. Using the body to make political claims is certainly not new, nor is the reliance on forms of biomedical diagnosis and classification to do so. Michel Foucault's (1978) notions of biopolitics and biopower help us understand the politicization of life, or the entry of life into the realm of explicit calculation. But in more recent literature, for instance, Adriana Petryna's (2002) concept of "biological citizenship" names the way that biology becomes a cultural resource through which citizens stake their claims for social equity in post-Chernobyl Ukraine; she traces the claims to health services and social support of those who were exposed to the radiation effects of the nuclear explosion in Chernobyl, in the name of their damaged biology.[9] For the sans-papiers, biomedical diagnoses of suffering become strategic resources as well, but there are several important differences from the practice of biological citizenship. Most notably, sans-papiers are not citizens making claims on a nation-state; by definition, they are legally outside the nation-state, and since the French nation-state has effectively closed its borders, their primary hope is to make a claim on a *non*-nation-state order, which may be translated into political recognition in the French nation-state context. While the European Union has been promising to introduce a common immigration and asylum system for some years now, at present no global legal or political system exists to adjudicate such claims.

So, when sans-papiers make claims based on their suffering bodies, they appeal not to a nation-state but to an understanding of humanity as a biological species, where suffering finds its universal measure in medical science. However, this book demonstrates that, on the ground, these universal claims are mediated by transnational regimes of care, grounded in a moral imperative. In this sense, the sans-papiers largely depend on a transnational, moral order and its local manifestations. While Petryna describes citizens mobilizing technical and scientific knowledge about their injuries to make claims on the Ukrainian state, in the case of the sans-papiers the claims require not only the mediation of science and medicine but of senti-ment. Those who enact this moral order imagine and respond to humanity as "ethical subject" (Laqueur 2009) as much as biological object. That is, biological claims must be mediated by embodied performances that make them recognizable to those who participate in these regimes of care—they must be recognizable as worthy of compassion. The state nurses explained to me, for instance, that when they felt a person's case was particularly noteworthy, rather than let the doctor simply read the medical file to decide whether or not the illness warranted papers to stay in France for treatment, they would bring the doctor in to meet the patient and to hear his/her story. One nurse said, "The *human* does not exist for them [the doctors] otherwise; they are just statistics to be manipulated." In other words, this is not just about a trade in biology or biomedical diagnoses; it is about a politics of benevolence and compassion for a *suffering* human—affective and biological registers must be combined. This is particularly interesting in the French context, since it requires a biological component to claims of political recognition, which the French republican model of citizenship, based on *jus soli*, does not explicitly acknowledge.[10] That is, universal humanity here is not simply about "fraternity" or solidarity, as in the French motto, but also about certain *kinds* of qualified bodies.

In this "new humanity," then, sentiment must be smuggled into bio-logical measurements; one's suffering must be configured as a particular biological form with affective resonance—enough to compel moral action. This can have serious consequences, as we will see; these range from bartering for membership with one's life and one's body, to situations where biological and political claims recombine in new ways, producing and protecting a very particular humanity. For instance, Dr. Amara, who worked at the medical clinic for undocumented immigrants that I had been observing, suggested to me that I might be interested in a paradox he had witnessed. He explained to me that several of his HIV+ patients had stopped taking their medication once they had received their papers, despite having received papers to gain access to the medication. In this scenario, it is not clear which is the more virulent form of suffering: no papers or no medication. Biological life and political life have taken on equal significance—life as someone sick is interchangeable with life as a politically recognized subject. Indeed, being sick is what is required to be a political subject. Here, a politics based on biology as a universal measure of humanity—without acknowledging that we live in worlds and bodies mediated by institutionalized forms of sentiment—produces all kinds of unexpected results.

Many scholars and activists have been compelled to explain this universal suffering body as "bare life," the concept used by philosopher Giorgio Agamben. I want to explain how and why I distinguish my focus from Agamben's, to make clearer what I take to be the meaning of the morally legitimate suffering body. For Agamben (1998), the Greek *zoe*, or "bare life," is life stripped of its political and social qualities, life that is not distinguishable as human. In his book *Homo Sacer*, Agamben suggests that the preoccupation of modern sovereignty is defining bare life, that is, who is included or excluded from the political and juridical realms; homo sacer is that which is abandoned outside the polis—someone who can be killed, but not sacrificed, in the sense that sacrifice gives death divine significance. Although Agamben helps us to recognize the central political role played by forms of life that are seen as apolitical and, more concretely, the importance of humanitarian organizations whose goal is to protect or liberate these forms of apolitical life, to call this figure "bare life" assumes that we can know what life stripped of all political and social features looks like, even theoretically; it assumes that we can all imagine it, and universally recognize it. This book suggests that this figure—be it the figure of the universal suffering body or that of bare life—is but a political device to create the conditions for care. Bare life does not exist beyond this; it always comes with political and social attributes allowing it to be identified as human, as bare, and as "life"—biology in the sense of this "biological life" is fundamentally political, including how we define and characterize physicality. What counts are the political choices that make us understand something as apolitical, as bare, and the political configurations that make this figure necessary in the first place. Similarly, to identify bare life as apolitical or outside of politics is to assume that one understands what *politics* looks like, a priori; it is, as French philosopher Jacques Rancière (2004) suggests, to close down the interval for action of those least likely to be seen as political subjects.

While I want to distinguish my focus from Agamben's, I find more kinship with certain forms of anticapitalist, transnational feminist theory, which have much to say about what I call the figure of the morally legitimate suffering body and how this kind of body only seems to be attached to certain kinds of people. In particular, transnational and postcolonial feminist literature is more attentive to the difference between the imagined figure and its enactment. Chandra Mohanty's famous "Third World Woman" (1988)—the suffering victim of oppressive patriarchal cultures, often equated with innocence, passivity and apolitical, corporeal existence—too often fits the mould of naked or bare life. Why is this so? This feminist theory pushes us to ask how the suffering body comes to be known as such: what does it look like, to whom, and why? Clearly, despite its supposed bareness, or its minimality, certain features are required for it to qualify as a recognizable sufferer, or in this case, to qualify as a member of the new humanity.[11]

Understanding that the suffering body is always produced by and a part of social and historical contexts gives us a place from which to ask when and for whom the body becomes the primary form of access to universal personhood. That is, not everyone is reliant upon it to prove their humanity. Historically, the body has been a source of authentication in situations where the subject is conceived of as unable to provide a reasoned, spoken truth. For instance, in her book on torture in fifth-century Athens, Page duBois describes the relationship between slaves' bodies and torture. The slave's body is constructed as a site of truth, according to Aristotelian logic: "truth is constituted as residing in the body of the slave; because he can apprehend reason, without possessing reason" (duBois 1991:68). In his analysis of trauma and memory in the context of South Africa, Allen Feldman places duBois's text in a longer line of analyses of slavery in the United States, where he suggests there is a cultural logic of testimonial authentication in the body. This truth, found in "the primordial landscape of the racialized body" (A. Feldman 2004:190), both designates and produces certain people as Other, as beyond and outside reason. If a suffering body provides the universal truth of humanity, it usually does so from a position outside reason—that is, it might provide proof of a certain kind of humanity, but it is not an Enlightenment, reasoning humanity. Immediately, then, this new humanity assumes a lower status.

Humanitarianism and Violence against Women

Two regimes of care in particular help to produce and protect the morally legitimate suffering body: humanitarianism and the movement against violence against women, the latter now also understood as gender-based violence. These are two languages of obligation not usually brought into conversation; that is, recent literature about suffering has been more likely to compare and contrast humanitarianism and human rights as both parallel and competing moral projects, or else to think of gender-based violence under the rubric of human rights.[12] While various human rights movements are also important players in the politics of care, I found that humanitarianism and violence against women occupy a special place in the politics of immigration in France, and for this reason I argue that we must read across them, all the while recognizing that there are other players. That is, I am not so much interested in limiting these as two separate regimes of care, but in recognizing them as two different ways to name and enact a politics based on care and produced as a moral imperative. Their centrality relates to the focus on the physical basis of suffering.

Humanitarianism, of course, means many things. Some call it a concern for the suffering of distant strangers;[13] others assert that it is defined by an ethics of intervention (Feldman 2007b). This book is most concerned with what has been called the new humanitarianism, which began with the formation of Médecins sans Frontières in 1971 by a small group of French doctors and journalists. While chapter 2 goes into this genealogy in detail, I want to note here that this new humanitarianism, run by doctors, focuses on health, suffering, and bodily integrity. The goal is not to improve the human condition but to alleviate suffering wherever it occurs, in the form of emergency medical care. Founded by Frenchmen, this type of humanitarianism holds a special place in both the French imagination and in the country's institutional structures.

If the notion of bodily integrity (or violation thereof) is central in determining who can claim to be a subject of humanitarian aid, so too is it central to the transnational discourse on violence against women. As a category of struggle, violence against women has only been in existence and use since the early 1990s; it was created as the lowest common denominator from the women's movements in the North and South, taking the issue of bodily integrity as a universal concern that they could rally around (Miller 2004; Keck and Sikkink 1998; Merry 2006). By way of a discourse on women's rights, it provided for the mainstreaming of feminism;[14] this happened especially in the context of war and genocide, which, provoked first in the former Yugoslavia and then in Rwanda, helped to establish persecution on the basis of gender as a crime against humanity.[15] In France, this set of discourses and practices only really took hold in the early 2000s. It was jump-started by the 1995 Fourth World Conference on Women in Beijing and furthered by the European campaign to raise awareness of violence against women. Drawing on mainstream human rights paradigms, the movement against violence against women took the body as the primary site of harm. It was able to come into being in large part because it was linked to health and humanitarian concerns—sexual harm could be spoken of in terms of death, for instance, in the case of HIV/AIDS, rather than in relation to "deviant" sexual practice. There was a shift from citizen to patient. What emerged was a victim-subject, particularly one of sexual harm, seen in isolation from other injustices or forms of exploitation—this was the only way to get around the tensions between feminist movements in the North and South and what each claimed to be the more significant forms of injustice: discrimination or lack of development. A focus on physical injury—believed to be a "transcultural value"—was looked to as a foolproof way to prevent cultural imperialism in the movement (Keck and Sikkink 1998:195).

While it may not be immediately intuitive that humanitarianism and the movement against violence against women should be thought about together, the combination of my different field sites across a period of several years helped me to think about these regimes of care as overlapping enactments of a politics focused on morally legitimate suffering bodies. Working with sans-papiers, medical officials, doctors, and state officials between 1999 and 2001, it became clear that the "best" position for someone without papers was to be gravely ill, since this was quickly becoming a primary—albeit exceptional—means of entry in the face of the closure of borders and zero illegal immigration policies. The sick body was, at that time, the most able to evoke compassion—it was the closest incarnation of an innocent, and hence morally legitimate, suffering body. Over the next few years, as chapter 3 explains, things gradually changed; the French state became more and more suspicious of both doctors and immigrants, questioning their honesty when they made requests for papers to treat life-threatening illnesses. But working with Rajfire, I noticed a parallel process at work as the interval for humanitarian exception based on illness was closing: women sans-papiers increasingly had to foreground their individual, gendered suffering—particularly, their experiences of violence—in order to garner basic rights. This became one of the more promising strategies, not their political or legal actions with community or activist groups, and it coincided with the new legitimacy in France of the transnational category "violence against women." As one long-time Rajfire activist exclaimed at a meeting about the category of gender persecution in asylum claims that emphasized the need to demonstrate victimhood above all else: "What price are we paying for the recognition of these forms of violence against women? The battle against sexist oppression must be a *political* one!"

My analysis at the time was that there had been a shift in the subject of compassion, from sick body to sexually violated body. But as I revisited my research material, I realized that the morally legitimate suffering body actually looked very similar across time, as did the mechanisms working to "save it." That is, these regimes of care use similar techniques, strategies, and logics and overlap in significant ways: if humanitarianism is associated with benevolence, compassion, and with making exceptions to respond to a moral imperative of emergency, the struggle against violence against women is often enacted through humanitarian measures, saving exceptional victims from violence in cases deemed of particular moral urgency. And if the face of the struggle against violence against women is still too often racialized, figuring women from the global South as primary victims, humanitarianism often responds more urgently to recognizably gendered, sexualized, and racialized bodies, that is, women and children of the global South. This intersection has a history: interestingly, before opposition to violence against women came into being as a movement, the only mentions of sexual harm in the international system were in humanitarian law and in the United Nations' antitrafficking convention (Miller 2004:23). In both, there is an emphasis on physical bodies and often on medical pathology as a way to render their struggle universal—physicality serves as common denominator. Both humanitarianism and those opposed to violence against women often use medical experts to address the problem; in this sense, both open the way to the medicalization of social and political problems. And yet, as this book shows, as part of a politics of care and protection, both humanitarianism and the movement against violence against women exceed a biomedical, rational logic; the biological is always mediated by the gendered and racialized narratives that allow certain people and bodies to be identified as morally legitimate, as worthy of being saved. In this sense, both humanitarianism and the struggle against violence against women foreground not only physical pathology but cultural pathology. What are the signifiers of innocent suffering? This book is about their embodied expression.

III. THE POLITICS OF ANTIPOLITICS

This book began as a search for the political; what I found was a politics—or rather, *antipolitics*—of care. By this, I mean two things: first, those who act in the name of the moral imperative generally claim to be apolitical—beyond or outside politics; second, rather than remaining outside the system in their desire to not engage with politics, they work to reinforce the status quo, the established order. Let me be more precise in what I mean by politics and antipolitics. Drawing on the French terms *le politique* and *la politique*, I want to make a distinction between what might be translated as "politics" and "the political." "Politics" refers to everyday politics, often to policy—that is, to the set of practices by which order is created and maintained. The second—"the political"—refers to the disruption of an established order.[16] Radical change is the result of *political* action, not politics. While a politics of care and compassion is a form of politics—it engages and reproduces a set of power relations—my argument is that it does not change the dominant order, it does not challenge established forms of inequality. That said, it is nevertheless productive—the question is, of what? What kind of politics is *this* antipolitics today? First, I want to put the idea of antipolitics in context and then turn to its specific contemporary effects.

In suggesting that a politics grounded in the moral imperative is antipolitical, I do not mean to suggest that we can (or should) separate politics and morality: the radical political change brought about by movements like those led by Gandhi or by Martin Luther King, Jr. were, of course, the result of a combination of the two. This book narrows the question of the relationship between morality and politics to inquire about situations where the moral order becomes a *primary* order; that is, where the drive to do what is moral, distinguishing itself from politics and the political—although not power—takes the upper hand in forms of government. The danger is that in pretending to be outside power, "unarmed," power is wielded without acknowledging it and therefore often without accountability. In this sense, I think of these moral struggles or "moralisms" as forms of "armed love," often instituting repressive measures in the name of care.[17] Moralisms happen in the urgency of the present, blind to the future; they lack direction for action. For instance, if, as a humanitarian, one saves lives, what kind of world does one save them into? This can result in what Friedrich Nietzsche called reaction posing as action (Brown 2001:40); it can be a form of *antipolitics*. In this sense, I refer to moralisms as antipolitical.

The tendency of humanitarianism and human rights to be restorative rather than revolutionary is not new, or for them to be "antipolitics" in the sense used by Hungarian dissident George Konrad; historian Samuel Moyn (2007) reminds us of this with reference to Eastern European dissidents in the 1970s. A number of other writers and scholars have made similar arguments about programs that seek to do good: James Ferguson in particular called the development apparatus in Lesotho an "antipolitics machine" in his book by the same name, by which he meant that it depoliticizes everything it touches while performing its own "pre-eminently political operation of expanding bureaucratic power" (1994:xv).[18]

In this particular case, however, as we will see, increased policing and criminalization of immigrants takes place in the name of care and compassion, along with a reproduction of gendered and racial inequalities, albeit through new, embodied means. Traces of the tendency to join moral imperative with repressive or oppressive measures are embedded in the histories of both the new humanitarianism and the movement against violence against women. Indeed, I want to briefly foreground parts of these histories here, to insist that—perhaps counterintuitively—practices of armed love were built into them from the start. What I describe in this book—the antipolitics of care—is not about the politics of care gone awry; antipolitics lies at its very core, and I want to be clear about this.

As I explain in more detail in chapter 2, then, while Médecins sans Frontières was formed in the heyday of May 1968, the new humanitarianism really came into its own as a reaction against *tiermondisme*, or "third-worldism"; the point here is that *anti*-third-worldism is ultimately moralist in tone. Briefly put, French third-worldism began in the 1950s, with the recognition of colonized peoples as political agents.[19] Fighting imperialism was understood as an essential part of the struggle against capitalism, and in this quest third-worldists supported national liberation movements against Western nations. In the years that followed May '68, however, the writings of the "New Philosophers"—many of who were former "gauchistes" themselves—helped dismantle third-worldism, arguing against a Marxist tradition.[20] In their texts, the "third world" was once again described as a place of misery and barbarism, and the people were pitied as victims of natural disasters and oppression. No longer were third world (or colonial) Others understood as political actors in their own right; the actors called into being by Frantz Fanon's *Wretched of the Earth* were reconfigured as victims of authoritarianism, famine, or flood, ultimately in need of salvation. Instead of politics, there were victims and their saviors—and a renewed civilizing mission.

Bernard Kouchner, one of the founders of Médecins sans Frontières, was a former third-worldist who subsequently turned anti-third-worldist. As head of MSF in the 1970s, he emerged as one of the primary spokespeople for those in the third world; but he was guided by the philosophy that, while one might denounce abuses of power, ultimately one could only support individuals against such oppression by drawing on the principles of human rights—there was nothing more, no collective struggle against imperial domination, no political. Rather, the global landscape was understood in the form of a "torturing state, and the martyred people" (Julliard 1978, cited from Ross 2002:161). In this landscape, "third world" people could no longer speak for themselves or argue for their rights—they were increasingly silenced. Guy Hocquenghem (1986), still a third-worldist, indicted his former May '68 comrades in an open letter, calling their turn to language of human rights the new "warrior moralism."

The figure of the heroic French doctor is certainly significant in the development of these warrior moralisms, or what I think of today as armed love. This is the doctor who has come to save the world—the contemporary cowboy. The French doctors of the 1970s were adventurers, fascinated with the French Resistance and with heroic war correspondents who braved danger to witness the truth (Emmanuelli 2005:29). One of their early slogans was, "In their waiting room, two million men: there where others do not go" (Emmanuelli 2005:47). This combination of heroism, machismo, and passion played a role in recruiting those who were interested in transforming the world. But in the process, it served to masculinize care, appealing to a new set of actors interested in war, violence, and emergency. These regimes of care are carried forward by warrior-saints like Kouchner, a self-described "mercenary of emergency medicine" (Caldwell 2009:7). Of course, masculinity need not be attached to specific types of biological bodies. Here I refer to masculine discourses that can be adopted by males or females, where the heroic warrior is a standard symbol (Eisenstein 2007; Hooper 2001). They draw on charismatic public figures who become heroes, often under conditions of emergency that only respond to the extreme, the exception, displacing all forms of politics to that limit.[21] Care here is often about rescue.

Just as the new humanitarianism arose from the ashes of the revolutionary moment of May '68, the language of those against violence against women is built on the back of feminist movements of the global North and South, pushing for political change and gender equality. However, it too has both its progressive and regressive guises (Miller 2004; Kapur 2002). The language of exceptional protection and care is an

integral part of the discourse of violence against women, even while it
also has its radical expressions, pushing for social justice (see, e.g., Incite!
2006, 2007; and Smith 2005); feminisms have long struggled with differences of race, class, and sexuality, and white middle-class feminists
have, at times, used this strategy of exceptional care and protection to
"rescue" nonwhite women (Spivak 1988; Mohanty 1988; Razack 1995;
Grewal 1998; Kapur 2002; Abu-Lughod 2002; Volpp 2006).

Some of these feminist practices of care can also be described more
precisely as armed love, where an interpretation of feminism is used to
encourage (often militarized) intervention, in order to "save" women,
and to condemn "their" men; this clearly has colonial echoes, where practices deemed violent to women were used to justify colonial rule. This
has occurred more recently in the form of "state department" feminism,
such as when former president George W. Bush and first lady Laura Bush
wanted to "liberate" Afghani women from the violence inflicted upon
them by the Taliban, by way of a military invasion; similarly, before the
occupation of Iraq, Bush suggested that the United States should attack
Iraq for the sake of its women (Volpp 2006; Viner 2002; Abu-Lughod 2002).
As Alice Miller (2004:17) recounts, in front of the UN General Assembly in
September 2003, then-president Bush pushed the global war on terror in
the name of saving girls from sexual slavery, among other moral projects.

Knowing these histories, what are the politics of antipolitics today—
how do these embedded practices of armed love reproduce extant
inequalities? Insofar as they are more concerned with moral legitimacy
than legality—meaning that the law may be used opportunistically[22]—
regimes of care have as their flip side regimes of surveillance and policing. What I will show is that those who are not worthy of compassion are
not simply ignored but are rather criminalized and condemned: they are
perceived as having failed in some important moral way. For instance, as
chapter 5 discusses, in the name of the fight against trafficking in women,
a French law on "passive soliciting" actually permits increased identity
checks by police, bleeding into a policing of undocumented immigrants.
In the name of saving a few innocent women, a widespread racialized policing and criminalization of immigrants is rendered legitimate.
Armed love takes many forms in this antipolitics; not only is it enacted

at the behest of feminists, but health officials too are reconfigured as border guards, choosing a few exceptionally sick individuals and excluding the rest. Thus, if this book demonstrates the unintended effects of a politics based on moral imperatives, it always simultaneously indicts the accompanying regimes of security and practices of violence to which they respond, and which they legitimize.

Ultimately, I argue that a politics of care reproduces a second-class status for immigrants in France, particularly those from the global South, exemplifying the "new humanity," worthy of rescue. It does so, however, in unexpected ways. Those undocumented immigrants who do get papers have inequality literally inscribed on their bodies, since their bodies are what they use to barter for their papers; they are forever marked as sick, as disabled, as violated. Their main value is their suffering, insofar as practices of care that respond to suffering mark the French as benevolent, as civilized, as humane. But finally, the politics of care maintains a racialized postcolonial nation-state, rendering immigrants visible in French society primarily in the form of gendered and racialized victims—they can never be equal.

.   .   .   .   .

I want to end—and begin—by acknowledging one of the biggest challenges of writing this book: to be attentive to the regulatory role played by suffering in this politics of care while still recognizing the deep injustices and very real suffering caused by transnational capitalism and other social and structural regimes of inequality. The literature on "social suffering" draws attention to these forms of structural violence (Kleinman and Kleiman 1996; Kleinman et al. 1997; Das et al. 1997; Das et al. 2001; Bourdieu 1999; Bourgois 2009). However, I want to suggest that there is a fine line between recognizing suffering and fetishizing it as the fundamental and only basis of a common humanity. While this book argues that an understanding of suffering as the basis of a universal humanity can result in the obligation to use suffering to barter for membership in the category humanity, we still need a language that can express the experience of pain in all its forms. In this sense, I hope this book opens the way to think about the shape of radical political change centered on equality, change that addresses the suffering of exploitation, oppression, poverty, and hunger as much as suffering from illness or gendered violence.

THE ORGANIZATION OF THE BOOK

This book is divided into three parts, reflective of the three aims and arguments just introduced. Part 1 draws on my research with the sans-papiers movement as well as the history of humanitarianism to provide the context for how the governance of immigrants increasingly takes place through practices of care. Chapter 1 tells the story of the political struggle around immigration. It focuses on the sans-papiers movement in order to analyze the context of its emergence and limits and also the rise of a competing complex of institutions and practices of care. Chapter 2 traces the genealogy of one critical regime of care—the "new humanitarianism"—in order to understand the transfer of political processes to a form of action based on the moral imperative, grounded in benevolence and compassion.

Part 2 discusses the on-the-ground workings of the politics of care, identifying the techniques that produce and protect the suffering body and arguing that its moral legitimacy is dependent on performances of both medical and cultural pathology. To this end, chapter 3 explores the humanitarian illness clause and the politics of compassion through which this exceptional clause is enacted, following doctors, nurses, and social workers as they become gatekeepers of the nation-state, and the sans-papiers as they configure their experiences as morally legitimate suffering. Chapter 4 traces the tension in the struggle against violence against women between a case-by-case approach that responds to a moral imperative to rescue and protect women from violence, and a stance that is grounded in a feminist political struggle for justice. As in the case of illness, where it is not always clear what qualifies as a humanitarian emergency worthy of exception, I explore what is understood as violence, worthy of exception. In each of these chapters, I am interested in the form the suffering body takes; what signifiers are used to render it morally legitimate?

Part 3 discusses the consequences and effects of a politics of care, arguing that they are, ultimately, antipolitical. Chapter 5 focuses on the struggle around human trafficking and a subset of this—that around modern slavery—which takes place in many of the same moralizing terms, through similar institutions and logics as other regimes of care. The chapter argues that the fights against modern slavery and against human trafficking produce victims needing to be saved, and I contrast this to the terms of the sans-papiers movement, which are based on solidarity and equality, not hierarchy. Finally, chapter 6 investigates the subjects produced by a politics based on care and produced as moral imperative; these, I suggest, are subjects of the "new humanity." The chapter begins with a discussion of the various contradictory subject positions I encountered in my ethnographic research, demonstrating how a politics of care produces diseased and disabled subjects who are more mobile than other so-called able-bodied migrants. It ends with a discussion of the circumstances under which we need to see a will to wellness as different from a will to biological life, and when we need to see this distinction as a form of violence inherent in a politics of armed love. The conclusion ends where I began: with a search for the political.

PART ONE

The Context

POLITICS AND CARE

ONE

Sans-Papiers and the Context
of Political Struggle

On October 27, 2005, responding to a call about a break-in, French police
chased three young boys of Arab origin in the *cité* (housing estate) of
Clichy-sous-Bois. The boys climbed the wall of a power plant in their
attempt to escape the police, and two of the boys, aged fifteen and sev-
enteen, died, while the third suffered from severe burns. Later it was
recognized that the police had chased the boys by mistake and that there
was no burglary. The boys had been playing soccer with their friends
in the neighborhood and had dispersed to avoid the all too familiar
police harassment. In response to this event, France erupted in what
were called urban "riots," which lasted for over three weeks, burning
ten thousand cars and causing the arrest of nearly five thousand people.
This was just three days after then–interior minister Nicolas Sarkozy
said that he would rid the *banlieue* area of Argenteuil of *racaille* (scum or

riffraff), by which he meant youth of immigrant origin. In response to the events, the government declared a state of emergency, using a 1955 law originally passed during the war of independence in Algeria—a move that rendered all too apparent how the borders between metropole and colony had never fully disappeared, but rather had been resurrected in new ways within the metropole itself.

These so-called riots—perhaps more accurately labeled "revolts" to recognize their political nature[1]—opened a space in France to discuss questions of economic inequality, racial discrimination, policing, and segregation for those of immigrant descent. Quite suddenly, it seemed, France's postcolonial status was no longer a public secret: it appeared in full view, in newspapers all over the world and, more importantly, in France itself. I open with this event as one of the most visible recent political eruptions in France of the tensions surrounding questions of immigration, labor, and their related colonial histories. In other words, this was not a sudden crisis; as the "banlieue film" *La Haine* (Hate) had already demonstrated in 1995, in its prescient fictional depiction of riots caused by police brutality against youth of immigrant origin, it is an ongoing, unresolved situation, where racial discrimination, police and state violence, and economic inequality simmer in what are also now called "ghettos."

In this chapter, I trace the shape of political action around immigration on the ground. In what context do regimes of care come into play— what is the larger frame? My own entry into this cluster of issues began with the question of the sans-papiers. While not the same struggle as the 2005 riots, which focused attention on the plight of French citizens— mostly children of immigrant parents, born in France—the struggle of undocumented immigrants derives from many of the same unresolved issues and overlaps significantly with the questions and problems that spurred the riots. Both are shaped by France's history of colonialism as much as they are by the current context of "neoliberal" reforms. Both are a product of racially informed technologies of exclusion, and both are shaped by the history of immigrant labor. In some ways, the sans-papiers struggle is an earlier incarnation of the riots; in other ways, it is a parallel and overlapping struggle. So, taking this as my jumping-off point, I explore the political eruption of the sans-papiers in order to think about the context of its emergence and limits, and about the rise of a competing complex of institutions and practices of care. Many scholars and activists have written about the sans-papiers precisely because of the significance of the movement for new practices of citizenship and belonging;[2] my goal is not to revisit this work, but rather to think about the nature and context of the sans-papiers political movement and why it has come to be challenged by a form of antipolitics. I say this at a time when sans-papiers are still marching, occupying churches, conducting hunger strikes, as they have since the 1970s; yet they are treated as individuals on a case-by-case basis by the state. Those who hope to be regularized must prove to be the exception—those who fit into the norm will remain undocumented. In exploring the context of the sans-papiers movement—from one of the foundational moments in 1996 to the challenges of global capitalism, colonialism, and changing practices of sovereignty—this chapter also asks, what kinds of resolutions need to happen, of past and present, for a new future to be accessible and imaginable?

THE SANS-PAPIERS

The Political Struggle

In August 1996, French riot police stormed Saint Bernard Church in Paris where three hundred or so undocumented Africans had taken refuge in their quest for papers and for basic human rights. The police broke down the church doors with axes, throwing tear gas on mothers and babies, and dragging people out. A few were deported that very night, one away from his wife and children. Madiguène Cissé, a woman of Senegalese origin and spokesperson for the sans-papiers, was strip-searched in front of her daughter, while one policewoman tried to humiliate her, taking her cell phone away from her, indicating that she, as a foreigner, had no right to it: "They've hardly come down from the trees, and they already have mobiles in their hands" (Cissé 1997, cited from Notes from Nowhere 2003:42).

The media coverage of this event prompted an immediate and vociferous reaction by the French public; they were outraged at the way the government had treated the sans-papiers. Paradoxically, polls showed that they did not object to the restrictive immigration policies that caused people to enter into situations of illegality; rather, they objected to the way these people had been treated—the complete absence of respect for basic rights. The government was chastised by all sides for breaking with France's history as the founder and home of human rights principles and, as one intellectual claimed, for breaking with the "founding principles of the social order."

The occupation of and eviction from Saint Bernard Church was the latest and most significant manifestation of a battle that has been ongoing since the early 1970s, including a series of hunger strikes.[3] Yet with the occupation of Saint Bernard, the existence of undocumented immigrants was brought front and center, "out from the shadows" as they claimed, in a new, mediatized and politicized way. Images of the sans-papiers, consumed by the public on TV and in newspapers, jolted movie stars, film producers, and intellectuals into action in support of the sans-papiers, for what they said was the sake of human rights. The intellectual Pierre Bourdieu and movie star Emmanuelle Béart were among those who joined in. Some came to stay in the church with the sans-papiers and some spoke out to the newspapers. Still others decided to become *parrains*, or "godparents," to the sans-papiers to help avoid heavy-handed treatment by the police—sans-papiers carried identity cards around with them made by their godparents as a form of protection. Demonstrations abounded with human rights rhetoric—this was about the protection of basic rights and equality, the reason for the French revolution. How could France of all places deny people basic rights?

This 1996 uprising of immigrants into public space was an attempt to show the French state and public that undocumented immigrants were not criminals in hiding but, as the spokesperson Ababacar Diop stated, "We wanted to remind people that we existed and wished to be free of the illegality that French laws had thrust upon us. There was something extraordinarily simple in this vision. We were humans confronted with immense difficulties. What could be more natural than to make known our distress and to ask for a framework of negotiation with the authorities so that we could see an end to the tunnel, without animosity?" (1997b:1).

The sans-papiers took control of their own situation; while associations and mediators helped, the sans-papiers led the way, refusing to let anyone speak on their behalf. In many ways, this marked their emergence as political actors. They coined the term *sans-papiers*, literally "without papers," to move away from the criminality and suspicion associated with clandestinity to a focus on people deprived of basic rights. Coming together under one identity was an extraordinary achievement, since sans-papiers are a remarkably heterogeneous group. Not only do they come from many nationalities, socioeconomic classes, ages, levels of education, and linguistic groups, but there are many different reasons for their lack of papers. Some began as refugees, others as students, and still others as spouses of French nationals. It is important to note that most entered legally and lost their papers due to changes in French immigration legislation (Fassin and Morice 2000). Most notable here were the Pasqua laws of 1993, which helped to enact the center–right-wing government's "zero immigration" policy. These created a set of often contradictory requirements for all persons filing a request for legal status, which ranged from proof of uninterrupted housing and employment for those wanting to renew visas, to an abrogation of *jus soli*, taking away the right of those born on French soil to French citizenship and making it contingent upon an oath of loyalty and a lack of criminal record. New policing practices (an intensification of the emergency security "plan Vigipirate") were instituted as a part of this legislative package, including identity checks of anyone who looked "foreign." This came with a penalty of three months of detention for anyone who could not provide valid documents. Aiding and abetting undocumented immigrants also became a criminal offense at this time (GISTI 1994; Iskander 2007).

The sans-papiers occupied the Saint Bernard Church as a last-ditch effort in a series of occupations that began with Saint Ambroise Church in Paris in March 1996. They made two demands on the second day of the Saint Ambroise occupation: the appointment of a mediator and a moratorium on deportations. The response was their forced eviction from the church by the police, with the complicity of the clergy. The sans-papiers subsequently moved from place to place, occupying locales from the Japy gymnasium in Paris to the Cartoucherie theater in Vincennes (just outside Paris), becoming more politicized with each move, each eviction.

In a stalemate with the government, despite growing domestic and international support, the group of sans-papiers established a committee of eminent personalities (lawyers, scientists, clergymen)—a de facto College of Mediators to act as intermediaries between the authorities and themselves. The government recognized this group, and negotiations began in May 1996.

The government, then under Jacques Chirac's right-wing party (Rassemblement pour la République, or RPR), promised to examine the cases favorably; but the government went back on its promises, saying it would only give temporary (three-month) acknowledgments of residence to parents of French children. In fact, not even this was true; the twenty-two people given temporary papers were chosen arbitrarily, and the majority of sans-papiers were left in the same position as before. The sans-papiers' answer was to occupy Saint Bernard Church.

This time, the clergy helped; the priest of Saint Bernard called for a peaceful settlement. Ten sans-papiers went on a hunger strike for more than fifty days. The church was consistently full, welcoming more than two thousand visitors and supporters each day. Political leaders such as the head of the French Communist Party, Robert Hue, and the widow of former president François Mitterrand, Danielle Mitterrand, went to show their support. The media kept a constant vigil. But on August 23, 1996, for the first time ever in France, the state gave the order to invade a church. The police broke down the doors with axes and tear gas in hand.

A few months after the Saint Bernard Church affair, the Socialists came into power, helped in no small part by these demonstrations against governmental abuses of human rights. Prime Minister Lionel Jospin's government promised to deal with sans-papiers more generously. Once in power, they passed a law that allowed for the legalization of sans-papiers who fulfilled certain conditions. France was finally lauded for living up to its reputation as home to human rights.

The Backlash: Policing and Detention

Despite this rhetoric, the promised reexamination of cases of undocumented immigrants in 1997 and the new law in 1998 on entry and residence of foreigners were both much less generous than initially promised by the Jospin government. The reexamination of cases on the basis of

more favorable criteria—an "amnesty" of sorts—only gave eighty thousand people papers, fewer than half of those who applied, and many
sans-papiers still found themselves without papers, despite fulfilling the
required criteria. People like the two Malian men who were deported
right after the Saint Bernard eviction while their children remained in
France were the flip side of the few legalized, and their deportations happened despite Article 8 of the European Convention on Human Rights,
which explicitly says that the state cannot deport someone with links in
that same country. The state's treatment of sans-papiers seemed as brutal
and arbitrary as ever.

When I arrived in France in September 1999, some were already saying
it was the aftermath of the sans-papiers movement. Although the social
movement was and is still very much alive, it no longer commanded the
national and international media and political attention it had in 1996.
Hundreds of associations still take it as their primary mandate, each
taking a different perspective, each lobbying for a slightly different con-
stituency. These associations, from labor unions to cultural and neighborhood groups, for the most part use the language of human rights in
a fight for equal citizenship, and they locate their struggles in the French
tradition of respect for human rights.[4] Yet these cries for human rights
fell on now-deaf state ears—a reality that has only been confirmed and
exaggerated with the turn to the right in France after the 2002 elections,
and ever more so with the election of Sarkozy as president in 2007. There
was and is still much violence and exploitation: I encountered many
people living and enduring such situations—at home, in the workplace,
and often in domestic service, for women in particular; these people had
often submitted claims with appropriate documentation and yet had not
been regularized.[5] Drissia, a fifty-year-old woman of Moroccan origin I
met through Rajfire, an activist network for undocumented and immigrant women, revealed to me the extent of the situation. Drissia had
been in France for over ten consecutive years, which qualified her for
papers according to the new law put into effect by the Socialists in 1998
(Article 12bis°3);[6] yet, despite what immigrant rights lawyers believed
was proof of her uninterrupted presence on French soil, her request had
been turned down multiple times. At the monthly meetings and regular

protest marches, I saw her alternate between tears and deep anger, often
in one sentence, at the sheer frustration of being treated as though she
did not exist. As Drissia's case illustrates, what counts as proof of uninterrupted presence is unclear—it depends on the interpretation of each
immigration official. For people who have been trying to erase any trace
of their presence so as not to be deported, providing official proof of each
month of residence for over ten years is a nearly impossible task—practi-
cally a contradiction in terms.

Many of the people who had not been granted papers found themselves ghettoized in the *banlieues*, which have a particular significance in
French immigration history. They are the result of discriminatory housing policies, aimed at structuring a formal outsiderness for the workforce
imported from the former colonies in the 1950s and 1960s.[7] Policing of
what constitutes "normal housing" has forced all types of immigrants
into this periphery; for instance, immigrants are not allowed to bring
in their families unless they first prove that they have "at their disposal
housing considered normal for a comparable family living in France"
(Scullion 1995:39, cited from Rosello 1997:242).

The sans-papiers were forced into the banlieues in a very particular
way. They would often end up living there, as it was the only place they
could find landlords willing to rent to them: it was a criminal offense to
rent to someone without papers. But most importantly, once in the banlieues, sans-papiers were often stuck there with no way out. This was
enforced by identity checks, first instituted by Interior Minister Charles
Pasqua with the Vigipirate plan but still in force under the Socialists and
reinstituted with even more vigor after September 11, 2001; that is, anyone can be stopped in a public place and asked for their identity papers.
Identity checks are perhaps predictably racialized and gendered—a
point to which I will return: Rachid, a man of North African origin I
encountered at various marches and demonstrations, explained to me
that he got checked four times a day. While, on the whole, young men
are policed more than women, as they have come to symbolize a certain
antimodern and ethnicized violence (Guénif-Souilamas and Macé 2004),
most people who are not Franco-French (i.e., white) have stories to tell
of identity checks and random arrests. I talked to a Columbian lesbian
couple, one light skinned, the other dark; they explained that Maria, the

one with the darker complexion, was regularly stopped by the police, while Valérie, with the lighter complexion, had not once been "controlled." If one does not produce papers, one can be taken into custody and deported, or given notice to leave the territory within a month. As it so happens, one of the most common places to check for papers is on the metro and, more specifically, on the RER—the trains going between Paris and the banlieues.[8] Most sans-papiers avoid the metro/RER for fear of getting "controlled." As Paul Silverstein (2004:111) writes, on the Parisian transportation network, race, space, and violence are intimately linked; that is, those taking the RER from the banlieue into Paris are understood and treated as especially prone to uncivilized, violent behavior. In this sense, policing is simultaneously linked to what people look like and where they are. The upshot is that sans-papiers are isolated in the banlieues, out of sight of the French mainstream.

But the violence against the sans-papiers is perhaps most powerfully illustrated by the increasing numbers of immigrants and refugees who are placed by the police in detention centers without trial. In France, these centers were initially instituted in the 1960s as a form of "administrative internment"; the centers coincided with the first waves of labor migration from the former colonies into France, targeting Algerians. Attention has been refocused on these centers because of their growing numbers and size and the increasingly important place they play, not only in France's politics of immigration, but as a global strategy of containment.[9] In France, there are three main categories: *zones d'attentes*, or "waiting areas," where people are put immediately upon debarking from planes or trains or boats before being deported; *locaux de rétention administrative*, or "administrative detention premises," which are found in places like police stations and where immigrants can be held up to a maximum of forty-eight hours; and *centres de rétention administrative*, or "holding centers," where people are brought before being driven back across the border and where they can be kept for thirty-two days by French law, or up to eighteen months under European directive.[10]

Zones d'attentes are spaces in airports and other ports of entry—spaces of nonliberty where those refused entry to France are detained.[11] In 2005 there were 122 *zones d'attentes* in France, and in 2008 the national association for border assistance to foreigners, ANAFE, reported close to 140 in France and the larger overseas departments and territories of France (DOM TOM), mostly in makeshift areas requisitioned by administrative authorities, such as in police stations and hotel rooms (Rodier 2003; de Loisy 2005). The decision to detain someone is purely administrative, although it is supposed to be monitored by a judge after seventy-two hours—the judge can choose to prolong the detention up until twenty days (crucially, the judge does not hear or decide on detainees' cases for asylum, simply on the right to extend detention).[12]

The most important *zone d'attente* is located on the premises of Charles de Gaulle Airport (Roissy), in Paris; otherwise known as "zapi 3," or *zone d'attente pour personnes en instance*, it was inaugurated in January 2001. French law states that those detained in *zones d'attentes* must be provided with "hotel-like service";[13] thus, the minister of interior rented rooms in the Ibis hotel, the well-known global chain of hotels. Unfortunately, rather than offering Michelin-guide quality, the Ibis hotel at Roissy has been transformed into a detention center cum prison, in which the law is effectively suspended and the police act as sovereign. Reports from the rare, controlled visits revealed that the windows were sealed shut, there was no air circulation or daylight, and, at one count, forty-two people were squashed into a room of forty square meters (approximately four hundred square feet)—and this included pregnant women. There were no bathrooms in the immediate vicinity, leaving the refugees and immigrants to be accompanied to the bathroom by a police officer, who often refused to perform this duty after a certain hour. These *zones d'attentes* have been condemned by doctors, lawyers, and activists for their insalubrious and inhumane conditions—the odors are described as suffocating and fetid, and people are crammed in "like cattle" (La Libération 2000).[14]

Only occasionally do the abuses committed in these centers erupt into public space: until 2005, NGOs were denied regular access to *zones d'attentes*.[15] During my primary period of research, from 1999 to 2001, the state allowed eight associations to visit, but each was only allowed eight visits per year, in controlled time periods; they required advance notice, and the association members were accompanied by border police at all times. These, in addition to visits by members of parliament and investigations run by the European Council's Committee for the Prevention of Torture, revealed that people's rights were regularly violated (Rodier

2003). Evidence of police violence showed up in the form of bumps, bruises, and torn clothes and was further supported by cases such as that of a woman from Sierra Leone who, eight months pregnant, miscarried in the center at Roissy due to alleged police violence. She was en route to the United States to join family members, having fled Sierra Leone after her husband disappeared. Her case became known because, with the help of an association, she decided to press charges against the police (see Associated Press 2000).

ANAFE spearheads the effort to get access to the *zones d'attentes,* particularly for lawyers and doctors; it publishes reports based on rare visits and telephone interviews, and the group documents repeated violations of fundamental rights.[16] During a one-month trial period in May 2002, which gave ANAFE regular entry into zapi 3, the organization documented hundreds of cases of abuse and violence.[17] The reports by ANAFE and undercover journalist Anne de Loisy illustrate that law has little bearing in these locales. Documented violations include moral and physical violence, humiliations, injuries at the hands of police, violations of the right to apply for asylum by refusal to register claims, and abuse of minors. ANAFE has documented hundreds of cases that go unpunished, like the Haitian who arrived at Roissy airport in December 2001 and tried to register his claim for asylum but was stopped from doing so by the border police in the *zone d'attente.* Two days later, he was beaten with a club when he tried to resist being put on an airplane and deported (ANAFE 2003). A similar case was revealed in a newspaper article in March 2001, about how a young woman from the Democratic Republic of the Congo had her legs crushed as French police attempted to drag her from a detention center onto an airplane for deportation. She had submitted a claim for asylum, which the detention center administrators simply refused to file. There are reports of Guineans, Chinese, Malians, Sierra Leonians—the list goes on—all of whom have been forcibly stopped from registering claims for asylum despite the law that refugee claimants cannot be deported without first having their claims reviewed. In the *zones d'attentes,* violations of the law are rampant: from sadistic police officers who like to kick detainees in the genitals (ANAFE 2003) to children being counted as adults, separated from their parents and detained.[18] Anne de Loisy, the undercover journalist who got access to zapi 3 as a Red Cross mediator, also documents a shocking brutality: "I was prepared for the violence regularly described by associations. Unfortunately, what I observed was worse than anything I could have imagined" (de Loisy 2005:10, my translation).[19]

The countless instances of violence in these detention centers occur with impunity—the police are rarely held accountable. The deaths of those forced from these centers onto airplanes are part of the same story: an Argentinean died in December 2002 of a heart attack after having been handcuffed by hands and feet to a seat and brutalized by the police; a twenty-four-year-old Ethiopian suffered the same fate in January 2003.[20] In this sense, those in detention centers qualify as what Achille Mbembe (2003) calls the "living dead," where civil death is on a short continuum with physical death.

While neither these centers nor these practices can be called "new," my point is that they must be located in a political environment where policing is ever more apparent and applauded. Already, in his first round as interior minister, Sarkozy was proudly dubbed the "top cop," and President Chirac garnered a similar title, "first cop of France," after he named himself head of the already extant Council of Domestic Security. Chirac and Sarkozy, and subsequently Interior Minister de Villepin, supported new laws on security that extend police power and were applauded for it by much of the French public, who see themselves in a crisis of law and order.[21] For instance, the 2003 *loi Sarkozy* promised to double the number of places in the *centres de rétention* over the subsequent five years, and the time of detention was increased to thirty-two days from the maximum twelve that previously existed (Tabet 2003). In these zones, the rule of law has been reduced to police rule and it functions along emergency lines.[22]

Struggles continue to this day for the basic right to freedom of movement in the new "borderless" Europe, the right to housing and autonomy, and the right to be free from violence and exploitation; I both participated in and witnessed a continuous stream of protest marches, occupations of buildings, and hunger strikes. Despite the proliferation of NGOs, and regardless of the protests that take place at a rate and level rarely attained elsewhere, very little ground has been gained. The question, then, is what else is going on? What is the larger context of the

Figure 1. Photos of *sans-papiers* with those who support them, by independent photographer Fabien Breuvart, plastered on the wall of the Bourse de Travail (Labor Exchange), 3rd arrondissement, Paris, May 2008.

struggle? Why were the sans-papiers able to command attention for a short period of time—to even take a stab at collective change—only to be rendered redundant, their continuing protests normalized and diffused to the extent that they are often simply a part of the French landscape (see figures 1 and 2)? We cannot answer this without understanding the interwoven stories of political economy, empire, and sovereignty.

THE CONTRADICTIONS OF CAPITAL AND LABOR

In France, as elsewhere in the global North, a significant tension has emerged: as increasingly restrictive legislation has forced borders closed, transforming the so-called open European space into Fortress Europe,[23]

Vas-y montre ta carte!

En soutien aux sans-papiers installés depuis début mai rue Charlot dans les locaux de la Bourse du Travail, venez vous faire photographier en compagnie d'un sans-papiers. Pour cela, munissez-vous de votre carte d'identité nationale française (ou d'un passeport) car vos papiers vous seront demandés pour poser devant l'objectif.
Les portraits à deux seront réalisés dans la cour de la Bourse du Travail tous les jours de la semaine de 13h à 14h, 85 rue Charlot, juste à côté de la Place de la République.

Pour en savoir plus : Fabien Breuvart, images & portraits, 35-37 rue Charlot Paris 3ᵉ. Tél. 06 65 23 95 03.

Figure 2. "Vas-y, montre ta carte!" ("Go ahead, show your ID!") "In support of the *sans-papiers* occupying the premises of the Labor Exchange on Charlot Street since early May, come get photographed in the company of a sans-papiers. For this, bring your French identity card (or your passport) because you will be asked for your papers to pose for the camera. These two-people portraits will take place in the courtyard of the Labor Exchange every day of the week, from 1pm to 2pm, 85 rue Charlot, right beside the Place de la République. For more information: Fabien Breuvart, images & portraits, 35–37 rue Charlot, Paris 3e, Tel. 06.65.23.95.03."

the black market and informal economies have grown, and labor conditions have changed to favor temporary, insecure forms of labor with no legal protection. These informal economies, largely shunned by Europeans, offer opportunities to those in the global South where conditions may be more precarious, encouraging migration. This tension is apparent in the increased demand for workers in the agricultural, garment, and construction industries in France, which is met by closed juridical doors—this was demonstrated to me clearly in conversations with sans-papiers. For instance, at a solidarity event run by a local sans-papiers collective, I met Ahmad, a thin, drawn-looking man of Maghrebi origin. The event revolved around the film *La Promesse* by the now critically acclaimed Dardenne brothers, which takes as its subject the sans-papiers in Belgium. After the film was shown, there was an open-microphone session for the sans-papiers in the audience. It was an opportunity for them to speak and share their experiences. Ahmad had been sitting behind me during the film, and we struck up a conversation afterward.

As I have already noted, I was identified as North African or *maghrébine* by nearly everyone I met, which gave me access to situations such as this—along with the attendant ethical responsibility not to abuse my power as researcher—but also denied me access to others. We exchanged information about our legal status, and then he explained to me, rather incredulously, that "it was so much easier to find work on the black market! I never had trouble. Now that I have papers, I can't find work." Ahmad is just one example of a tension between industry wanting and needing labor and the state refusing to let people in legally. Stated otherwise, he exemplifies the contradictions between capital and labor, where capital flows relatively freely while labor cannot. One might say that undocumented immigrants are desired precisely because they can be denied all rights. The French state is complicit in this process, having passed laws that produce a category of person who is neither legalizable nor deportable.[24]

I turn to these contradictions to suggest that they are significant in creating the liminal spaces in which sans-papiers often find themselves, and they have been an important element in driving the sans-papiers to political action. At the same time, these contradictions pose a very difficult challenge. In their discussions of migrant labor in contemporary Europe, Jon Gubbay (1999) and Gareth Dale (1999) explain that capitalism is at once cosmopolitan and transterritorial and yet simultaneously creates and relies upon territorial structures, specifically states. States actively organize the forces and relations of production and manage and control property and populations, both within their territories and beyond, when possible. Capitalism engenders tendencies toward labor mobility and toward the generalization of political rights and citizenship, but it simultaneously depends on the establishment of economic, political, and cultural infrastructures through which the management of social reproduction occurs. These processes in turn curtail free mobility of labor and encourage the limitation of rights (Dale and Cole 1999). Saskia Sassen (1996) has described this tension as one between *denationalizing* economic space—where practices and institutions such as global financial markets, international business law firms, NAFTA, GATT, and WTO all push for border-free economic spaces—and *renationalizing* political discourse, where the drive is to intensify border control to keep immigrants and refugees out. These contradictions and challenges posed by global capital, growing economic disparities between the North and South, and an aging European population (the United Nations reported that Europe would require 700 million immigrants by 2050 to keep the same ratio between active and retired members of society)[25] lay the groundwork for labor mobility and France's need for immigrant labor— yet they also increase France's need to assert control over its territory, enacting sovereign power by restricting access to immigrants.

The power of global capitalism—much of which derives precisely from its contradictions—is what the sans-papiers movement has bumped up against, and the strategies mobilized thus far have not been entirely suc- cessful in challenging it. The sans-papiers struggle has been most vocally and explicitly one for basic human rights, yet it would be wrong not to highlight, within this, their demand for the right to work free from exploitation. In their manifestos, they ask for the regularization of work- ers already in place, rejecting the vulnerability (précarité) that comes with either temporary or no work permits. Rather, they have argued that since there is an important relationship between the French economy and irregular migrant labor, they—and their labor—should be recognized.

Natasha Iskander goes one step further to argue that the sans-papiers movement that began in 1996 was at base a labor mobilization (Iskan- der 2007). With a study of the garment industry in the Sentier district of Paris, she suggests that the anti-immigrant policy initiatives, particularly the restrictive Pasqua laws, shut undocumented immigrants out of the informal labor markets where they held good jobs and enjoyed oppor- tunities for advancement through informal social networks. With the new laws, firms dependent on informal labor for their flexibility ended up developing hybrid forms of informality, with one part above board. This required legal work permits for the better off-the-books employ- ment, and those without papers, while flexible, were increasingly seen as a liability since if caught, their employers could be fined and firms shut down. After this crackdown on undeclared work, those without legal permits were relegated to working in underground production sites, in which they worked in both physical and social isolation, on extremely temporary terms, and in jobs that required low-skill, with no opportunity for advancement. With the isolation enforced by an increased policing of immigrants and identity cards, forcing them into the *banlieues,* they had no opportunity to challenge their substandard working conditions, and no social networks that could protect them from exploitation. Iskander therefore suggests that the labor code enforcement that came as part of the new anti-immigrant laws resulted in a new underclass of workers with few rights, and without power, who were pushed to collective action; and this came to fruition in the sans-papiers social movement.

Even while the social movement challenged rights that affect employment, rather than work arrangements themselves—such as the right to freedom of movement—the sans-papiers have made no attempt to hide their protests as driven in a critical way by labor conditions. They protest around symbolic buildings such as La Bourse (the French stock exchange) and have occupied areas such as the French Federation of Construction (NoBorder Network 2005, cited from McNevin 2006:145). They have strong links with the trade unions: at the majority of protest marches that I attended, the trade unions were present in full force, understanding the struggle as a shared one, and many of the other French activists who joined the struggle either labeled themselves as Marxists or communists, understanding this as part of the class struggle. The sans-papiers' own literature identifies them as autonomous but in solidarity with a broader movement of opposition to "neoliberalism," such as that represented at European Social Forums (McNevin 2006); here, neoliberalism is taken to mean a set of economic policies favoring marketization and moving the locus of government outside the state. As the former sans-papiers spokeswoman Madiguène Cissé told me, explaining her own role in the process, she felt it was essential to organize on the European level because of the 1985 Schengen Agreement, which coordinated border control for the European Union. She and the French sans-papiers spearheaded a European-wide network for the rights of undocumented immigrants—other nascent movements in different nation-states looked to them to lead the way. She spoke of her role as a leader with the sans-papiers in Germany, for instance. She acknowledged that their struggle took place at the level of the global political economy; she explained that this was about

North-South relations and about new forms of imperialism. That is, if the global North gets richer, it is at the expense of the global South, which produces the raw materials and absorbs the excesses of the global North. It is no wonder, then, that this has produced greater flows of migration out of the global South to escape the ever-growing poverty. As Cissé wrote, "We believe in the struggle, in Senegal and elsewhere, against structural adjustment programmes, and our struggle is one and the same struggle" (Cissé 1997, cited from News From Nowhere 2003:43).

If, as I am suggesting, the sans-papiers struggle should be understood as one against global capitalism and the economic reforms grouped under the heading "neoliberalism," and if labor rights figure high on the agenda of the human rights that they demand, we cannot ignore the echoes of the immigrant rights movements of the 1960s, which made similar claims yet explicitly linked capitalism to France's status as imperial power. I turn now to trace the connections with these earlier movements, which bring us face to face with France's status as a former imperial power and its current reality as a postcolonial state. This again proves to be both impetus and challenge for the sans-papiers movement.

REVEALING A POSTCOLONIAL STATE

The "immigrant question" in France is grounded in post–World War II migrations from the French colonial empire. The postwar period of rapid economic expansion required cheap labor that could not be recruited in great enough numbers from the carefully selected "culturally compatible" European immigrants that France desired; there was stiff competition from other European countries. France's ties with its colonies—even as the empire was being dismantled by independence struggles—ensured that an influx of immigrants came from what was coming to be known as the third world;[26] and in the 1950s and 1960s, mass migration from the colonies began to supplant European sources of labor. The single most important region of origin was North Africa: Algeria, Morocco, and Tunisia. By 1982 there were nearly 1.5 million immigrants from North Africa in France, with increasing numbers of immigrants from former sub-Saharan colonies, and Africans constituted 43 percent of the foreign population (Blatt 1997). The understanding in the 1960s and 1970s was that immigrants were purely migrant laborers who would eventually return to their countries of origin.

The sans-papiers movement not only challenges the inequalities of capitalism, but insists on a critical understanding of France as a post-colonial state, shaped both materially and ideologically by the histories and hierarchies of colonialism. The movement helped open the way to think about the colonial past and what Ann Stoler (2008) calls "the impe-rial debris" of the present. In the 1960s, in the immediate aftermath of decolonization, no link needed to be drawn between immigrants, labor, and colonialism; it was plain to see. May 1968 was a movement that recognized anti-imperialism as an essential part of the struggle against capitalism. But with the failure of May '68 to disrupt the social order in any meaningful way, the various connections to colonialism—"its mate-rial and social afterlife" (Stoler 2008:194)—were buried, even as the rem-nants have seeped out to shape the present in often unacknowledged ways. This process of erasing or forgetting the structures of the past was encouraged by the turn from the class-based struggles of the 1960s, where the typical actor was the Algerian worker—unskilled, a man without his family, a foreign national expecting to return eventually to Algeria (Wihtol de Wenden 1995)—to a politics of difference, which was ushered in by the new generation: the primary actors were the children of North African immigrants, the self-designated "Beurs."[27] They mixed ideas of universalism and citizenship with references to ethnic identity and multiculturalism, and they focused on issues of racism and police harassment as well as community and cultural services.[28] As sociologist Sylvie Tissot (2008) argues, the shift from a socioeconomic approach to an ethnoracial perspective resulted in the loss of the link to economic problems that profoundly shape immigrants' lives. From the perspective of the state, this new political language produced an understanding of immigrants and their children as the "dangerous classes," defined by unsurmountable cultural and religious differences. They were no longer people with rights to defend. In other words, the history and origins of their inequality were now viewed through the lens of cultural difference.

The sans-papiers forced this relationship between migrants, labor, and colonial history into the visible present once again, albeit in its new, reconfigured form. As Madiguène Cissé explained when asked where the sans-papiers of Saint Bernard come from: "Where do we come from, we Sans-Papiers of Saint-Bernard? It is a question we are often asked, and a pertinent one. We didn't immediately realize ourselves how relevant this question was. But, as soon as we tried to carry out a 'site inspection,' the answer was very illuminating: we are all from former French colonies, most of us from West-African countries, Mali, Senegal, Guinea and Mauritania. But there are also among us several Maghreb people (Tunisians, Moroccans, and Algerians); there is one man from Zaire and a couple who are Haitians" (Cissé 1997, cited from Notes from Nowhere 2003:1).

The postcolonial history haunting the sans-papiers' predicament was rendered explicit through the evocation of their parents' service in wars to save France, their motherland.[29] Ababacar Diop, another key spokesperson for the sans-papiers, and also of Senegalese origin like Cissé, claimed in reference to these soldiers, "This sacrifice, willingly undertaken by foreigners to defend the land of the 'rights of man and of the citizen' must be remembered. To those tempted to blame us for all the degradation of suburban public housing projects, we answer that our grandparents lived in much worse socio-economic conditions when they helped fight and defeat France's enemies" (1997b:2).

Not only did the sans-papiers evoke their service and hence France's debt to them, but as those familiar with France's civilizing mission, and its universalist language, the sans-papiers played on the notion of France as home to human rights in order to hold the French state accountable. As Diop stated, "We needed to reaffirm not only our attachment to France as the fabled land of refuge and human rights, but also our determination that the authorities should take account of our aspiration to live in France in dignity and equality" (1997b:2). The sans-papiers claim to human rights, then, was simultaneously a nationalist strategy, daring France to live up to its own self-image; a transnational claim, appealing to an international community to hold France accountable for its violations; and a postcolonial evocation of the sans-papiers' intimate knowledge and relationship with their former motherland.

While France's colonial history has grown into a troubled present, with increasing unrest in the *banlieues,* a violent backlash against Islam that Vincent Geisser (2003) has called "islamophobie,"[30] and an everyday form of racialized policing, the particular and uneven role of France's colonial past in shaping its racialized present has been—until recently, with an explosion of academic interest in the topic—selectively ignored, suppressed, or rendered invisible. Stoler (2001, 2011) calls this a "colonial aphasia," an occlusion of knowledge, a disremembering or a difficulty speaking about the relationship between empire and immigration, race and nation. This aphasia has resulted in misrecognitions, locating the idea of race inside metropolitan France as an aftermath of empire rather than an integral part of what made France in the eighteenth and nineteenth centuries, and thus central to what it means to be "foreign" or French in France today. Crucially, Stoler argues that such colonial aphasia obscures how the "interior frontiers" of the nation-state have been tied to its "exterior" ones. In a similar manner, Laurent Dubois finds it necessary to point out that, from its inception, French universalism was a complex mix of inclusion and exclusion, such that while everyone was theoretically equal, certain people were deemed "not ready" for citizenship; this argument served to justify slavery in the Caribbean. He calls this deferral of the application of universal ideas "Republican racism" and suggests that it haunts contemporary discussions around immigration in France (Dubois 2008:18). The recent surge in French scholarship engaging colonial history and postcolonial studies takes on the idea that French colonial history is a vital foundation for an engagement with contemporary debates about race, immigration, and national identity in France.[31] However, as Stoler (2011) points out, it does so without necessarily tackling the complicated relationship of French scholars to this history, for whom it has been selectively available and out of reach.

Clearly, not all sans-papiers in France come from former colonies. One notable exception in the earlier years of the sans-papiers movement was the "third collective," composed of Chinese sans-papiers. After the occupation of Saint Bernard and the regularization of some of the Africans who occupied the church, they spoke out about work conditions of "semislavery" and their lives in "prisons without bars," breaking a code of silence in the Chinese community; they subsequently formed several collectives that made demands for papers (see Les Chinois de France n.d.). Yet the history of colonialism is of primary relevance for them, too, insofar as it has helped to structure French society; those who come from places such as China or Sri Lanka still enter into a system of racial hierarchies sharpened in the history of empire. These inform where people can and do "choose" to live, and they shape the contemporary practices and logics of security, which require segregation and confinement for certain racialized populations (Stoler 2011); certainly, these practices are of concern to all sans-papiers today.

The fact that the French state has not faced the injury of colonialism head-on means, again, that the predicament of the sans-papiers cannot be recognized and addressed in its complexity. While I am not suggesting that the varied situations of the sans-papiers are determined in any easy or straightforward way by colonial histories, I do want to suggest that they must be understood as part of the "ruins" of the imperial project on which France is built—with inequality, racism, and exploitation at its base. As scholars of the colonial and postcolonial have argued, the modern French state was constituted by and through its colonies—the colonies were at once the experiment for modernity (Rabinow 1995) and the ground on which the categories of race, nation, and citizenship were determined (Stoler 1995, 1997; Silverman 1992; Dubois 2000; Conklin 1997, 2000; Lebovics 1992; Lorcin 1995; Shepard 2006). The separation of colonial bodies is what enabled the production of the French body and the French nation.

Perhaps it is unsurprising, then, that the French state has put enormous energy into reformulating the colonial narrative to both recognize and tame it, and to avoid accountability. Two years after the 2005 riots, which brought the history of colonial law into the present through the enactment of the original 1955 law on states of emergency, Sarkozy gave a speech in Dakar to "the youth of Africa," which at once acknowledged France's colonial past and yet unabashedly repeated the underlying tropes of the civilizing mission: that Africa and Africans were backward, uncivilized, outside of history. Sarkozy began his speech with acknowledgments such as, "The colonizer came, he took, he helped himself, he exploited. He pillaged resources and wealth that did not belong to him. He stripped the colonized of his personality, of his liberty, of his land, of the fruit of his labor." But then he quickly retreated from taking responsibility for this violence by saying, "The colonizer took, but I want to say with respect, that he also gave. He built bridges, roads, hospitals, dispensaries and schools. He turned virgin soil fertile. He gave of his effort, his work, his know-how."[32] From there, his speech descended into themes drawn from what Mbembe (2007) aptly calls "a colonial and racist library." A few words are sufficient to show that Sarkozy's approach to Africa is one that dates from the nineteenth century, taken almost word for word from G. W. F Hegel's *Reason in History:* "The tragedy of Africa is that the African has not fully emerged into history. . . . In this imaginary world where everything starts over and over again there is no place for human adventure or for the idea of progress. In this universe where nature commands all, man escapes from the anguish of history that torments man, but he rests immobile in the center of a static order where everything seems to be written beforehand" (Sarkozy 2007).

Many African intellectuals, writers, and politicians spoke back and expressed how the new French ruling elites "were trapped in a frivolous and exotic vision of the continent" (Mbembe 2007) that revealed both their fears and fantasies of Africa as an ahistoric, undeveloped world, beholden to nature rather than history, and the cause of its own present misfortunes. While many found Sarkozy's words shocking and violent, they reveal only too clearly France's attitude to its colonial past, which, while riddled with contradictions—both making a show out of acknowledging the injury and simultaneously repeating it—ultimately refuses accountability. Rather, as historian Mamadou Diouf states, it assumes the arrogance and contempt of the master for his slave—taking the liberty of both defining and reprimanding the slave (Ndoye 2007, interview with Diouf).

In another speech a few months later in December 2007, Sarkozy began a three-day visit to Algeria by denouncing colonialism as "profoundly unjust," but he again avoided apologizing for the violent crimes the French are accused of committing during the period of French rule from 1830 to 1962, and particularly during the bloody war of independence from 1954 to 1962 (see New York Times 2007). This approach fluctuates between trying to erect firm borders between France and its former colonies, assuming colonialism is a thing of the past, and acting as if the French metropole and its former colonies are still part of one political space. For instance, when he was interior minister, Sarkozy made several visits to African countries such as Mali and Benin to discuss issues of immigration and security and to promote his new, highly restrictive immigration bill. (He was greeted with people shouting, "Racist, go home." Mali is the sub-Saharan African nation-state with the highest number of immigrants in France, but only half of them have papers.)[33] On the one hand, he was there to demarcate the borders of France (and French responsibility) from Africa. On the other hand, the underlying message of his visit was that the French empire was intact: in most other contexts, it would have been the foreign minister who went to meet with high-ranking officials in a foreign country, not the minister responsible for *domestic* affairs.

In the face of these contradictory French policies, there have been new social movements cropping up since 2005 to fight for recognition of the relationship between immigration, racism, sexual violence, and colonialism. Groups like Les Indigènes de la République and Le Collectif Féministe pour l'Égalité have put out calls to women who experience racist and sexist violence to come together to form an indigenous, anti-imperialist feminism, one that recognizes the imperial legacy of contemporary French political formations. Les Indigènes de la République's first public statement in January 2005 begins, "Discriminated against in employment, housing, health, school and leisure, people whose origins lie in the colonies, former or current, and in post-colonial immigration are the first victims of social exclusion and precariousness. Independent of their real origins, these populations from the vulnerable neighborhoods are indigenized, relegated to the margins of society" (Mouvement des Indigènes de la République 2005, my translation). With these statements and their actions, they are rewriting the accepted links between past and present, and between groups of people, joining those not previously imagined as part of one narrative. While I was in Paris in May 2008, I witnessed their *marche antiraciste et décoloniale* (antiracist and decolonizing march) as I was walking through the largely immigrant 18th arrondissement, past Montmartre. What struck me most were the protesters' signs, invoking the legacies of diverse figures such as Frantz Fanon, Che Guevara, Zapata, Nelson Mandela, James Baldwin, Aimé Césaire, Angela Davis, and Jean Genet (see figure 3). While the rest of the march felt very familiar to me, an echo of the many marches I participated in with the sans-papiers, this transnational, multigenerational legacy of oppression was not one that I had seen invoked before. These protesters were laying claim to the visions of leaders who had fought the legacies of colonialism, and they were marching for all those whose lives have been affected by this history—the sans-papiers included.

That said, Les Indigènes de la République are far from popular; they have been critiqued and outcast by mainstream Franco-French feminist groups and by many on the political and academic Left. All indications show that the French state and much of the French public are still not ready to claim responsibility for the migration patterns and racial formations that issue from the colonial restructuring of the global landscape. There is still a difficulty acknowledging that the very concept of French citizenship—which depends on exclusion as much as inclusion in its universalist principles—cannot be divorced from the exploitation of labor and resources that happened in the colonies and by the racialization of this process. The sans-papiers movement, then, is both borne of and circumscribed by this enduring public secret.

THE CHALLENGES OF LAW AND SOVEREIGNTY

In addition to the challenges of contemporary capitalism and the history of colonialism, the sans-papiers movement has been shaped by changes in the nature of sovereignty. These changes have already been well-documented and analyzed theoretically—in particular, the tension between national and transnational sovereignty and a tension between state and popular sovereignty (Balibar 2004; Ong 1999; Sassen 1996, 2006). I want to point to some of the specific manifestations of the changes in sovereignty and law in France when I was there and the resulting types of insecurity.

Figure 3. Marche antiraciste et décoloniale (antiracist and decolonizing march), organized by Les Indigènes de la République, May 2008, 18th arrondissement, Paris.

European integration gives concrete form to the tension between sovereignty at the national and transnational levels and to the way people actually experience this as instability. The Single European Act of 1986 first instituted a common European space without trade borders. This was then integrated into the Maastricht Treaty, which envisaged a common space without internal borders in which goods and capital could circulate. Creating a common space, however, raised the question of the circulation of people who were not European Union nationals; in other words, the question became how to control the movement of *certain* people in a space with no borders. The tension was one of free circulation for some and not others and the coordination of national legislation, which controls borders, with European legislation, which opens national borders.[34]

The Schengen Agreement was created for this purpose in 1985—to reconcile the opening of borders to capital with security concerns about people. It helped enable the movement of capital and the control of people, with a coordination of border controls and policing. But it is important to note that the Schengen space does not map directly onto the European Union: while the EU adopted the Schengen Agreement as part of EU law in 1999, certain states opted out of parts of the agreement, such as the United Kingdom and Ireland; on the other hand, non-EU members such as Norway and Iceland opted in. The agreement was thus accompanied by a series of different statuses for (a) members of the Schengen states, (b) EU citizens from non-Schengen states, (c) non-EU citizens who are residents in a Schengen state, and (d) non-EU, non-Schengen citizens. Not only does this system of differential status challenge key aspects of the French republican ideology, which refuses to distinguish between people on the basis of nationality, but it has led to a broader anxiety about how to control and patrol space. For instance, it is impossible to distinguish between citizens, residents, or Schengen members simply by looking at them—it is impossible to know whom to check at borders. The uncertainty has resulted in racial profiling and, in general, increased policing and increasingly harsh immigration policies and controls (Rodier 1997; Hollifield 1994). One example of this in France was the creation, in 1994, of a commission within the Ministry of Interior with enormous police powers over entry, residence, and employment.[35] It was the first time an institution had been created with the sole purpose of policing immigration, and it became responsible for coordinating all activities of the national police force against undocumented immigration (Samers 2003).

In this climate of insecurity, the harmonization of immigration and refugee policies in Europe was proposed to avoid the negative effects of the policies of member states on each other. This issue has taken tentative shape through the Treaty of Amsterdam (which entered into force May 1, 1999). This treaty gave the European Union responsibility to introduce a Common Immigration and Asylum System—also a priority of the Lisbon Treaty, which entered into force December 2009—but this common system has yet to be realized. Harmonization touches on the most sensitive questions of national sovereignty: borders and policing. In this sense, member states have been loathe to touch these issues.[36] Thus, while the European Parliament and European Commission should be more involved in this process, their roles have proved to be largely symbolic; their positions are taken into consideration but most often elicit antagonism. In the absence of democratic procedures at the European Community or national level, it has been the governments who decide among themselves on the general contours of migration control. Thus, while there is some secondary European law to harmonize immigration and asylum policies, largely instituted since 2004, earlier decisions were coded through "resolutions," "recommendations," or "position papers," none of which have clear legal grounding and do not formally link states. The European Parliament earlier called this "pseudo-legislation" that "leaves much to be desired" (Rodier 1997:229–30). The resulting policies have taken the lowest common denominator of the EU member states, sidelining questions raised by the European Commission about the equal right to freedom of movement. Instead, uncertainty has led intergovernmental cooperation to privilege policing as the way to manage migration flows. Jurist Claire Rodier (1997) suggests that, paradoxically, not involving EU institutions has led to the increasing autonomy of the politics of immigration; while escaping democratic controls by these institutions, the pseudo-legislation of immigration does not always follow the desired outcome of the member states. This has increased the situation of instability and insecurity.

These conflicting drives to establish sovereignty at the national or transnational level, illustrated by the process of European integration, do not undo the rule of law, but they blur its boundaries, creating partial or graduated legal regimes, which have led to legal voids for many.[37] In other words, it is no longer clear who can claim to be a subject of the law, or which law one should claim to be a subject of. It requires a body of new laws, policies, mechanisms, and institutions that are still in formation. This uncertainty is felt by EU citizens and residents at all levels: where and how they can travel; their status at home and abroad (and the meaning of "abroad"); where they can find employment; where, when, and on what to vote. This same inability to ascertain one's status is particularly true for immigrants and refugees in Europe. As just one example of this, immigration law falls under European jurisdiction, while citizenship is still the prerogative of the nation-state. There is no clear or circumscribed juridical realm—there are overlapping realms, accompanied by legal voids.

I had my own experience of this legal uncertainty. I had asked for a research visa while a graduate student at Stanford in California, and I was told by the French embassy to ask in Canada since I am a Canadian citizen. When I arrived in Montreal en route to Paris, the French embassy told me that because I was a student at an American university, I should apply in San Francisco. It was too late; I already had a ticket and was on my way to Paris, so my only option was to enter on a tourist visa. The tourist visas allow stays of three months, after which one must leave the country. One is free to return after that, although how many times, no one could tell me. I also did not know what constituted leaving the country; what with the European Union, did it mean leaving the EU or just France? Did it mean going outside the Schengen space—and since Britain had opted out of it, did it mean I could just go to London on the Eurostar, through the Channel Tunnel? Did I need to return to Canada, or to the United States? Could I keep coming back indefinitely, as long as I left whatever constituted the French space every three months? No one could answer all these questions. This is just one small example of the spaces of juridical indeterminacy that help ground the new emphasis on regimes of care, which are less reliant on law than on moral legitimacy.

I end with the words of the interior minister at the time, Nicolas Sarkozy, to reveal the clear anxiety around sovereignty.[38] In a statement on the sans-papiers published in January 2003 in the French national newspaper, *Le Monde*, Sarkozy explicitly blamed the European Union for the problem of illegal immigration in France (Le Monde 2003). He stated that the large number of short-term visas delivered by member countries of the European Union was the origin of illegal immigration, constituting an overturning of procedure. For instance, he explained that visas for Algerians had increased from 48,000 in 1996 to 277,000 in 2001. To solve the "problem" of illegal immigration, he claimed that France needed to take control over its own visas and should encourage other EU members to do the same. His statement is a call for a reestablishment of sovereign power at the national level and, when this proves infeasible, for the coordination between EU partners on a common policed border that will keep immigrants out. In other words, it admits to a reconfigured notion of sovereignty, one that leaves many gaps and uncertainties; and these gaps and uncertainties form the groundwork for the new and shifting forms of government.

·   ·   ·   ·   ·

It is in the context of the challenges of global capitalism, the "ruins" (Stoler 2008) of colonialism, and a fluctuating system of law and sovereignty that the sans-papiers struggle must be understood. These factors provide the drive to migrate, and they simultaneously make it nearly impossible to live in conditions that are nonexploitative or nondiscriminatory. In this sense, they create the conditions for political struggle, and yet they also circumscribe it. This context is critical in order to understand the growth of regimes of care; for one, regimes of care allow us to ignore painful histories, entrenched inequalities, and our complicity in these by blocking out all but the present.

These challenges help explain why the group of primarily African men who participated in weekly marches around the statue at the Place du Châtelet in the center of Paris, chanting "papers for all," were seen as a tourist curiosity rather than as people who live in conditions where exploitation and violence are part of daily life. I joined these sans-papiers in demonstrating several times—they were there every week without fail—and I remember thinking that anywhere else we would be noticed, we would disrupt public space. Instead, the chants were recuperated into a narrative about exotic African rhythms as they sang and played the drums. Even while in the center of Paris, the sans-papiers were effectively out of sight—invisible to the state for whom they do not officially exist, invisible to the public except in their occasional eruptions into the space of Paris proper with demonstrations that are quickly quashed or subdued. I realized, gradually, that they had become more visible in another guise: as suffering bodies, as victims. That is, they were more visible to the state and to the public in their suffering and thus less visible as political actors, both in the sense of a threatening or potentially liberatory mass and as individuals with pasts and futures—individuals who imagine and desire. I turn in the next chapter to the development of the politics of care and its central figure of the morally legitimate suffering body, focusing on the "new humanitarianism."

TWO   Genealogies of Care

THE NEW HUMANITARIANISM

With the effects of severe economic recessions in the late 1980s, Médecins sans Frontières and Médecins du Monde decided to bring their missions back "home" to help those excluded from systems of social security in France. In 1993 Bernard Granjon, the president of MDM-France, asked, "Must we accept, in this rich country which is France, in the homeland of the rights of man and of the citizen, the ineluctable spiral of poverty which results in what more and more resembles professional and social apartheid?" (Granjon 1993, cited from Fox 1995:1614). These medical humanitarian organizations joined with other NGOs in what they called Mission Solidarité France, a network of centers across the country instituted to ensure that the socially excluded received free medical and social services, and to help reinsert the excluded into the mainstream social security system. This same impetus to bring humanitarianism home led MSF and MDM to advocate for the sans-papiers.

RESO, which in English stands for Health Access Network for People in Vulnerable Situations),[1] was just one of these medical humanitarian organizations, composed of former and current MDM members. I interviewed one of the main doctors of RESO, Daniel. I visited him in the central RESO office, located behind the Hôpital Rothschild in the 12th arrondissement of Paris. He was young and clearly passionate about his work. In addition to running RESO, he had various trips planned with MDM missions. He opened charts and computer programs to explain how RESO functioned, demonstrating how he kept track of all the network doctors and participants, while avoiding a parallel system that duplicated services of mainstream medical and social organizations. He answered a few calls while I was there, speaking to patients, diagnosing them as best he could over the phone in order to determine if they needed to see a doctor in person. Daniel admitted that he chose to be a doctor precisely to do humanitarian work and to travel. He explained that it was the best entry into the kind of political work he wanted to do. This was striking to me: When did it become true that humanitarianism was the best way to do politics? What kind of politics? If in the last chapter we saw how the sans-papiers movement has struggled to change the exclusionary politics of the French state, here, I turn to think about how humanitarianism and other "regimes of care" have come to play a greater role in the governance of immigrants. This despite the fact that such regimes of care do not purport to be about politics, but about emergencies and about protection, care, and compassion.

My goal is to understand the transfer of political processes to a form of action based on the moral imperative and grounded in benevolence and compassion. To this end, I trace the genealogy of one critical transnational regime of care—what has been called the "new humanitarianism," referring to the movement of *sans-frontière-isme* that started with Médecins sans Frontières in 1971. I suggest that, in practice, this shift to the moral imperative occurs through a conflation of the social, the political, and the medical: for instance, illness becomes one of the primary ways not only to render visible but to *experience* forms of alienation, isolation, malaise, inequality, hardship, violence, or disability. And rather than cure people, the goal—grounded in a medical logic—is to care for them in the immediate, to treat them, regardless of whether they can be cured. As Xavier Emmanuelli (2005:121–22)—a cofounder of MSF and the founder of the French SAMU Social, or social emergency service, a spin-off of France's emergency medical assistance service, SAMU—so revealingly states, it is the difference between *soigner* and *guérir:* caring and curing.[2] He suggests that a doctor's role is to care, first and foremost; to ease immediate suffering rather than to dispense with the reasons for the suffering. This is certainly true; but translated into the sociopolitical realm, this has meant that, rather than change the conditions in which people live and thereby improve human life on a broader scale, the focus is on alleviating pain in the present moment. While most would argue that we always need both responses, albeit at differing times, the problem here is that all too often only one is put forward for the most disenfranchised—longer-term improvement in life conditions is displaced in favor of emergency response.

I explore the increasing emphasis on doing politics through regimes of care by discussing two movements born about twenty years apart, but brought into the world by many of the same actors: Médecins sans Frontières and SAMU Social, the social emergency service just mentioned. I am interested in their histories, but it is not accidental that both play important roles in the management of immigrants in France today. MSF is more internationally acclaimed, while SAMU Social is largely known as a domestic program, yet they each have both international and domestic ambitions; and while MSF exemplifies the notion of humanitarianism and SAMU Social is more focused on what it calls "social emergency," they each do both humanitarian and emergency social work, revealing the continuum between the two. To me, these organizations exemplify the contemporary medicalization of the social, where an emphasis on the suffering body guides all action. My goal in this chapter is to understand some of the characteristics of what I see as this sociopolitical logic of caring rather than curing, and the context and history of its development, in order to better understand how it later comes to bear in the realm of French immigration politics. I want to be clear that I am not making an expansive argument about MSF or SAMU Social as the founding "fathers" of this type of moralist antipolitics. Rather, I am working with an assumption that both medical humanitarianism and SAMU Social are nodal points, helping to bring the idiom and the actors of medical emergency to sociopolitical situations in a context simultaneously shaped by many other factors. Perhaps even more importantly, they have brought the temporality of medical emergencies to social and political problems.

MSF has clearly played an important role in spreading this form of discourse and practice around the world; winning the Nobel Peace Prize in 1999 is just one example of its role as global moral leader. But I suggest that its increasingly significant presence has also worked to silence more explicitly political responses. Indeed, scholars have shown that humanitarianism has become a central feature of democratic politics in the West, one of the characteristic modalities of globalization (Calhoun 2008, de Waal 2007). Of course, its constituents are clear that it will not—and should not—save the world. It does not act with longer-term political consequences in mind. It avoids precisely this, in the name of immediate, urgent, and temporary care and in the name of political neutrality. Set against a different vision of humanitarianism that sees itself as part of a larger project of social transformation and improvement of the human condition, this new humanitarianism—which MSF spearheaded—is grounded in the ethical and moral imperative to bring relief to those suffering and to save lives, regardless of political affiliation—and that is it.[3] Proponents of this form of humanitarianism argue that it is precisely the ability to isolate victims in their present crisis, outside of politics and history, that allows humanitarian organizations to do their work, to render borders irrelevant in the name of a higher moral injunction to prevent and relieve the suffering of others. Yet, in the absence of other types of long-term structural responses (i.e., curing) coordinated or enacted by political movements, or even by institutions like the state, humanitarian NGOs end up filling in the gaps; the result is a conservative management of social and political problems, one that works to retain what is already there, rather than to change it or to plan for a different future. This leaves no room to imagine a better world, no place to ground hope that spans more than the time of an emergency. It also often entails parallel systems for different populations and immediate and urgent care for the most disenfranchised only when their suffering becomes unavoidably visible.

In what follows, I give a brief history of MSF and of SAMU Social, focusing on a few defining characteristics in order to better understand this particular form of emergency governance, its contradictions and tensions, and how it embeds a form of antipolitical moralism. The two groups' stories are interrelated; I tell them together here to emphasize the larger context of which they are a part. But first, I give a brief description of the roots of humanitarianism in Catholic charity; in particular, I describe the specificity of the French context and its history of mixing the medical, the social, and the political. I want to emphasize that the compassion driving humanitarianism is a hybrid form, simultaneously religious and secular. Throughout the chapter, I focus on the French context while making clear that humanitarianism has been both a way to create a new internationalism as well as a new international role for France—in other words, French humanitarianism is practiced simultaneously as a form of nationalism and universalism, with international significance.

HUMANITARIAN ROOTS: THE HISTORY OF FRENCH CHARITY

The ties between the social, the medical, and a universalist politics underlie humanitarianism. But these specific linkages have their French genesis in Catholic charity. Indeed, as we will see, contemporary humanitarianism brings together the ideals of the Rights of Man with an inheritance from the Catholic Church: in some sense, republican and clerical traditions find their reconciliation here.[4] I take France's history of charity in hospitals to be relevant in terms of the structural similarities and continuities with the new humanitarianism, but most importantly I trace it here because those who helped form the new humanitarianism look to French Catholic charity either as inspiration and forerunner or as a set of ideologies and practices to distinguish themselves from. Xavier Emmanuelli illustrates the former position. Daniel, the RESO doctor, exemplifies the latter; he claimed to find Church-based charity abhorrent because it treats people like objects, not human beings, while humanitarianism involves a form of exchange between human beings. Either way, both positions invoke this history of charity. What follows, then, is in many ways an ethnography of this history in the present, a history powerfully summoned by those involved in humanitarianism to explain who they are and what they do.

French notions of health have a history of explicitly mixing the social, medical, and religious, such that France had the largest system of medical charity in Europe in the late eighteenth and early nineteenth centuries; in 1791 France had the largest hospital population of any European state, with 120,000 hospital inmates, while England had mere 3,000 in comparison (Jones 1989:8). Of course hospitals were very different establishments in the ancien régime; they were primarily social rather than medical institutions, catering both to *pauvres malades* and *malades pauvres*—the paupers who were sick and sick individuals who, incidentally, were poor. However, we can see continuity in France in the ambiguity between poverty and illness, the social and the medical, compassion and repression, in both how charity functioned then and how state social services function now.

I conducted interviews with three doctors who worked for Paris's SAMU and SAMU Social. All independently evoked France's history of charity in hospitals when speaking about their own work and how they combined medical and social issues. In describing SAMU Social—which functions in many ways like France's early hospitals, taking the poor off the streets with the double-edged task of caring for and disciplining them—Dr. Ibanez, one of the primary SAMU Social doctors, drew on his own version of the history of French hospitals, the Hôtels Dieu, and their role in caring for both social and medical needs. The moment I walked into his office in Paris's emergency service headquarters, which adjoined Hôpital Necker in the 15th arrondissement, he launched into a passionate history of France's hospitals, drawing diagrams on the blackboard to make sure I understood. According to Dr. Ibanez, the French Hôtels Dieu were Catholic institutions that housed and protected the poor when the poor symbolized God. With the rise of Protestantism, the poor were abandoned by God and no longer cared for. He claimed that this was also the beginning of capitalism, when the poor became bothersome to the bourgeois and were thus put in prisons rather than hospitals—in other words, the hospitals were transformed into prisonlike institutions and the poor were criminalized. A new emergency medical service was started by religious orders to give shelter to those in need; but again, with Protestantism, the poor found themselves out in the cold. With the French Revolution, the priests were no longer welcome in the hospitals, and doctors replaced them, but in the interest of caring for the rich. He said that, while there is public assistance today, it is of a different character. He made a distinction between *aide* (help), *assistance* (assistance), and *secours* (going to someone's aid): The first he explained as the grounding of medical ethics—medicine serves whomever needs help. The second derives from Protestantism, and he qualified it as an investment that must be profitable. And the third he explained as Catholic charity, given freely. His version of the history of French hospitals embeds a critique of capitalism that informed the founders of medical humanitarianism—as we will see, they rejected a professionalized medicine that only feeds and serves the rich.

While this is clearly Dr. Ibanez's version of history, and while it was obviously simplified to make a point to me, according to most historians the connection between the medical and the social is indeed grounded in the first hospitals. In medieval France the hospital was a place for the suffering poor, which included the sick; they were seen as holy, close to God. The Reformation brought a new rationalized and laicized form of assistance to the poor that, according to historian Colin Jones, actually spanned the Catholic and Protestant divide (contrary to Dr. Ibanez's version). It encompassed a new form of compassion to the deserving poor, leaving the undeserving—beggars and vagrants—out. The desacralization of poverty led to the involvement of governments in poor relief, perhaps most importantly because it was an issue of public order. As Jones (1989:3) notes, the movement of reform may be characterized overall as one of social discipline. Because of France's early centralization of political authority, the relief schemes for the poor were implemented on a far larger scale than anywhere else in Europe. However, respect for the Catholic Church's autonomy stopped plans for a secular nationwide system. Instead, the earlier hospitals were refurbished by the Church, and new ones established at the end of the seventeenth century proliferated nationwide, called the Hôpitaux Généraux. They were oriented around religiously inspired charity—yet this charity encompassed both compassion and repression. Foreshadowing the consequences of the medical humanitarianism built into France's contemporary illness clause (see chapter 3), Jones describes what he calls the "charitable imperative" of the ancien régime: "Just as the charitable donor acted out of moral compunction, so the recipient of charity might have to be forced to play out the role of the grateful pauper" (1989:7).

The Hôpitaux Généraux were oriented to the helpless poor, including the homeless, old people, the disabled, orphans, and foundlings, whereas the Hôtels Dieu were created early in the seventeenth century for the paupers who were sick *(les pauvres malades)*. However, the distinction between the poor and the sick was difficult to make. Jones writes that the Hôtels Dieu persisted in serving social rather than medical requirements. Interestingly, he writes that they often served as a staging post for itinerant or migrant workers, providing them with a roof over their heads and solid food to tide them over. An eighteenth-century hospital physician suggested that these people were not really ill but resting. This definition of illness, however, begs the question (Jones 1989:10–11)—again, this resonates with the contemporary situation. Both types of ancien régime hospital served as a surrogate family for individuals whose biological family could not support them; we see echoes of this in the contemporary hospital clinics for the marginalized and underserved.

The change from charity hospitals as the basis for dealing with the poor sick (the wealthy sick were treated in their homes) came with the establishment of the welfare state, when social services were rendered the domain of the secular state and were systematized. "Government of the social" is another name for this transformation in French democracy, dating from the Revolution of 1848, which separated moral duties from legal rights in the process of dealing with inequality (Procacci 1989; Donzelot 1991). Government of the social, which made moral and ethical concerns central to forms of government, was a response to the 1848 revolutionary movement, where the poor claimed a *right* to labor as the political solution to their poverty. This implied state intervention in the market to ensure the right of each individual to work. Social economists subverted this popular demand on the state by proposing philanthropy as an alternative framework to economic and juridical intervention. Instead of labor being a right, the problem was recast as one of society having a secular, moral duty toward its members by encouraging work. Social sympathy was stressed and cultivated over all other sentiments, including religiously inspired charity. This was meant to counter the self-interest of the modern, economic subject, while leaving the economic system intact. These technical practices of care managed the newly identified "social" needs of the population by marking each problem as discrete—health, or the regulation of housing—and addressing them administratively, each with their own set of experts: psychologists, social workers, public health workers, teachers, and so on.

We are at a moment now where the reconfiguration of the welfare state and its system of social services has led to a renewed need for help or support to treat the marginalized and excluded, categories that are incorporating more and more of the population. This has set the stage for the development of medical humanitarianism, which as we will see enacts its own form of government, drawing on the techniques developed through social government while simultaneously rejecting of the idea of bureaucratized charity. These new humanitarians looked instead to emotive responses, not rational or institutionalized ones. In this sense, religiously inspired charity is not only a forerunner but a contemporary; even in the French republican context, it never fully disappeared. In particular, while the French Catholic Church was attacked by secularists at home, missionary medicine found a home in the colonial empire. Catholic doctors in the 1920s and 1930s attacked great endemic diseases through their work in the colonies (Taithe 2004); and later, many compared the "French doctors" of the new medical humanitarianism to medical missionary Albert Schweitzer, even if the MSF founders themselves had a less clear relationship to this history, sometimes claiming, sometimes distancing themselves from it.[5] In the contemporary global context, faith-based humanitarianism is perhaps the most rapidly growing form of humanitarianism (see also de Waal 2008). In this sense, it is worth recognizing that the commitment to "humanity" at the heart of the new humanitarianism is not so different from that of its religious counterparts; that is, according to some of its founders, this is a "modern expression of the same religious fervour" (Taithe 2004:155). It also serves as a reminder that charity incorporates both a form of help and a mode of social control—a way of disciplining a population no longer fully disciplined by the nation-state. But let us now turn to the development of this new humanitarianism.

THE NEW HUMANITARIANISM: INTRODUCING MSF AND SAMU SOCIAL

Humanitarianism has a long and sometimes ambiguous history, largely because it is not easily defined. Religious orders dispensing charity and abolition efforts to ban slavery are early examples, but the direct precursor to the new *sans frontières* medical humanitarianism—and an important player ever since—is the Red Cross movement, which was started in 1864 by a Swiss businessman, Henry Dunant, concerned by the plight of suffering soldiers.[6] The mandate of the International Committee for the Red Cross (ICRC) was the protection of, and rendering assistance to, victims of war. During and after the Second World War, a number of humanitarian organizations were born, such as Oxfam (Oxford Famine Relief Committee), some of which also fell under the rubric of the United Nations, such as UNICEF. French humanitarianism, however, was conceived considerably later.

Médecins sans Frontières was founded in 1971 by a small group of French physicians, "adventurers . . . mercenaries of health,"[7] the most vocal of which was Bernard Kouchner, in conjunction with journalists writing for a medical journal called *Tonus*. In the context of the civil war in Nigeria, these physicians served as volunteers in Biafra doing medical relief work among the Ibo. The founding of MSF grew out of their reaction to the International Red Cross's strict approach to neutrality in war zones, which involved a high degree of confidentiality because the emergency work of such international organizations was both made possible and constrained by agreements between states. The Red Cross and other international organizations had been providing equal amounts of relief to both sides in the Nigerian conflict, but in the spring of 1968 the government of Nigeria withdrew support for relief in an attempt to force the rebels into negotiations. A few NGOs like Oxfam decided to break with the tradition and airlift in food without the government's permission.[8]

Kouchner was one of the volunteers for the Red Cross who decided to flout its policy on confidentiality and to talk to journalists about what he had seen: "By keeping silent, we doctors were accomplices in the systematic massacre of a population" (Koucher 1986, cited from Allen and Styan 2000:830). Returning to France from Biafra in 1969, he started an international committee against genocide in Biafra; but it was in 1971, when the Biafra physicians met the *Tonus* journalists who were independently calling for a *secours médical français* (French medical rescue team), that this group was constituted as a new species of NGO called Médecins sans Frontières.

MSF emphasized four key principles that, while constantly subject to the organization's own self-critical examination, still largely hold true for the group today: "the most important principles of humanitarian action are humanity, which posits the conviction that all people have equal dignity by virtue of their membership in humanity, impartiality, which directs that assistance is provided based solely on need, without discrimination among recipients, neutrality, which stipulates that humanitarian organizations must refrain from taking part in hostilities or taking actions that advantage one side of the conflict over another, and independence, which is necessary to ensure that humanitarian action only serves the interests of war victims, and not political, religious, or other agendas" (de Torrente 2004:5). As Nicolas de Torrente, the executive director of MSF-USA, writes, these "embody humanitarian action's single-minded purpose of alleviating suffering, unconditionally and without any ulterior motive" (2004:5).

SAMU Social was created twenty-two years later, in 1993, by Xavier Emmanuelli, a cofounder of MSF—and subsequently a rival of Kouchner[9]—with the help of several of his former MSF comrades. SAMU Social functions as an addition to the French emergency medical assistance service, SAMU, with a mandate to manage social emergencies, that is, to help people on the street who are either in physical or social distress and to respond to calls from homeless people. SAMU Social workers either take people to medical services, to an emergency shelter, or to a day-time shelter; they transport them and ensure that they are properly cared for. It is no accident that many of those now served by SAMU Social are sans-papiers. They compose the majority of the disenfranchised, itinerant population.

Here I want to note that SAMU proper—that is, the original emergency medical service—predates both MSF and SAMU Social, and it arguably played as critical a role in the development of MSF as it did in its namesake, SAMU Social. The practice of medical intervention in emergencies, on which MSF is based, developed with the SAMU movement in the late 1950s and 1960s. The idea to bring medical help to the site of the accident was new, rather than to rush victims to the emergency rooms of hospitals. MSF was made thinkable and possible by the technical skills and logic of emergency medicine, which was grounded in the idea of moving the treatment to the victim, rather than the victim to the treatment; and these were developed by SAMU, which functioned on a semivoluntary basis until it was instituted by the French state in 1972 (see Taithe 2004).

Emmanuelli writes in his memoir, *L'homme en état d'urgence* (Man in a State of Emergency), that the same concerns that drove him to help found MSF motivated him to create this social service for those who are suffering. He envisioned them as sister institutions; early on he dreamed of an association called Emir, or Équipe Médicale d'Intervention Rapide (Rapid Medical Intervention Team), which he said was a combination of what later became two separate organizations: MSF and SAMU. While MSF works on the international scale to intervene in wars, disasters, and displacements of people, SAMU Social works on the domestic scale to address the crises brought about by gaps in social services, particularly for those most excluded, such as the homeless. That said, while each branch of SAMU Social works locally, Emmanuelli has exported the idea of an emergency social service to an international arena, because, as he explains, as the global North exports capitalism and its model of development, it exports the corresponding forms of exclusion. He created SAMU Social International in 1998, which now has a worldwide presence.[10]

In the rest of this chapter, I elaborate on three defining and innovative features of MSF and SAMU Social. I see these as laying the groundwork for the regimes of care that have come to occupy such an important place in managing those who are disenfranchised. While many may be familiar with MSF's founding, I work in each example to reveal that the translation of political problems into the antipolitics of care is an inextricable part of the new humanitarianism.

CHALLENGING BORDERS: UNIVERSALISMS AND THE SUFFERING OF HUMANITY

I begin with the way that MSF infused universalism with new meaning and substance, most notably, by breaking down barriers and challenging notions of state sovereignty. Yet I suggest that MSF's new universalism marks a shift from the universalism imagined in May 1968—a form of leftist solidarity—to a universalism based on the individualism of human rights, grounded in a moral, *not* a political, imperative and enacted in the temporal present. In other words, this universalism also produced a different vision of humanity and a new strategy to protect it.

The organization's name itself—Médecins sans Frontières—indicated a desire to put aside conventional borders of nation-states, to challenge sovereignty. While MSF never purported to suggest that borders are irrelevant—the name is about overcoming barriers more than borders (Redfield 2005:20)—the group disavows any political or religious affiliation or identification and assert its independence from political and governmental bodies. It does not agree that a nation should be free to determine its own destiny. Its vision is a global one, guided by a belief in human dignity and liberty. Its vision of medicine is also transcendentally universalistic: it claims that because "illness and injury do not respect borders," neither should medical care (see Fox 1995). Despite the extant mandate instituted in 1948 by the Universal Declaration of Human Rights to put aside the rules of sovereignty in cases of human rights abuses, this mandate was never insisted upon, let alone acted upon in so clear a way. MSF in many ways spearheaded a group of what international affairs scholar James

Rosenau has called sovereignty-free actors that include Greenpeace and Amnesty International, each positioning itself on an international stage previously reserved for states (see Brauman 2004:406).

This universalistic aspect of MSF has a distinctly French flavor; that is, the French have long grounded their politics on a paradigm of universalism.[11] Yet I want to focus on the specificity of the universal humanity that developed with MSF. Certainly the uprisings of May '68 were driven by a commitment to universalism; May '68 was a political moment that deeply influenced the founders of MSF. It was the biggest strike in the history of the French workers' movement and the biggest mass movement in French history. The strike was not just about pay and conditions; it was a social movement that nearly brought down the government, one that sought to disrupt the social and political order. While the official crisis lasted just one month, the political movement of which it was a part encompassed a period of twenty years: from the mid-1950s to the mid-1970s. This was an era shaped by strains of Marxism and utopianism: Maoist, Trotskyist, and anarchist theories and groups found their place, along with Althusserianism in the university context. Universalism here was about equality and solidarity. A member of the Communist Party and a medical student at this time, Bernard Kouchner was shaped by this era. But one might say that those who joined MSF a few years later, and ultimately took charge of it from Kouchner—Rony Brauman and Claude Malhuret—were even more identified as *soixante-huitards*. They were university students during May '68, and Brauman in particular was a "professional revolutionary," involved in the ultraleft groups of the time. Indeed, the French medical sociologist Claudine Herzlich (1995) argues that medical humanitarianism rose out of the context of 1968, where the School of Medicine in Paris was a place of high activism. The medical students drafted a "white book" containing a radical reform of medicine, medical education, and the practice of medicine, trying to make a break with "capitalistic medicine."

Despite MSF's origins in a revolutionary moment, it blossomed into and helped to shape an era of moralist antipolitics. As we already learned (see the introduction), Kouchner and many of his comrades actually changed their views quite radically after the failure of May '68, turning from "third-worldism"—a critical part of the movement, to which I will return—to holding that, while one might denounce abuses of power, ultimately it is impossible to engage with injustice on any other level. Politics in terms of the anticapitalist, anti-imperialist revolution dreamed of by the *soixante-huitards* was replaced by a defense of the principles of human rights, and by a view that separated victims from perpetrators, heroes from villains, in order to side with and defend the powerless (Ross 2002). Koucher and MSF brought a form of action that was appealing in its purported ability to avoid Machievellan politics (Caldwell 2009). This is an ideology grounded in individualism, in life itself, one that no longer sees the possibility of larger political change. As Kouchner said, in defense of his mission to rescue the Vietnamese "boat people" fleeing the Communist regime in 1979, "One must be on the side of the victim, it's clear, whatever his/her political identity" (La Libération April 23, 1979, cited from Vallaeys 2004:283, my translation).[12] MSF helped forge the ideological path for human rights and humanitarian organizations to respond by intervening and speaking for the suffering masses. Indeed, calls for human rights by anticommunist dissidents in Eastern Europe at the same moment also relied on the fact that "human rights" were anti-revolutionary. As Sam Moyn writes, "human rights arose on the ruins of revolution, not as its descendent" (2007:3).

Looking at humanitarianism through the lens of SAMU Social brings this shift in universalism—and its notion of humanity—into relief. MSF and the *sans frontières* movement legitimized the breakdown of state sovereignty, allowing for intervention in the name of suffering anywhere that states were not protecting their own citizens. In light of this, both MSF and SAMU Social often fill in gaps in social services, in the absence of a state or governing body; but they only do this in the context of emergency. That is, they can only provide care in very limited conditions. Their universalism is of the temporal present—beyond that, no universal promises are upheld, no long-term human condition supported. Though not without its own early debates on this issue, MSF made clear that it was not there to treat the chronic shortages in the third world; it fought hard to enforce its paradigm of emergency. As Kouchner said, again in the context of the Vietnamese refugees, "Finally, we were no longer going to ask these questions, but simply extend a hand to those who were drowning; this was extreme urgency" (Vallaeys 2004:285, my translation).[13] Here, he refers to a moment when he forged a consensus between long-time intellectual and political rivals Jean-Paul Sartre and Raymond Aron, putting aside questions about whether the violence refugees were fleeing from was committed for or against national liberation, by or for the people. Instead, he succeeded in narrowing the focus to the immediacy of urgent suffering; this in turn enabled a rapid response in the name of the moral imperative.

Xavier Emmanuelli is clear that SAMU Social also manages social problems through idioms of crisis and public health, in other words, it medicalizes sociopolitical problems, at least temporarily, until the problem can be treated in "posturgent" care. Both SAMU Social and MSF urge the state to step up to do its job postemergency; this involves longer-term structural change, including reintegration of people into social systems and codes of life. But Emmanuelli is honest when he writes that his plan for those who leave urgent social care has never been realized: they remain cared for only in the temporal present, in their state of emergency. While he has dedicated his life to emergency response, he admits that, today, people confuse emergency and the long term, crisis and its context, believing that measures taken to respond to emergencies can actually solve the long-term problems (Emmanuelli 2005:13–14). He is also clear that the temporality of medical and social emergencies is different; that is, the time it takes to recover in each case is not the same. Social rehabilitation requires a series of individual, political, and social changes that may span years; recovery from a medical emergency works in a very different time frame. In general, the options are death or survival, after which one leaves the space of urgent care. While medical and social emergencies are always connected, they often come to be conflated, and treated as one and the same, by both MSF and SAMU Social—intentionally or not. In other words, the end point is a politics of life, where life is about physical survival in one circumscribed moment.

Central to this new universalism, then, is a focus on the urgency of individual suffering and a concomitant category of humanity composed of suffering victims, seen through this limited temporal lens. This focus—through the subsequent development of a whole apparatus of humanitarian government—has gradually worked to appropriate the resources for longer-term political responses, limiting our ability to even imagine them.

THE RIGHT TO INTERVENE: THIRD-WORLDISM VERSUS THE NEW CIVILIZING MISSION

The second defining feature of MSF, *le droit d'ingérence,* or "the right to interfere," is based on the universal conception of the human condition just discussed; sovereignty is challenged in the name of this universal human-ity. This invokes a moral obligation to interfere in the name of suffering. And yet, when placed in its historical context, developed against "third-worldism," we see that the right to interfere is haunted by the "civilizing missions" that preceded it; more broadly, it threatens to reenact them.

The right to interfere is a particularly interesting idea, because *le droit d'ingérence* can be translated into English in several different ways: it can mean the "right to *intervene,*" but it can also signify the "right to *inter-fere,*" and the latter translation is preferred by Kouchner. In fact, the pre-ferred translation is the "*duty* to interfere," which again plays with the word *droit.* In English, *droit* could signify the "*law* to interfere," but in French the preferred meaning has a connotation of moral obligation. In English, the idea of a duty carries more weight than that of a right. Yet, as Tim Allen and David Styan (2000:828) point out, Kouchner takes the *duty* to interfere as a given—one is morally obligated to interfere if others are suffering. As a result, he has spent his time fighting to institute the legal *right* to interfere. Again, this draws from a French political and legal tra-dition: the French practice of international law regarded intervention as technically legal, while others interpreted it as infringing on the rules of sovereignty (Guillot 1994:31). In this sense, MSF suggested that *ingérence* be more actively developed in the wider international community. The 2005 "responsibility to protect" doctrine of is a direct descendent of this right to intervene, asserting that the international community has the duty to assume the protection of a state's citizens if the state is unable or unwilling to protect its own citizens—I will return to this.

France's colonial history haunts the debate over *le droit d'ingérence*, shaping the present in a decisive way. As we will see in the next chapters, regimes of care—inadvertently or not—often work to perpetuate colonial hierarchies, and the following history should help to explain why this might be so. French colonial policies were highly interventionist and were involved in nearly all aspects of life, from health to education to sexuality. With the war in Algeria and the independence movements of many French colonies in the 1950s and 1960s, the New Left led by student youth espoused a Marxism that identified and sympathized with the international proletariat in the third world. This movement was called *tiermondisme*, or "third-worldism," and took a position of solidarity with revolutionary movements in the third world, rebuking any criticism of these independence movements and any type of interference with their regimes: this was in reaction to the previous interventionist colonial policies. Leading figures included Frantz Fanon as well as his French allies Jean-Paul Sartre and Simone de Beauvoir. In the broadest sense, third-worldism was an attack on the capitalist system, from aid programs to multinational corporations.

In the late 1970s and 1980s, however, many former third-worldists—including Kouchner—changed their tune, dismantling their own former movement in the face of the anticolonial revolutionary Marxist movements that did not deliver on their promises. They watched as newly "liberated" nation-states like Cambodia, under the Khmer Rouge—whose leaders were trained in France, and associated with the Parti Communiste Français (PCF)—turned into totalitarian regimes. Claude Malhuret and Rony Brauman, both of whom later became presidents of MSF, turned their backs on third-worldism in the context of the suffering they witnessed in refugee camps on the Thai border, where they were stationed by MSF to provide medical aid to those fleeing the Cambodian regime. As Brauman claimed, "Some 90 percent of refugees in the third world were fleeing this kind of regime, and we were working in camps where they had been gathered. . . . We were ferociously critical of third worldism and what [Raymond] Aron called the 'lyrical illusion' that it permitted" (2004:410). Intervention again became an issue. Specifically, a division emerged between those who reaffirmed the original

anticolonialist position (the original *tiermondistes*), and those who wanted
to promote a new *mission civilatrice,* or "civilizing mission," in the name
of human rights. MSF fell into this latter category, as did the broader *sans
frontières* movement (Allen and Styan 2000). In other words, a form of
universalism based on rights explained the "moral obligation" to once
again interfere, walking in the footsteps of the colonial legacy.

As in the case of colonial humanitarianism, it would be too simple to
categorize this form of humanitarianism as a mere legitimating screen
for new imperial gestures; rather, MSF echoes its colonial precursor in
its attempt to challenge military discourses through the propagation
of a new global ethics. The point is, of course, that the French civilizing mission was an intensely violent regime—a violence perhaps all the
more brutal in its attempt to teach others a form of Enlightenment ethics.
Intentions, that is, are not always relevant.

I want to reemphasize that this anti-third-worldism was and is moralist in tone: it is driven by a moral imperative to intervene based on suffering, not by a political or democratic movement. Because of the new
humanitarianism's unwillingness to take a political position except in
extreme circumstances (such as the Rwandan genocide), it can and has
been incorporated into other political frameworks and used toward various political ends, including imperial ones. For instance, the "need for
defense of human rights in the third world" was endorsed by President
Mitterrand in 1987, and his government included "humanitarianism
of the state" in its policies. Clearly, this was no longer a revolutionary
movement. Indeed, there was a place for the emerging humanitarianism in the French state itself: the minister of human rights from 1986 to
1988 was Claude Malhuret, ex-president of MSF. And in 1988, Bernard
Kouchner was named French minister of health and *action humanitaire*—
the latter being a position created especially for him by the newly elected
government. And from 2007 to 2010, Kouchner was the French foreign
minister in Nicolas Sarkozy's right-wing government. It is worth noting
that while Malhuret and Kouchner were both integrated into the French
government, they represent two sides of the humanitarian spectrum,
with their rivalry leading to MSF's split in 1979, when Kouchner and
many of the founders left to found Médecins du Monde (see Guillot

1994; Fox 1995; and Brauman 2004). Rony Brauman, the president of MSF from 1982 to 1994, was among this younger and more powerful group allied with Malhuret, and he writes that, while the split happened in the context of whether or not to charter a boat to rescue Vietnamese refugees fleeing Cambodia, the disagreement was more broadly about whether to forge an independent organization of doctors with technical know-how, specific guidelines, and limits (later called private humanitarianism), or a series of symbolic actions to expose the suffering of others that ultimately remained state-affiliated (state humanitarianism). What is interesting is that despite this split, and despite different ideas of humanitarianism, both leaders affiliated with the French state at one moment or another, demonstrating how the moral legitimacy of this apolitical organization was increasingly seen and used as a political resource. The overlap of humanitarianism and government is by no means new, despite claims to the contrary.

Of course, humanitarians are aware of the potential to appropriate their moral legitimacy toward nefarious ends; from the beginning, Rony Brauman was highly critical of Kouchner's attempt to institute humanitarian intervention as a legal right and duty, suggesting that international jurisprudence can be used by states when they find it convenient or in their interest to interfere. In a manner that anticipated the contemporary debates about the responsibility to protect doctrine, Brauman pointed to the inevitable mix between military and humanitarian aims in a "humanitarian invasion" (or a legal intervention supported by United Nations or national military forces to help with transportation or supplies). Brauman suggested that mixing medical humanitarianism with military interventions runs counter to the idea of allowing NGOs access to victims and counter to medical humanitarianism's purported vocation of healing. Indeed, there is evidence that relief activities reinforce war economies.[14] In his position as foreign minister, Kouchner himself illustrated how mixing humanitarian and military ventures can lead down a slippery slope. He supported *le droit d'ingérence* in Iraq in 2003, backing the intervention that eventually turned into war and the American occupation. For such decisions, he has been labeled "neoconservative," demonstrating the potential consequences of moral posturing.[15] We are in an interesting position today, able to see many of these warnings play out; as Mariella Pandolfi (2008) argues, the new doctrine of the responsibility to protect merges the benevolent responsibility to intervene in times of suffering with a right to employ force in the protection of global citizens, conflating militaristic and humanitarian perspectives. This has become one of the preferred foreign-policy tools of the post–cold war order, creating a humanitarian industry with its own form of "mobile sovereignty."

The shadow of the civilizing mission in this work—"using the hardware of the world's most powerful states to pursue philanthropic goals" (de Waal 2008:184)—also has its religious echoes. As we have seen, for many in the humanitarian world, Catholic charity is claimed as a forerunner; yet the religious impetus is not just historical—it blends into the contemporary moral imperative, creating a form of compassion that cannot be called either religious or secular. Xavier Emmanuelli and many of those who work for SAMU Social are explicit about its religious inspiration and precedents. Emmanuelli speaks of his own work—with MSF, SAMU Social, and even as a country doctor—as sacred; he imagines himself as assisting in a resurrection when he saves those who are on the brink of death (Emmanuelli 2005:21–22), and he admits that as he gets older he feels he is saving his own soul through his humanitarian work, "taking care of my own good works, my own poor" (2005:75). He describes the work of humanitarian NGOs as "messianic missions of unconditional aid" (2005:49), even as it calls itself universal humanism. Clearly, for him, the compassion that feeds medical humanitarianism is not simply about a secular Enlightenment rationality. In fact, many from MSF looked to the priest Abbé Pierre as a model of humanitarianism at home; Emmaüs, the movement launched by Abbé Pierre in 1954, used similar techniques of moral indignation and media appeals to draw attention to the suffering of the homeless and, later, the sanspapiers, which MSF and MDM both turned to address in the 1980s. While much of the new humanitarianism is driven by the moral imperative to *stop* suffering, the logic whereby victimhood is considered sacred is still an integral part of the compassion that drives humanitarianism. As cultural historian Bertrand Taithe (2006) argues, humanitarianism cannot be separated from its religious sources and emotional responses to pain.

Taithe (2004) also reminds us that the ideologies of universal Christian love and of universal rights both emphasize the opening of borders to expressions of care and compassion. The right to intervene, then, is a composite form, a mix of civilizing, messianic, and philanthropic mission, interfering to protect those in need—yet always risking a form of domination in the process.

THE DUTY TO BEAR WITNESS: NEUTRALITY AND POLITICS

The third guiding principle I want to address is the desire to bear witness to the violations of human rights and human dignity that doctors encounter in the field. This resolve grew out of the finding that the International Committee of the Red Cross did not speak out against atrocities taking place in the camps in the Second World War, despite witnessing them through its deliveries of food and medicine: the Red Cross responded that its silence enabled it to continue doing relief work in the holocaust setting (see Fox 1995). Kouchner and MSF's real innovation came in the way that they ruptured the silence: they informed a vast world-scale public about human rights abuses and evoked public indignation about them, making sophisticated use of the mass media. They called this a "duty to bear witness."[16] There have been two downsides to this innovation: first, this professionalized command of the media has led to humanitarians speaking *for* the "suffering masses," rather than with them; and second, the duty to bear witness, in constant tension with the principle of neutrality, has led at times to a form of antipolitics, or conservation of the status quo.

The mediatization of missions was considered essential to the new humanitarianism; not only did it publicize the findings of doctors as part of a moral duty to bear witness, but the publicity helped to secure funding and provide a degree of immunity from governments and other political interest groups hostile to the new humanitarians' interventions. Media publicity crossed borders and built solidarity. MSF quickly learned that official funding as well as private donations were most effectively secured when international media covered acute suffering. Kouchner had an intuitive sense of the role of media in politics, and NGOs all over the world have since followed his lead. Early on, MSF became a key source representing the "third world."[17] In this newly moralized landscape, however, this meant that the so-called third world people could speak less and less for themselves and still be heard. It is not simply that they did not have equal access to the circuits of media, but that professionalized NGOs from the global North created and used new types of media to produce knowledge about places they felt were underrepresented, circulating and managing images in new ways; political action soon required engagement on this terrain. Those with fewer resources had less room to represent themselves and hence to politically engage on their own terms.[18] This inequality in representation is all the more potent in light of the fact that a colonially derived racial hierarchy inadvertently underlies many medical humanitarian missions, where the doctor has been until very recently predominantly a white male, and often a European expatriate. In the name of protecting human dignity, he speaks for and represents nonwhite, non-European victims. There is, then, a colonial legacy in humanitarianism generally and for MSF specifically, which recalls the exclusions and contradictions of universalism.

Perhaps the most important tension in the debate over the duty to bear witness is how this affects the purported political neutrality of humanitarian NGOs.[19] As Kouchner himself states, "If you are humanitarian . . . this is not politics, you must be neutral, taking care of all."[20] Neutrality, to reiterate, is the duty to refrain from taking actions that advantage one side of the conflict over another. While this tension is as old as MSF itself, it is far from being resolved. MSF holds an Annual International General Assembly to which all members from all sections around the world are invited to discuss and evaluate the year's successes and failures. I attended the 2005 meeting, and the question of political neutrality as related to the duty to bear witness was again the key debate. To what end does MSF bear witness? To advocate for justice, for policy changes, for an end to the impunity of certain actors? This, the representatives realized, quickly ran into the dangerous terrain of political engagement and intervention, which MSF prides itself on avoiding. Yet one representative brought up the issue of the slippery slope between political neutrality and irresponsibility—this too was fiercely debated. As Peter Redfield states, "MSF responds with a defense of life that both recognizes and refuses politics. It forcefully claims an independent right to speak out and act without regard to considerations other than conscience, yet it never quite abandons neutrality in its insistence that final responsibility for alleviating suffering lies elsewhere" (2005:343). The MSF charter does not mention *témoignage* (the duty to bear witness), in an attempt to avoid suspicion by local authorities that missions have an element of political intent. Instead, bearing witness is framed as a choice for members, rather than a moral duty, even as the charter suggests that the organization itself feels morally bound to speak out.[21]

In a challenge to MSF, Paul O'Brien (2004:31), then CARE's advocacy coordinator in Afghanistan, points out that neutrality is a political value. Redfield (2011) puts this slightly differently: neutrality is a strategy. The way it works and what it hopes to achieve depends on the context. In this sense, the balance between neutrality and the duty to bear witness can be thought of as a *political* strategy: When does it make sense to emphasize neutrality over all else? When must one leave neutrality and speak out? The danger of speaking out too forcefully is that one can be seen to be taking a side—a political position—and thereby can lose access to those who need help. The danger of too much neutrality is irresponsibility; this can mean that the status quo is protected, even if the urgency of suffering is temporarily relieved. If nothing is done to address injustice, one indirectly participates in its reproduction.

SAMU Social demonstrates how an organization based solely on this logic of urgent yet neutral care can actually function as a reactionary force, protecting the status quo. In fact, many of Emmanuelli's MSF colleagues were against his idea of an emergency service specially designated for the poor, which they argued would encourage ghettoization, but Emmanuelli defends himself by saying that the state had already failed these people. It was too late to say that SAMU Social would get in the way of universal health care or undermine a system of social equality. He claimed that we live in a world where equality is not a reality, and SAMU Social is there to respond, to pick up the pieces in the face of this reality. Yet this leaves in place a failed system. Despite the horror of some of Emmanuelli's MSF colleagues at his proposed plan, MSF functions similarly; it responds to situations of suffering brought on in large part by inequality, injustice, and war, without addressing the causes of suffering. When acting alone, that is, without counterparts who do address these issues (whose aim is to "cure"), this can perpetuate inequality in ways that get entrenched, limiting imaginable futures. It is no accident that humanitarian interventions are not equally distributed: in 2002–3 MSF spent over half its funds in Africa, keeping it the center of humanitarian activity (Redfield 2006:350).

SAMU Social has been accused of creating or at least maintaining two-tiered medical and social systems, where some people get basic health care and social services and others only get them in situations of crisis or emergency. In this sense, it is not surprising that Emmanuelli was only able to actualize his idea under conservative politician and former French president Jacques Chirac, then mayor of Paris. Similarly, MSF sustains a world in which some people have regular health care and others only get it in situations of emergency. This has become a real dilemma in places where, for instance, AIDS has a high prevalence rate: In the Republic of the Congo between 1998 and 2000, MSF addressed sexual violence as a humanitarian emergency for the first time. But by providing prophylactic antiretrovirals to survivors of rape, MSF ended up creating a two-tiered system in reverse, in which only the survivors got access to these medications; they were virtually nonexistent for the rest of the population, despite an 8 percent HIV+ rate in the country.[22] MSF is highly aware of these contradictions, and troubled by them (Le Pape and Salignon 2003); the question is what to do about them and whether they must be accepted as part of the intractable tensions of the humanitarian enterprise. If they are indeed irresolvable, then expecting or allowing these NGOs to respond to the more profound inequalities of our time—allowing care to do the job of curing—creates a complicity in reproducing them.

CONCLUSION: MEDICAL HUMANITARIANISM
AND ITS DIASPORA

As we saw with the opening example of RESO, and the desire to bring humanitarianism "home," medical humanitarian NGOs have expanded in several directions since their founding. This does not mean that the logic of emergency has been altered; what it does mean, however, is that the goals of medical humanitarianism have grown to encompass new political territory, all in the name of a moral imperative to relieve suffering. These goals have moved beyond immediate disasters to focus on longer-term projects such as MSF's Campaign for Access to Essential Medicines, which is a sustained effort to attend to the difficulties of poor people in obtaining medicines for conditions such as HIV/AIDS, malaria, and tuberculosis. These developments pose constant challenges to the conception of medical humanitarianism, adapting and readapting the French tradition: for instance, while the Access to Essential Medicines Campaign grows out of a frustration over drug shortages in MSF's work, it borders on playing an advocacy role in the realm of policy, again, something MSF has strictly refused, acknowledging that it cannot save the world by itself. The British humanitarian organizations see fewer problems with this combined approach, and their organizations tend to be organized more thematically than professionally (i.e., made up of doctors). Thus, for instance, Oxfam is organized in opposition to poverty and hunger, which allows both emergency and long-term responses: human rights and development approaches are both part of Oxfam's mandate.[23]

That said, this multipronged approach brings its own set of problems, such as the dependence on states and their funding; or the well-known challenges of development, which have their own problem of "antipolitics" (Ferguson 1994; Escobar 1995). But in the transnational arena, we see a growing convergence between these two forms of humanitarianism and between human rights, development, and humanitarianism.[24] What this means in practice, however, is that social problems are often covered as emergencies, as humanitarians become involved in problems that used to belong only to nation-states—and for which they clearly do not have the resources. The following chapters explore this broadening emergency mandate and how various social and political problems have ended up being managed by an expanding humanitarian diaspora—a complex of institutions and practices that function on the basis of care and protection, enacted under the threat of emergency, as solutions to global problems of inequality, exploitation, and discrimination.

PART TWO   On the Ground

COMPASSION AND PATHOLOGY

THREE

The Illness Clause

LIFE AND THE POLITICS OF COMPASSION

One late afternoon in the spring of 1999, I went to a workshop for NGOs on the theme of the sans-papiers and health. It was held just outside Paris in the *banlieue* and organized by an NGO that focuses on AIDS and drug addiction. A representative from a medical humanitarian organization had been invited, and there were debates about what the new scheme for universal medical coverage in France entailed for those without papers.[1] Most striking was a discussion of the 1998 provision of the Conditions of Entry and Residence of Foreigners, which grants legal permits to those already in France who have pathologies of life-threatening consequence, if they are declared unable to receive proper treatment in their home countries.[2] The discussion revolved around one particular tension in what I have called this "illness clause": was it simply for people with very serious pathologies, or could others use it to obtain legal status by pointing to their structural location in France, which inevitably involved pathologies like depression? In other words, what does "*life*-threatening" mean—how does one define "life"? One doctor insisted that it was only for serious pathologies such as HIV or cancer, while another stated that there were more opportunities than first meet the eye: by way of example he said that a few sans-papiers hunger strikers had received temporary permits for illness after their hunger strike, but these were then renewed indefinitely for "psychiatric reasons." This must be understood in a context where hunger striking, a primary form of protest for illegal or undocumented immigrants since 1972 (Siméant 1998), no longer holds the same power it once did, and hunger strikers may now be deported. Following up on this discussion at the end of the workshop, a woman who worked for one of the major immigrant rights associations said to me, "Isn't it terrible? We almost wish for illness when we talk to sans-papiers." The wish for illness, of course, was not born of malice, but of a desire to better help the undocumented, and it was one I was becoming increasingly familiar with.

How did illness become a primary means to attain papers and rights for those on the margins? In this chapter, I examine what I see as a defining moment of the politics of care: a focus on the universality and legitimacy of the suffering body, here manifest as the sick body. The illness clause was put in place to protect biological integrity as the manifestation of a common humanity. Yet how does this work on the ground—how is this common humanity identified? In what follows, I demonstrate that what gets taken as universal—the stripped-down truth of life, common to us all, whether it be our suffering or our dignity—is actually an intensely political, historical, and cultural creation, one that is recognized through the frame of moral legitimacy. In this case, the universal truth of the suffering body gets produced through discretionary power: both institutional and affective.

First, then, I introduce the illness clause and illustrate how it institutes and protects what is considered an apolitical suffering body. Second, I turn to examine the factors influencing how bureaucrats and health officials actually translate claims about human suffering into state recognition; in what ways do they become gatekeepers, not only of the nation-state, but of a concept of humanity? Third, I focus in on compassion as a critical mediating force between suffering of various forms and biologically based injury. That is, I examine the narratives that sans-papiers must rehearse in order to elicit compassion, matching an understanding of humanity based on affect to a biological "universal" one. With affect as a driving force, I argue that the suffering body that gets recognized as universal actually has historically grounded racialized, gendered, and sexualized contours; this is what helps define its moral legitimacy. Finally, I end by discussing the demise of the illness clause and what this reveals about how and when claims to universality function.

THE ILLNESS CLAUSE: PROTECTING APOLITICAL SUFFERING

The illness clause, to reiterate, is a provision of the French law on the conditions of entry and residence that grants legal permits to those already living in France who have pathologies of life-threatening consequence, if they are declared unable to receive proper treatment in their home countries. The goal is to permit them to receive treatment in France.[3] The logic behind this was humanitarian and exceptional: the French state felt it could not deport people if such a deportation had consequences of exceptional gravity, such as their death. This "illness permit" was instituted formally in 1998, after much lobbying by the Collective for the Rights of Sick Foreigners in France, which brought together thirty-five associations or NGOs, and included medical humanitarian groups like Médecins sans Frontières and Médecins du Monde.[4] That is, only in 1998 did the Ministry of Health officially become involved in the immigration process, which normally falls under the rubric of the Ministry of Interior. Nevertheless, the *banlieue* outside Paris that receives the highest number of claims for legal status began the practice of taking illness into account in 1990. I conducted my fieldwork primarily in this banlieue and in Paris.

My ethnographic work demonstrates the increasing importance of the illness clause, but statistics back this up, and I turn to those first. The

Table 1   Recommendations for "illness clause" permits from the state medical office (DDASS) in a *banlieue* outside Paris, 1998, 1999, 2000

Recommendation	1998	%	1999	%	2000	%
Negative	233	23	97	10	325	20
3-month permit	71	7	145	15	266	16.5
6-month permit	102	10	158	16	314	19.5
1-year permit	127	13	174	18	265	16.5
Long-term permit	422	42	412	41	442	27.5
No opinion (lack of information)	52	5	0	0	0	0
Total	1,007	100	986	100	1,612	100
			889		1,287	
			accepted		accepted	

local statistics from the state medical office (the DDASS),[5] where I did my research, show that applications for the "illness residency permit" increased seven times over the course of the 1990s, and three-quarters of the applications were given positive responses. Indeed, the more recent statistics are even more striking: From 194 patients treated in 1993, the number of those treated rose to 4,000 in 2003. Table 1 shows that, in the time I was conducting fieldwork, the number of positive responses increased by 44 percent just in that particular *département*, from 889 in 1999 to 1,287 in 2000. If we look at the statistics for a range of *départements* across France, we see an increase in the number of cases considered for illness permits, from 1,500 in 1999 to 36,008 in 2004.[6] And again, the number of actual permits given increased ten times over the course of six years: from 1,045 in 1998, to 12,109 in 2003 (see Bénévise and Lopez 2006). The numbers are staggering. Table 2 gives the statistics on the types of illnesses admitted and the type of permit granted in the local state medical office in which I worked—top among them is HIV, but cardiovascular illnesses, cancer, diabetes, and TB are all included.

These figures must be contrasted to the statistics on political asylum; of key importance here is that, as the number of permits for medical reasons increased, those granted under the title of "refugee" significantly

Table 2   Most frequently encountered pathologies in the state medical office
(DDASS) in a *banlieue* outside Paris, 1998, 1999, 2000

Pathology	1998	%	1999	%	2000	%
HIV	113	15	124	16	156	12.6
Cardiovascular	74	10	88	11	139	11.3
Rheumatology,						
trauma, orthopedics	67	9	81	10	144	11.6
Cancer	49	7	50	7	57	4.6
Diabetes	44	6	41	5	89	7.2
Psychiatry	42	6	44	6	87	7
Urinary, nephrology	26	4	39	5	61	5
ORL (ear, nose, and						
throat), opthalmology	54	7	53	7	89	7.2
Tuberculosis	36	5	40	5	67	5.4
Gastroenterology	24	3	26	3	47	3.8
Pneumonic	32	4	22	3	44	3.6
Hepatitis	25	3	48	6	45	3.7
Gynecology	25	3	15	2	44	3.6
Neurology	29	4	22	3	42	3.4
Endocrine	36	5	27	4	25	2
Hematology					17	1.4
Sterility					26	2.1
Diverse (multiple						
pathologies)	62	8	52	7	56	4.5
Subtotal	738	100a	772	100	1,235	100
In process	53		82		89	
Accompanying adults	46		85		211	
Undiagnosed					29	
Absence of pathology					48	

[a] Figures are copied from the DDASS table; the percentages listed here for 1998 in fact total 99%.

diminished (D. Fassin 2001a, 2001b). Figure 4 illustrates that, as the
number of people admitted for political asylum went down, those let
in under the auspices of medical humanitarianism went up.[7] Indeed,
from the end of the 1980s, the number of asylum seekers granted refugee status decreased by six times to 2,000 per year. This was due to

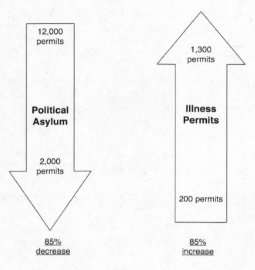

Figure 4. Entry and residency permits in France: medical humanitarianism versus political asylum, 1999–2000.

increased surveillance of borders and harsher treatment of refugees by administrators (D. Fassin 2001b, 2005); more broadly, it reflects the attempt to coordinate refugee policy across the European Union, instituted initially by the Treaty of Amsterdam in 1999 and still up for debate despite the ratification of the Lisbon Treaty in 2009, which prioritized this issue. In practice, this has meant pushing all EU members toward taking the fewest number of refugees possible, or settling for the lowest common denominator in terms of refugee numbers. Differently stated, the decreased numbers reflect a shift from a universal conception of the refugee to a restrictive juridical and political concept that is "independent of the reality of dangers incurred" (Legoux 1995, cited from Delouvin 2000:69). Refugee status has been increasingly determined by the politics of immigration, not by the circumstances of the individual seeking asylum: the grounding assumption is that asylum seekers are making fraudulent claims, and they must do their best to prove otherwise. This link between refugee claims and immigration policy was actually made explicit in France: as Hubert Védrine, the minister of foreign affairs, stated in 1997 with regard to asylum policy, "The practice followed must maintain a just balance with our desire to control migration flows" (Delouvin 2000:70).

Thus, with the possibility of papers effectively closed to immigrants and refugees—who are seen as either criminal or economically burdensome[8]—those already in France without papers turned to the illness clause as a means to ease the exploitation that is a regular part of being undocumented, believing, rightly or wrongly, that papers would solve all their problems. I met an Algerian woman named Safia who exemplified the magical quality attached to residency papers, for which she would do almost anything; she refused to go to any gathering or event that did not relate to this quest. Papers had become her driving goal—the solution to all her problems. As we sat in her home, she explained to me that she would have the rest of her life to do other things, but only if she dedicated all her energy now to getting papers. She showed me an enormous binder that documented her struggle, which had begun in Algeria many years prior. Papers have become a talisman for equality, and people are willing to go far for this—the power of the illness clause must be understood in this context. I say talisman, unfortunately, because they do not necessarily end the suffering nor the struggle. Immigration legislation has been so volatile that one can have papers one day and none the next, without one's situation having objectively changed (see Fassin and Morice 2000). Similarly, difficulties often arise with maintaining legal status once one has received papers—one has to prove consistent and stable employment, which structural conditions make difficult every step of the way.

As I mentioned, those who work to help immigrants obtain basic rights also realized that illness was the most promising way in. Not only did social workers in hospital clinics ask if their undocumented clients were sick, suggesting it as a means of entry, but this was happening increasingly in the NGOs I worked with. This said, we must certainly inquire how the French state reconciles the denial of papers to immigrants because they are perceived to be criminal or economically burdensome, with the decision to give papers and social services to immigrants who are sick. Stated otherwise: Why is it that illness can travel across borders while poverty cannot?

The framing of the illness clause helps to explain this. Although the French state instituted the illness clause out of "respect for human dignity," drawing on its history and identity as a nation committed to universal ethico-moral standards, the illness clause was only ratified because it was perceived as outside the political realm. That is, it was instituted in May 1998 under the right to "private and family life." Placing this clause under the aegis of the "private" exempts it from debates about the politics of immigration, citizenship, and notions of the French nation, and it ignores the structural problems and economic demand that may have caused the immigration in the first place. Instead, the clause focuses attention on what is construed as an apolitical suffering body. In conversations that I had with state officials and doctors, they confirmed that the space of "pure" life honored in the illness clause is conceived of in opposition to political community—in this sense, the boundaries of the political are demarcated from a purported universal, and hence legitimate, biological realm. One such example came in a conversation I had with M. Bonnet, a member of the Conseil Constitutionel, the highest legal body in France; M. Bonnet explained to me that one cannot intervene in the political matters of sovereign nations—except when it concerns violations of bodily integrity. Similarly, health care officials found ways to subvert politically charged immigration laws for the higher, moral cause of the suffering body. Indeed, despite increasingly restrictive legislation that has managed to alter and limit the right to health care, that right remains the most extensive of all those granted to immigrants, whatever their legal status—more comprehensive than any civil, political, or social rights.[9]

As proof that this clause is humanitarian and apolitical in nature, and that it remains in the realm of the private, the French state does not automatically include a work permit with the illness visa—initial attempts to do so rendered the clause too politically contentious. When an amendment to the law was first proposed through a published ministerial instruction, or circular, on June 24, 1997, the local state medical office was given permission to determine whether the patient was fit to work and should be granted a work permit.[10] The state medical office gradually realized, however, that its suggestions were not being followed. That is, the work permit for those with illnesses is subject to the same arbitrary treatment as the rest of the legalization process—sometimes people are granted it, more often they are not. I watched as immigrants returned to the medical office, complaining that they had not received the promised permit. The medical officials said that, in conversations with administrators at the prefecture level, they were made to understand that those at the prefecture did not want the sans-papiers admitted for illness to enter the system of state benefits (*sécurité sociale*, including welfare and pension benefits)—these administrators felt that being part of the system of benefits would encourage sans-papiers to stay longer. They protected the suffering body—but only that.

The visa given for illness is thereby isolated from all other aspects of life; it is narrowly focused on the healing of suffering, injured, or disabled bodies, disqualifying its recipients from taking any economic, social, or political role in French society. Consequently, those who gain entry on the basis of chronic illness, such as those who are HIV+ and capable of sustaining a full-time job, are for the most part not given the right to work. While their papers formally allow them to rent apartments, open bank accounts, and travel on the metro without the risk of being arrested and deported, they do not have the substantive means to do any of these things.

Ironically, this means that the French state, in the name of human dignity, indirectly sanctions working on the black market. In this sense, a doctor named Isabelle who worked at one of the clinics for undocumented immigrants where I conducted fieldwork, suggested that, in her experience, the illness clause was "a curse." It was worse than nothing because it gave people hope, and yet, because work permits were not granted with the residency papers, it paved the way for greater exploitation of their misery, making them work in situations of virtual slavery or prostitution. She suggested that politicians and those who supported them got rich off the backs of those working on the black market. "Why else are they not deported?" she asked. "It must mean that it is profitable for the state to keep them." Drawing on her experience working with sans-papiers, she made an interesting and provocative point: she felt that it would be better to have a two-tiered system of citizenship rather than full "equality" because there is more room for exploitation in a system that grants people either all rights or no rights at all. In this, she gestures to a characteristic utopian quality of policies of the French state, built as it is on ashes of revolution; and yet, these nevertheless may open the way for ever greater forms of discrimination and violence. We see this, for instance, in the French state's refusal to permit any official recognition of racial or ethnic differences, the goal being to avoid racial categorization and institution- alized discrimination. The principle of color-blindness is incorporated as Article 1 of the 1958 Constitution, which institutes equality as a fundamen- tal principle of French society. And yet, without acknowledging a category called race, the very real practices of racism cannot be confronted.

Economic profitability of undocumented immigrants aside, the ill- ness clause is also productive of a particular *moral* economy, in which a new hierarchy of morals and moral legitimacy takes shape and certain ethical configurations gain credence.[11] Here, humanitarianism functions as politics (or antipolitics, as the case may be) and inevitably has unan- ticipated consequences. The threatened body associated with political asylum has been recast as suspect, conflated with that of the economic immigrant—or in the words of former Socialist minister Michel Rocard, "the misery of the earth" (1996), which, he claimed, France could not absorb. With humanitarianism as the driving logic, only the suffering or sick body is seen as a legitimate manifestation of a common humanity, worthy of recognition in the form of rights; this view is based on a belief in the legitimacy, fixity, and universality of biology.[12] Indeed, what are considered basic human rights are themselves now circumscribed to fit the limited understanding of human life. It is in this sense that I speak of the space of the apolitical suffering body as the very center and founda- tion of the new politics of citizenship in France, a space at the intersec- tion of biopolitical modernity and global capital, in which contradictory and unexpected diseased and disabled citizens emerge. How, exactly, do these citizens emerge? The next section discusses how an apolitical uni- versality is made on the ground.

ON THE GROUND: DEFINING "LIFE"

One of the cruel ironies of being "without papers" is that one must inevitably walk around with a tell-tale pile of papers: medical, legal, bureaucratic. This is all in an attempt to gather the "right" papers. Yet it is nearly impossible to know which documents one might need at any given time. What proof of one's humanity does one need for each office, for each administrator? This ambiguity holds true for the illness clause, which is based on evidence of an illness of life-threatening gravity. What qualifies as "life threatening"—what is the meaning of "life" embedded in this phrase? Biological life is more malleable in its abstractness than those who insist on its universality may realize. There is room for play. In this section, I demonstrate that life is ultimately defined quite pragmatically, reliant on factors such as institutional structures and cultures of expertise; the discretionary political and moral views of doctors, nurses, and social workers; and the location and know-how of the sans-papiers themselves. What is clear, however, is that life is not a consistent or easily identifiable concept.

The illness clause was at first put into place informally, in response to what was seen as an urgent and unethical situation: the deportation of sick and dying undocumented immigrants. While precisely to address the immediacy of suffering and imminence of death, it was nonetheless dependent on the institutions enabled to recognize this urgency. This recalls a dilemma faced by Médecins sans Frontières early in its life, one that ultimately led to its bifurcation into MSF and Médecins du Monde, as chapter 2 relates; former MSF presidents Rony Brauman and Claude Malhuret argued for creating an independent institutional structure with technical know-how that could effectively respond to emergencies. Bernard Kouchner, on the other hand, warned of the encumbering aspects of bureaucratic charities. With the illness clause, we encounter a similar dilemma: How does one address the urgency of suffering without appropriate structures in place? And yet, how does one act on the urgency of suffering *with* bureaucratic structures in place? My goal here is not to discuss bureaucracy, but rather to point to the challenges of a politics of care when it is charged with greater powers of government. More broadly, I am interested in how this common humanity is actually produced and protected in practice.

The process of giving residency permits for illness was initiated in 1990 in various prefectures in France, beginning with the one in which I conducted my research.[13] The 1998 law came after the fact—after these medical offices had already been granting temporary authorizations for medical purposes.[14] But in general terms, the process goes as follows: To benefit from an illness permit, one needs an official medical certificate (from a doctor) saying that one is sick and that one's pathology should be taken into consideration as the basis for granting residency papers. This doctor's note must be presented to the immigration office (in the prefecture), although its contents, that is, the medical condition, should remain confidential. If the doctor requests it, the immigration office should refer the patient to the state medical office—the DDASS, or in the case of Paris, the Préfecture de Police, where the state doctor is based.[15] The state public health doctor should either meet the patient or read his/her file, issue an opinion about whether the patient needs papers and for how long, and this should be sent to the immigration office again, who puts it into practice. But there are many, many hoops to jump through to get here— almost none of which are about law or procedure. They are about moral and ethical stances, political positions, and deeper understandings of health and life. So while represented as universal, as "outside" politics, the body and its production are deeply embedded in political, spatial, and bureaucratic structures.

Isolation

Whether an immigrant has access to the illness clause depends from the beginning on their knowledge of their rights and their milieu. Are they in contact with immigrant rights or local community associations, or are they completely isolated? Do they have a way of learning about the law? At a Paris Women's Center community meeting, I met a lesbian couple from Colombia who had been in France for nine years. This was the first time they had been in contact with an immigrant rights group, which happened to operate out of the Women's Center. They had lived undercover for the previous nine years. They worked under the table; they went to and from work without stopping, one doing child care, the other cleaning homes, terrified of being arrested and deported. They had applied for papers during the 1997 amnesty (Chévènement's circular) but were refused on the grounds that they were single—célibataire—and their fear only increased. Indeed, their lives were typical of sans-papiers in their trepidation and isolation and in the exploitation they experienced for lack of power. Valérie explained to me that she had come to France when she was thirty; she and her partner Maria had left home in large part to escape discrimination against gays and lesbians in Colombia. At age thirty-two she became amenorrheic, that is, she stopped having her period. She went to a doctor whom she paid out of pocket. She explained to me that without properly examining her, and without asking her even one question, he had said to her, "You have premature menopause; what do you want *me* to do about it?" With that, he ushered her out of the office as quickly as he could. Since that humiliating experience, she had been afraid to go to another doctor about the problem. And she still had not had her period—when I met her, she was thirty-nine.

The evening we met, the three of us sat and talked while we ate a dinner provided by the Women's Center. There was a debate on prostitution scheduled that evening, and the food was part of the event. Valérie and Maria explained how they had spent all their money on their health problems—again, they are typical of sans-papiers whose lives are so difficult both emotionally and physically, their material conditions often so harsh, that they inevitably suffer from a variety of pathologies. Valérie had had two "nervous breakdowns." She said that the doctor she went to see had charged them double the regular price, knowing that they could do nothing to protest. She did not realize that everyone in France had access to medical care, free of charge, documented or undocumented. Again, like many sans-papiers, she did not want to go to a state building such as a hospital for fear of being discovered and deported. That evening I gave Valérie and Maria the numbers of Médecins sans Frontières and a few other hospital clinics that cater to sans-papiers. It was only because they had stumbled on an association based in the Women's Center, ARDHIS—specifically for lesbian, gay, and bisexual sans-papiers— that a whole new world of possibility opened for them.

Doctors

As we can see from Valérie's situation, if sans-papiers make it to a doctor, the operative question becomes, what kind of doctor is s/he? Doctors might know the law, but how do they apply it? Perhaps more importantly, doctors might understand the moral imperative to help, but do they adhere to a similar set of moral values about what suffering merits immediate relief? Where and how do their politics and morals meet? There were no rules about any of this. First, it was not clear at that time what pathologies were deemed "serious" and whether patients might have access to care in their home countries. There were no statistics, no guidelines for this. Dr. Amara, one of the doctors at a hospital clinic for sans-papiers, explained to me that even in "purely" medical circumstances, much interpretation is involved. For instance, with cases of hepatitis, a liver biopsy can identify the presence of hepatitis, and yet it can stay dormant for years. Only 40 percent of chronic cases become active. Does one give papers to chronic sufferers? Or how about cases of cancer that are in remission? At what point does one consider that remission definitive?

Second, the political leanings of the doctor writing the certificate are of critical concern for sans-papiers. The role of doctors' political inclinations was made clear to me when I was sick in Paris. I went to a doctor who initially thought I was *maghrébine*—he asked me this directly. When he realized that this was not the case, he let his views be known: he was fiercely anti-immigrant. He lived in the *banlieue* and explained that his neighborhood was "overrun." He said that people who did not have to deal with immigrants in their daily lives could pretend to be sympathetic, but anyone who did would understand his sentiments. I can only imagine that his racism had consequences for his immigrant patients: I doubt that he would have helped any of them to get papers, whatever their medical condition. In a similar vein, Dr. Amara spoke of a friend of his who refused to write a medical certificate that would open the way for an "illness permit" to a patient who was HIV+ because he simply did not want more HIV/AIDS patients to be able to get care in France. Dr. Amara explained that he could have reported his friend for acting illegally; but he did not feel this was an option, personally or professionally, since it was rarely done.

If, on one end of the spectrum, there are doctors who are anti-immigrant, on the other end there are doctors who are committed to more progressive combinations of medicine and politics. These doctors espouse a broader understanding of the meaning of health and feel a moral obligation to help those who are excluded by society. I encountered one such doctor—Dr. Girouard—who volunteered his time for a well-known immigrant rights organization. I met him in one of the Parisian banlieues where he saw patients, in a small building beside the local church. This banlieue, like most others around Paris, was largely built of drab concrete—a stark contrast to the architecture of Paris itself. He received patients a few days per week. I sat in with him as he attended to his patients, and then he agreed to answer a few questions. I could see he was helpful and kind to the sans-papiers, and he did what he could to help. He spoke to me about the "sans-papiers syndrome"—by this he meant the hypertension, ulcers, depression, and so on that were the result of the structural violence of immigrants' daily lives. With this syndrome in mind, he told me that he had written medical certificates for undocumented pregnant women whose partners or husbands did not have legal status. This helped them to avoid the medical costs of the birth and follow-up. He explained that one can exaggerate the complications of pregnancy enough to make women eligible for free pre- and postnatal care, which they would not otherwise have access to. Dr. Girouard had taken on sans-papiers hunger strikers as patients, making sure that they were medically fit. But because of this, he said, the immigration officers hated him. The result was that, if they saw his name on the medical certificate, they doubted his word. He admitted that he had made the mistake earlier in his career of writing a certificate for someone with hypertension, which was not a serious enough condition to warrant papers. The act compromised his credibility and revealed his political inclinations. Indeed, it broke the cardinal rule of humanitarian "neutrality." Interestingly, adhering to the principles of neutrality in this case might have better advanced his political beliefs, demonstrating that neutrality is not outside politics; rather, as Peter Redfield (2011) has argued, neutrality is a strategy.

Dr. Girouard's dilemma echoes that described by Susan Coutin (1994) about private citizens becoming enforcers of the law. Classifications performed by citizens, like judgments rendered by immigration officials, help create the legal discourse that defines individuals as juridical or nonjuridical beings. In this case, an individual's juridical status could depend on the relationship between a doctor and an immigration officer:

political sympathies on both sides come into play, in a complicated dance that is officially about "objective" medical opinion. This illustrates again that the illness clause is a discretionary practice, in which *who* makes the decision is crucial.

Medical Teams and Social Workers

So far, we have seen that the enactment of the illness clause depends in part on the isolation or community experienced by sans-papiers, and on the political positions of the doctors and immigration officials. But the urgency of suffering meets yet another challenge: not everyone in the business of health, medicine, or humanitarianism is driven by a desire to save the world or by a moral imperative to relieve suffering. Rather, as Liisa Malkki has written with respect to Red Cross workers, some are there simply as professionals, to earn a living, and to this end they exercise different types of expertise and respond to different imperatives.[16]

In the hospital clinics set up to help sans-papiers, the care depended on much more than the doctors: it was contingent upon the medical team as a whole. In one of the clinics where I observed, the team consisted of a nurse, a social worker, and several rotating doctors. The social worker did her job, she was professional, but she did not go out of her way to help people; she was not inspired by a larger mission to help those who were disenfranchised. It was a busy place, and she seemed overwhelmed by their need rather than inspired by it. Her manner did not encourage patients to share stories or hardships, it did not elicit information that might illuminate their condition, but she did her work nonetheless; she knew the rules. On the other hand, the doctors at this clinic were clearly driven by passion for the injustices of their patients' situations. They each had other jobs and came to help out in the clinic one or two days per week. They cared deeply about the situation of the sans-papiers and learned as much as they could about them as people. While they wrote medical certificates for the patients they judged sick enough (which each did slightly differently), they were each aware of the ethical dilemmas involved in their acts. In talking to me, several raised concerns about the unintended consequences of the illness clause—the false hope it instilled when the permit was only granted on a temporary basis, or the way it forced people to work under the table while they were receiving treatment because their papers had not been accompanied by a work permit. In working with the team, I realized that patients would need to adjust their mode of interaction, changing what they emphasized from doctor to social worker in order to be heard. The social worker functioned in a more rule-bound manner; the doctors responded more to an idea of moral urgency.

In a different clinic in Paris, another type of expertise was operative. There I interacted primarily with the social workers, who played a much more significant role in the process of giving medical certificates. In both clinics, it was commonplace for those who came for medical appointments to see social workers simultaneously: for marginalized populations, the possible treatments for medical conditions are inevitably complicated by social realities and living conditions. The doctor who started this service had held an important position with Médecins du Monde; he started the clinic when he realized that people had trouble accessing hospitals. When the service began, the patient population was 60 percent French people, 40 percent foreigners/sans-papiers. When I was there, 99 percent of the patients were without papers.

The head social worker, Mme. Julien, was an extremely efficient woman—she had a tough exterior, and she moved and spoke quickly, abruptly. After a few interactions with her it was clear, however, that she was kindhearted. I sat with her and another assistant in a room with a big round table as they received patients. The patients would sit on one side, she would sit beside them, and I sat across the table. She had their medical files in front of her, and early in each meeting she would ask each new patient if they had a serious illness; this was her attempt to help them by way of the illness clause. Most responded with a vigorous "yes," although it quickly became clear that they did not necessarily know if they did or not. Her question was a leading one—her voice suggested that severity of illness correlated with severity of suffering, and patients obviously wanted their suffering recognized.

On the first day I sat with her as she received patients, I listened to an Algerian man with a knee problem and a housing problem, a couple from the Republic of the Congo who told a long story about their lives, an older woman from the Congo who had a legal problem, and another Congolese woman who had refugee status but explained that she had had "her insides taken out" and thus wanted to be declared disabled so she would not have to work anymore. Before the next patient came in, Mme. Julien closed the door and said to me, "They all talk so much when you're here, I can't pick out the information I need! They look at you and talk and talk, I have a whole hall of people waiting!" When I replied apologetically—completely taken aback—that I was not asking them questions, she answered, "I know it isn't your fault, you're trying to observe but it's making my work harder." She asked me to come back in a few days, when she had another social worker on hand to help. I apologized profusely, but she responded by saying, "You have something—you're perhaps made for this kind of work—they turn and talk to you, they can tell you're listening, attentive."

I did go back, but it was clear that I was still disrupting her work, and she tolerated me begrudgingly. I tried to figure out what I had done the first time to elicit this response—what did my body language reveal? I had talked with the sans-papiers when she left the room, but only because they kept talking whether or not she was there. When for a large part of their daily lives they were invisible—undocumented and hence unrecognized by society, as they were quick to point out—listening became a powerful act. As Hannah Arendt so insightfully writes, "The fundamental deprivation of human rights is manifested first and above all in the deprivation of a place in the world which makes opinions significant and actions effective" (1951:293). I was positioned very differently than Mme. Julien. She dealt with stories of suffering and pain everyday and had done so for years. She had learned to be pragmatic; she knew what to look for and what to ignore in the quest to get people papers. What became apparent was that she was looking for a particular type of humanity in these people—were they *very* sick? If not, she went through the other criteria that would enable her to help them with their papers. Everything else was superfluous. I was disturbing this process, disrupting the work of expertise with a different kind of listening, revealing the patients to be more than the mould they were required to inhabit in order to get help. It was making everything messy.

At each step of the way to papers, a performance is required on both sides, from both parties. The illness clause sets up a legal category of sick sans-papiers, but similarly, it sets up a category of medical officials imbued with a new sort of power and responsibility. In each performance, a particular subject is both revealed and produced: a particular doctor, a particular social worker, a particular immigrant, a particular victim. If the immigrant is not allowed to speak as a multifaceted subject, only to exhibit injuries, a particular nation and a particular humanity also get produced in the process.

The State Medical Office

This new configuration of patient-victim and medical gatekeeper was exemplified in the state medical offices. These subject positions were created by the structural situation—as we will see, it had little to do with intentions. But let me reiterate: it was only after the sans-papiers made it to doctors who wrote them medical certificates, and only after they had presented themselves to the prefecture and after the prefecture had in turn referred them to the state medical office, that they showed up at the medical office.[17] Each level involved a series of decisions, sometimes politically motivated, sometimes morally motivated, and sometimes simply about luck. It was in the state medical office that the crucial decisions were made as to who got papers and who did not. The state public health doctor (*médecin inspecteur de santé publique,* or MISP) gave her/his opinion about whether the patient should be granted papers and for how long, but it was ultimately at the discretion of the immigration officials to confirm or deny this.

Much of the decision making was defined by the structure of the state medical offices—this is yet another active factor in defining "life." In the office where I did my research, state nurses operated on the front lines, receiving sans-papiers face-to-face: there were only a handful of *départements* where this was the case. The rest received medical files by mail. The nurses at the DDASS where I did my research received sans-papiers two days per week, to allow them to present their cases. The state medical office building was an imposing concrete edifice, set in the midst of the concrete *cité* (housing estate); it was grouped with the other regional administrative buildings, such as the immigration office, the city hall, and the police headquarters. Yet it did not have the same threatening structure as the prefecture; it was lined with windows that looked out onto the concrete playground below. The nurses' office was a small but friendly space, with photos of children from all over the world pinned on the walls (taken by one of the nurses on her travels), bringing color and life to an otherwise sterile atmosphere.

On the second floor, the sans-papiers lined up on seats outside the nurses' office, and the nurses called them in one by one. There were usually two nurses on duty, and one listened to the sans-papiers' request while the other dealt with other public health issues. They both sat in the office, however, and if the story being told was particularly heart-wrenching, or someone needed specialized help, there was always another nurse to turn to. I sat with the two nurses, behind their desks, and faced the sans-papiers as they came in. I remained silent; I sat and listened, and I occasionally wrote in my notebook to look busy so that they did not direct questions to me. I did not want to disrupt the nurses' work. The nurses spoke to the sans-papiers patients, and after the patients left the nurses would tell me the specifics of each case. I observed the interaction and the body language.

The nurses listened to the stories recounted and took notes about relevant information such as the sans-papiers' family lives, if they had family members left in their countries of origin, and why, besides illness, they wanted to stay in France. The nurses looked at the details of the medical certificate and then passed the file to the state public health doctor. In theory, the state doctor made the decision on his/her own, after reviewing what the nurses noted about the patient in question—a point to which I will return. Again, this was one of the few *départements* that functioned with the help of nurses. In the other offices, the state public health doctors reviewed the files and made their decisions without ever meeting the sans-papiers (Delettre 1999).

One nurse at the state medical office where I observed explained to me that they continued to receive sans-papiers in person because they had been doing it since 1990. She suggested it was also because they had more available nurses. I realized quite quickly, however, that the persistence of face-to-face interactions owed as much to the biographies of the nurses as to the practice's longevity. The nurses insisted on maintaining their role because they believed passionately in what they were doing and in treating people as human beings in a broad, humanist sense—not simply in the medical realm. One of the nurses explained to me her reasons for doing this job: "For me," she claimed, "there are no borders." She had brought up her children in a *cité* where children from all backgrounds played together. The interactions with sans-papiers (whom the nurses called *les étrangers,* or foreigners) made her work worthwhile, she said. One of the other nurses worked part-time in prisons and with drug abusers. The nurses each believed that the social and medical were intimately intertwined and hence felt a moral obligation to play a role in the immigration process.

The role of the nurses was critical in determining who received papers: they fought to keep the process a face-to-face interaction. But at its heart, as we have already seen, was a tension between "medical" views about the value and meaning of life and health and political views on immigration. The medical officials were concerned about each patient before them and responded to what they often thought of as a moral obligation; the immigration officers, by contrast, were the appointed guard dogs of the nation-state. And as it so happened, the immigration office had more power to institute its view, since the illness clause came under the jurisdiction of the Ministry of Interior—the ministry responsible for immigration. The medical officials, as part of the Ministry of Health, had to ingratiate themselves with the immigration officials in order to influence the immigration process.

The medical officials' role was subject to a continuous power struggle. They admitted to being constrained by their relationship with the prefecture; despite acting out of a desire to further a notion of social justice, they could not simply let everyone in, because they were being monitored. They had to provide their statistics to prefecture officials at meetings every few months; and, as the nurses said to me, at the end of each meeting there was a deadly serious statement couched in the language of joviality, in which medical personnel were warned to drastically reduce the numbers of sick people they let in. The nurses and doctors realized that, to be kept in the decision-making circles, they had to maintain legitimacy—and their legitimacy depended on only letting in people who suffer from pathologies that have life-threatening consequences.

But again, we return to the question of how to identify such pathologies, how to protect "life"—the broadest of concepts.[18] There were no lists of life-threatening pathologies, nor was there easily accessible information on whether people could receive treatment in their home countries. The doctors were urged to contact the Office of Populations and Migrations for information. But no source of information took into account people's substantive ability to access medical treatment: Did they live far away from city centers? Did they have a means of transport to hospitals or doctors? Did they have the money to get treatment, or to continue treatment if it involved subsequent trips to medical facilities? These questions were not included in the guidelines. These were asked at the discretion of the medical officials receiving each case.

There are documented differences in how the state medical officials understood what it means to be in a "life-threatening" situation, and these different understandings evidently resulted in different strategies by both medical officials and sans-papiers. Of the state medical offices in three different *départements,* one gave papers to immigrants for nearly every pathology—the percentage of overall positive responses was 96.7 percent. The other two gave papers 90–100 percent of the time to those suffering from fatal or terminal illnesses such as HIV/AIDS and cancer, but they differed on giving papers to those suffering from chronic illnesses such as diabetes (24 percent vs. 84 percent) and heart disorders (24 percent vs. 92 percent); and finally, they differed radically on psychiatric problems (0 percent vs. 80 percent) (see Delettre 1999; and D. Fassin 2001a).

What this means is that different understandings of "life" were being played out and that the structure of the particular state medical office was a major factor in outcome. In the particular state office where I observed, the face-to-face interaction between the nurses and sans-papiers largely determined how "life threatening" was interpreted and, thus, who was granted permits for illness. The personal interaction allowed for compassion to be evoked—it allowed the sans-papiers to appear as people, not simply as files or pathologies. It allowed for their social realities to be included in the judgment. Yet a face-to-face encounter allows for performances on both sides, and if one does not perform in the desired manner, one may be penalized and excluded. The nurses recognized this; compassion formed the basis of their struggle with officials at the prefecture, who also recognized the power of the personal interaction. Afraid that such interactions would elicit compassion more often than not, the prefecture wanted to eliminate the phase where sans-papiers came to the medical office, and the medical officials wanted desperately to keep it.

PRACTICING COMPASSION, CULTIVATING THE BONDS OF HUMANITY

Let me be clear: compassion was not always a determining event. In the majority of cases, compassion did not figure in the nurses' decisions or opinions. Certain cases were more straightforward than others. On my first day sitting in with the nurses, an Algerian couple came in with a little girl who was perhaps five years old. The girl had clearly been undergoing chemotherapy; she had no hair left. As one nurse, Felicia, said to me, it was a "horribly easy" case. The family was there to ask for papers for the mother so that she could stay with her daughter during treatment. Felicia joked with the little girl, trying to keep the spirit of the interaction light, and promised the mother that the nurses would recommend that she receive papers. There were also cases in which it was easy to give a negative reply: one man explained that he was allergic to eggs, for example, and another had an itchy scalp.

The dilemmas and the evocation of compassion came for nurses and doctors with the more complicated cases—often chronic or psychiatric, as indicated by the earlier statistics. More broadly, if as we have just seen, institutional structures, political positions, and cultures of expertise play an instrumental albeit unacknowledged role in defining life, then compassion, too, enacts a critical form of discretionary and mediating power, helping to define the universal truth of suffering, health, and humanity. When I first asked the nurses about difficult or ambiguous cases they

had encountered, Felicia gave me a few examples. She spoke of Algerians who had seen their families killed or tortured before their eyes. She
said they suffered from trauma, but it was unclear whether she thought
this was an illness or not. In such cases, the medical offices found themselves picking up the slack for OFPRA (the French office for the protection
of refugees and stateless people), because very few refugees were being
accepted. The state medical officials would thus declare such people ill
if at all possible, again, for "humanitarian" reasons. Felicia also told me
the story of an African woman I will call Latasha, whose friend desired
Latasha's husband. As the story goes, the friend threw sulfuric acid on
Latasha in order to steal her husband. Latasha was completely disfigured.
She came for reconstructive surgery, and it took a long time for her to be
presentable enough to go out in public—"She'll never be pretty," Felicia
said. Unsurprisingly, Latasha did not want to return home. I never found
out what kind of permit the medical officials gave her; but the nurses
clearly felt for her and did what they could to help.

Gradually, I learned of other such difficult cases—the ones where the
definitions of life, dignity, and suffering were being written and rewritten
on the spot, mediated by compassion. One doctor involved in the issu-
ance of illness permits raised the difficult question of pregnant women,
echoing the concerns of Dr. Girouard that I mentioned earlier. What if the
pregnant women were deported away from their husbands or partners?
Could being pregnant alone be considered an illness with life-threatening consequences? The answer had occasionally been yes. There were
also cases of African women in polygamous marriages who were infer-
tile or unable to conceive and yet whose marriages depended on them
bearing children—or so the story from the medical officials goes. They
came in asking for papers for sterility treatment because their husbands
would otherwise divorce them, leaving them alone in a foreign country.
Such women, too, had occasionally received papers for treatment.

Compassion Training

These stories reveal the cases that the medical officials found to be particularly compelling, difficult, or memorable, the cases that elicited

compassion and that help to draw the contours of the category of "life" and of humanity. But why these stories and not others? Compassion is not a fixed or essential emotion; while Arendt (1990) argues that compassion, in contrast to pity, is directed toward particular individuals, possessing a practical character in that it can only be actualized in particular situations in which those who do not suffer meet and come face-to-face with those who do, nevertheless, the emotional commitment involved in compassion is dependent on the ability of the person called on to imagine the suffering. That is, even if they are face-to-face, for imagination to play its role in the coordination of emotional commitments, people must make a case for it, nourishing their imagination from the same referents; their claims must be shaped by the same ideas of what suffering is and where the threshold of the bearable is drawn (Boltanski 1999:50). Indeed, compassion is a practice that all are trained in (Berlant 2004).

This is where the nurses come into the picture: they were experts in the practice of compassion. One might also call this training in "humanity"—in producing and feeling the sentimental bonds of this category of universal solidarity. Humanity in this sense involves cultivating a particular ethical sensibility that conjoins the human and the humane (Laqueur 2009). Several of the nurses who worked at the office where I observed had been there for a long time: twenty years for one, ten years for another. They had watched the rotation of many state public health doctors and had seen how each handled cases differently. I started doing fieldwork at the state medical office at a transitional moment—when one doctor was being replaced with another. I was therefore able to watch the training process—that is, the multileveled initiation process of the doctor by the nurses. The nurses used their experience to help the doctor learn the ropes, to teach her how to fill in the forms and to read the files in order to decide which illnesses—and from which countries—were most serious. The doctors were trained in public health and employed by the state, but insofar as they were often transferred from completely unrelated state services, they frequently knew nothing about immigration legislation or about the conditions that could be deemed serious enough to warrant papers. In addition to teaching the doctor about immigration laws and public health conditions in different countries, then, the nurses also used subtle techniques to train the doctor to take the same political approach as they did. Most importantly, they taught compassion.

A few weeks into the tenure of the new state public health doctor, the nurses presented her with a "test" case to see what she would do. The following story is real, but they presented it to her without their conclusions. In the late 1990s, a young Algerian woman I will call Fatima came to Paris after having been raped and disfigured by her uncle. The background to this violence was the death of her primary caretaker, her grandmother, which forced her into the care of her uncle and aunt. Both her uncle and aunt blamed her for the rape and thought it was normal that the uncle would be tempted to engage sexually with her if they were living under the same roof. Fatima was therefore sent to France where her mother was living. The nurses said that she had looked terrible. They decided to give her temporary papers to allow her to receive medical care. When the treatment was finished and her papers were about to expire, Fatima returned to the state medical office to ask for a renewal of her papers. As they later explained to me, the nurses understood that she would return to a "pitiful" life in Algeria where she would be forever shamed because of her rape and would thus be unmarriageable. According to them, her life would be one of ostracization and loneliness. They decided that in the face of this reality, they would rather grant her authorization to stay in France for treatment for an indeterminate period—which means, effectively, forever if she so chooses, renewing her illness permit until she could apply for citizenship. The treatment the doctor prescribed was psychological—Fatima was considered to be suffering from trauma. The nurses were very clear when talking to me that this decision crossed over into the realm of social justice. But they saw themselves as inevitably implicated in moral decision making, which they believed was required at a fundamental level in caring for people's health and well-being. Health, they explained to me, was about the social and political as much as the physical and emotional.

As part of their compassion training, the nurses presented this case to the state public health doctor; "Thank goodness!" they exclaimed, that the doctor agreed Fatima should be given papers. However, there were other cases in which the doctor did not exhibit the "required" compassion. For instance, a woman with serious diabetes came asking for papers for her husband; she herself had a ten-year residency permit and she asked that he stay to help her. The state doctor responded simply that she did not need her husband. The nurses reacted to her opinion by saying, "Come on, we all need our husbands and all the more when sick!" This convinced the doctor to change her mind. The doctor had come to a similar "wrong-headed" conclusion (according to the nurses) in the case of a woman who came in with a twenty-day-old baby who had a cold; the mother wanted to stay with the baby until the baby recovered. The doctor's response was that the baby did not need her mother. The nurses were horrified—they realized that "these are questions about human rights, not about medicine; that is why she has trouble." The nurses agreed that obviously a cold is not sufficient grounds to give papers; but, they argued, reprimanding the doctor, the negative response should be based on the fact that the illness is not serious enough, not on the fact that the baby does not need her mother! They had no choice but to engage in an ongoing training process. For example, this involved inviting the state doctor to meet patients whose cases went beyond the "purely medical," so that she too could meet them face-to-face, feel compassion, and understand them "as human beings."

Compassion in Action

The nurses' job was to translate stories into pathologies when they felt it was appropriate, trauma narratives into biologically based injury; this translation between regimes of truth was in many ways the essence of their job and what they themselves saw as their moral calling. I was present in the medical office for several encounters that culminated in a decision by the medical officials to give papers on compassionate grounds—I saw the process at work. Again, the cases reveal that compassion is not simply about responding to suffering based on the premise that all life is equal and all suffering must be eased. Life is never devoid of its particularities or its histories, and compassion is evoked more strongly by some stories and images than others, rendering only some kinds of suffering morally legitimate. One case involved a Moroccan man who had come to France at age twenty-three and had been in the country eleven years without papers. He had had polio and was partially disabled because of it. He had had three temporary illness permits but had been turned down in his application for papers in the 1997 amnesty because the prefecture claimed that he was not "really sick." While the nurses were going through his papers, they discovered that he had been granted disability benefits *(allocation aux adultes handicapés)* for the next two years by some fault of the prefecture; unfortunately, he could not access the benefits unless he had a *titre de séjour,* that is, residency papers. The doctor who had provided the medical certificate argued that because the state had granted him benefits he could not now be refused papers—clearly the doctor was appealing to the state medical officials on humanitarian grounds. The nurse realized that the man did not need urgent health care. He was disabled but not acutely or "life-threateningly" sick. Yet it did seem unfair to deny him papers when everything else was in place and he had been in France for so long.

The state public health doctor walked in just as the young man left; Annette, one of the nurses, showed her the papers and explained the situation. The doctor said, "It's a horrible situation, but he doesn't need medical care. What do we do? Give him papers for an indeterminate duration? We're entering into the social now, not the medical!" They wondered how to do it and decided to ask the doctor who had originally written the medical certificate if the patient required some type of surgical care. "We're cheating a bit here aren't we?" said the doctor. Nodding "yes," one of the nurses offered her view that sometimes one had to "cheat" in exceptional cases for humanitarian reasons. She reassured the new state doctor, confiding in her that the former state doctors had done this as well.

Later, Annette explained to me how meeting people face-to-face made all the difference to her. She was deeply aware of the ethical dilemmas they faced in granting permits, which involved a continuous reinterpretation of the meaning of both "health" and "life." She took the Moroccan man's case as her example, stating that, on paper, his situation might have looked different; but here we could all see him, "young, good-looking, came when he was twenty-three and now is thirty-four—he wants to be able to get on with his life!" Clearly, compassion was in play.

Another such case occurred while I was present. Interestingly, it was initiated by a phone call from an official at the prefecture. Felicia, the nurse on duty, was wary at first; but later she described this particular official as more sympathetic than the rest. The official spoke of a young man from Eastern Europe who had tried to claim refugee status but had been refused by the prefecture because this official's boss would not acknowledge the claim that the young man made; namely, that he had been forced into a prostitution ring, one that was linked to drug smuggling. More specifically, this young man, whom I will call Boris, had claimed asylum to escape a prostitution-drug ring in which he was being held against his will. The official had clearly been moved by Boris's story and was calling confidentially to ask if the medical office could help; he suggested that Boris might have hepatitis. Felicia was excited and intrigued but nervous that it was a trap designed to catch her in devising pathologies for papers. "No problem, we'll take care of it," she told him. Whatever this young man had in the way of pathology, they would find a way to help him.

We waited and waited for Boris to show up with his file; I was there when he did. He was young and appeared very nervous and uncomfortable. One nurse asked him a few questions in a kind voice, trying to put him at ease; she was hoping to hear his story, but he revealed only the minimum. The nurses were disappointed, wondering why they were not able to elicit his story while someone at the prefecture had succeeded in doing so. They prided themselves on creating an environment where people shared their experiences and cried if they wanted to cry. They identified themselves as compassionate people. Despite the young Eastern European's silence, they did help him. Here, it was the compassion of an immigration official translated to the medical officials that led to papers being granted at the behest of the medical office. It was not the result of the face-to-face interaction with the nurses: in the right circumstances, compassion can also work in translation.

Compassion can be the key to making an exception, but its lack can be just as fateful. There were people who were not able to elicit compassion, whose stories of suffering did not strike a chord in the nurses or doctors. I had heard the nurses explicitly say that their job required them to

perform humanitarian gestures, but I also heard them say just the opposite, explaining that they were there to enforce a "medical" agenda. This
comment reveals that the distinction between the medico-scientific and
the humanitarian is a strategic one. That is, the medico-scientific realm
does not stand outside politics, despite being represented as universal
and objective; rather, its claim to be outside is revealed here as in itself
political. Some examples of how the medical is demarcated from the
humanitarian are instructive. An Algerian man came in one day accompanied by a white French man. The Algerian explained his case: he had
been in France for ten years but had been refused papers at the prefecture because he did not have enough proof of his uninterrupted presence on French soil. It was not clear if he was slightly mentally disabled
or if he was simply terrified, desperate; he acted as if this were his last
chance at life. He said he needed an operation but did not know when
he would need it, and he answered the nurse's questions vaguely. The
nurse explained to him kindly but firmly that she needed more medical information, that this office responded only to medical need: "not
to the social, not to the humanitarian; it has to be a serious illness, not
just a prolonged one." He looked upset and asked beseechingly, "You
don't help with papers?" Without hesitation, the nurse shook her head
and answered, "No, only when it's medical." He looked distraught. Here
was a case that did not convince the nurse to make an exception. Something failed to evoke her compassion.

Similarly, a twenty-five-year-old Algerian man came in one day, and
not long after he entered the office he started crying. He claimed that he
had had a heart attack a few days ago, which Felicia pointed out was
not true. He had had a heart *murmur,* she said, looking down at his file.
He said that he could not go on. If he was sent to Algeria, who would
take care of his wife and his mother? "Last week I was going to commit
suicide," he said. "I've never done anything to anyone, I haven't committed a crime and still they do this to us, they break up couples!" I
could tell Felicia was getting impatient. Her tone of voice changed. She
said, prodding, "Oh suicide would really help your wife. How long
have you been married?" "Nineteen days," he answered. Felicia then
got more annoyed. "How can the state break up your marriage when

they don't even know about it? Be fair," she said. He told a long story about his mother who was a healer and his wife who was sick; and he kept saying how unfair it was to have a heart attack at his age! He was very agitated and kept repeating himself. When he left, Felicia said, "Son nez est grand comme un bec" ("His nose is as large as a beak"), gesturing toward her own nose, pretending it was growing, insinuating that the man was lying. She claimed his marriage was one of convenience because the wife was thirty-nine and he was only twenty-five. Why Felicia was immediately so suspicious was hard to say. The man certainly exaggerated, and his story did not make complete sense. But then he was distraught and crying. At the time, I was surprised by her reaction because she rarely lost patience, and I concluded that the man must have elicited a negative feeling in her—nothing concrete, because to me, the message he conveyed largely rang true.

THE COLONIAL CONTOURS OF THE MORALLY LEGITIMATE SUFFERING BODY

The illness clause is premised upon the notion of a universally recognizable suffering body. However, if institutional structures, political positions, and the discretionary power of compassion help to shape its enactment, we must also understand that it is profoundly shaped by broader global economic inequalities and colonial histories; these influence who shows up at the state medical office, and they determine the character of the relationship between nurse and patient. In other words, the activity in the state medical office—while sometimes couched as exceptional, humanitarian, and apolitical—nevertheless reflects and reproduces global inequalities on a local stage.

Most explicitly, those who came to request papers for illness were primarily from former colonies (see table 3). The largest group of claimants were from Algeria, then Mali, Morocco, and Congo-Zaire. Similarly, building on histories where men initially came alone as migrant laborers, *sans-papières* (undocumented women) were overrepresented in the borderline cases at the state medical office because they tended to be

Table 3   National origin of patients (most prevalent nationalities) applying for
"illness clause" permits in the state medical office (DDASS) in a *banlieue*
outside Paris, 1998, 1999, 2000

Rank[a]	1998	%[b]	1999	%	2000	%
1	Algeria (150)[c]	15	Algeria (207)	21	Algeria (323)	23.7
2	Mali (140)	14	Morocco (122)	12	Mali (162)	10
3	Zaire	8	Mali (110)	11	Morocco (158)	9.8
4	Morocco (70)	7	Ivory Coast (59)	6	Rep. of the Congo & Zaire (DRC) (122)	7.6
5	Pakistan (59)	6	Rep. of the Congo (52)	5	Ivory Coast (99)	6.1
6	Rep. of the Congo (55)	6	Cameroun (45)	5	Cameroun (86)	5.3
7 & 8	Cameroun (50)	5	Pakistan & Tunisia (36)	4	Tunisia & China (64)	4.1
9	Ivory Coast (43)	4	Zaire (DRC) (31)		Pakistan (44)	2.7
10 & 11	Senegal (32)	3	Haiti (28)	3	Haiti & Yugoslavia (38)	2.4
12	Tunisia (31)	3			Senegal	2

N O T E S : There are no national statistics on illness permits; these figures come from the
département with the highest number of claims for legalization.

[a] Rank is based on an average of the years.

[b] Percentages are calculated based on the total number of files (including all nationalities, not
only those most prevalent).

[c] Numbers in parentheses are the total number of patients of that nationality; not available for
all nationalities.

the ones joining already present husbands. In this sense, the dynamic
between nurse and patient goes beyond the usual power difference in
medical settings, informed not only by the difference between citizen
and foreigner but by the history of gendered and racially marked colonial hierarchies.

But the illness clause is also shaped by images and narratives and their
histories. To be accepted as a French subject on the basis of compassion,

one must be accepted as plausible; and images present in the national imagination inform the legitimacy of one's performance. As Judith Butler writes, "affect depends upon social supports for feeling" (2009:50). Was the Algerian man turned away because Algerian men should not cry? Was it because Algerian men are depicted in the French public imaginary as violent and deceitful and as oppressive to women? These images are the colonial legacy and have become all the more intense since the bitter war of Algerian independence from French colonial rule. Since the recent backlash against Islam in France and Europe, they have been reinvoked with increasing frequency. If the nurse's suspicion of the Algerian man had anything to do with representations of Arab men as emblems of "antimodernity" in France (Guénif-Souilamas and Macé 2004), it is similarly plausible that, in Fatima's case, compassion was based on a familiar Orientalist narrative about pitiful Muslim women. In other words, compassion depends on circulating narratives, images, and histories—on evoking a historically located moral legitimacy—and often on maintaining this unequal power relation between nurse and patient, citizen and foreigner.

Furthermore, as critics of the humanitarian movement have noted, for a person to be helped, humanitarianism often requires the suffering person to be represented in the *passivity* of their suffering, not in the action they take to confront and escape it (Boltanski 1999:190). Whether the Algerian man who claimed to have had a heart attack was indeed lying or not, his performance was not convincing because it was too active, he was perceived as strategic—not a suffering, passive (and therefore innocent) body. His personality took up too much room in the narrative. Worthy or not, one must perform innocence, and again, this requires that one seem above or beyond politics. It is perhaps not surprising, then, that gender plays an important role in who will be accepted: gender configurations suggest that women are more easily understood as victims, as apolitical, and hence they are more easily interpellated into the position of moral legitimacy. Indeed, the passive feminized subject is compassion's ideal.[19]

Interestingly, compassion seems to be most consistently evoked in cases revolving around sexuality or sexual violence. That is, issues around sexual violence or sexuality are privileged as the most basic form of suffering: from Fatima who was raped by her uncle, to the Eastern European who was fleeing a forced male prostitution ring, to the sterility of African women in polygamous marriages—these situations are deemed most worthy of humanitarian exception. As Eric Fassin (2007) writes, violence is a language, and while sexual violence can speak of sexual order or disorder, it can also simultaneously speak of various types of borders: race, class, nationality, and so on. More importantly, perhaps, it can serve as a weapon to divide people along the lines of race, class, or ethnicity, for instance, by associating certain kinds of violence with certain kinds of people. The way sexual violence stands in as the most morally legitimate form of suffering is characteristic of the larger politics of care I discuss throughout this book; it brings together the languages of humanitarianism and violence against women, drawing on shifting understandings of vulnerability that are often expressed through sexualized bodies.[20]

Gender and sexuality are of course both highly racialized performances, as Sherene Razack (1995) has demonstrated in her work on the gender persecution law in Canada; certain women are better positioned (i.e., stereotyped) to take advantage of images of innocence. In the French case, as in the Canadian context Razack describes, one becomes a more sympathetic character if one's experience plays into the familiar narrative that Gayatri Spivak (1988) has termed "white men saving brown women from brown men." As I will further discuss in chapter 6, a key element of this dynamic is that, with the illness clause, one must *remain* sick to keep one's papers. If one recovers, one loses one's papers and a chance at life as a citizen in France. One must remain in some way disabled, diseased, or a victim. In other words, one must maintain the unequal power dimension—one that is embodied in new ways, bringing a new twist to extant racial, gendered, and geopolitical hierarchies.

THE REENTRY OF HISTORY
AND THE END OF COMPASSION

As we have seen, the illness clause was instituted to protect undocumented immigrants whose suffering is identified as exceptionally grave, worthy of compassion, and outside politics. To truly exist outside politics as an undocumented immigrant, however, is an impossible proposition, not least because the classification of "undocumented" or "illegal" is political. Restrictive immigration laws forcibly intervene in one's daily life in any number of ways: they make it dangerous to travel on the metro for fear of identity checks; they make employment in nonexploitative conditions hard to find; they make it difficult to find housing, to get schooling, to get medical care. The apolitical status of the "successful," sick subject of the illness clause—outside time, space, and history—is required for humanitarian intervention, which eschews any form of longer-term political change or solution in the name of being able to respond, unfettered, to emergencies. But as we have seen, the neutral humanitarian space is itself a fiction, fraught with tensions, and much work goes into maintaining it as such. As soon as historicity enters the picture, the humanitarian impulse is unable to function; it is transformed.

The truth of the apolitical, innocent subject—in other words, its status as fiction—started to come to light several years into the practice of the illness clause. From 2002 to 2006, as I returned to the state medical office where I did my primary research, I watched as the situation became increasingly politicized. When Nicolas Sarkozy was appointed the interior minister in Chirac's government in 2002, he tightened the immigration laws, and conditions of life deteriorated rapidly for the sans-papiers. This was evident at the level of policy as well as at the local level, and I will turn to this latter first.

With very few other means of entry, word eventually spread about the illness clause, and lines of immigrants filled the halls at the state medical office and trailed down the stairs. As already mentioned, the number of cases considered for illness permits across France rose precipitously, from 1,500 in 1999 to 36,008 in 2004. In this climate, the public health staff came face-to-face with the sans-papiers in ways they had not anticipated. When confronted with large groups of immigrants in their halls and bathrooms and stairways, they could no longer circumscribe their encounters to meeting with individual, atomized suffering bodies. Dealing with this situation was no longer a question of compassion, but one of politics: the suffering was suddenly visible as a collective experience, part of a larger context. And with groups of sans-papiers in public spaces, the issue became racialized; the nurses said that they heard racist remarks circulate among the public health staff. They were shocked to learn that their own colleagues, with whom they had worked for years, were unabashedly racist. They blamed the climate of fear instituted by Sarkozy for authorizing the racism.

But if this were not enough, the nurses discovered a trafficking ring in medical certificates for very serious illness such as cancer and HIV/ AIDS as well as the increasingly common diagnosis of PTSD or trauma, with proof of torture. The patients came from all over: the Maghreb, Haiti, the Republic of the Congo, the former Yugoslavia. The nurses explained to me that, one day, when Annette left the room to photocopy the documents of a patient with a serious type of cancer, she forgot a document and returned unexpectedly to the office, where she found the patient half snickering, half laughing. It made her concerned; so she looked through the file more carefully. She began to see a pattern in the files: there was an increasing number of serious illnesses like cancer and HIV/AIDs, but the patients did not look very ill. For instance, they had not lost their hair with chemotherapy, and Annette said to me, "I remember thinking, these new chemo drugs are amazing! People really do not look as sick." When examined more closely, the certificates all had the same grammatical errors, and often the doctors' names were fabricated. When real doctors' names were used, the nurses investigated and determined that the doctors had not actually signed these affidavits.

Annette told me that because they had always tried to be helpful, they really did not anticipate this; it took them several years to figure it out. During that time, the trafficking ring gathered more and more confidence, and the applications with false documents grew in number. In one sense, this was quite predictable; such forms of "fraud" are not specific to the French context, but rather they are embedded in humanitarianism more broadly, where the logic of aid renders such "corruption" almost inevitable. This is because humanitarianism takes place in the context of unequal relationships between aid givers and recipients, and yet humanitarianism is framed as only an ethical—not a political— practice. As Ilana Feldman (2007a, 2007b) suggests in the context of early relief projects in Gaza, acts such as exaggerating the number of people registered for food rations might be political claims, but they are considered fraudulent because they are made in what is considered to be a circumscribed, ethical field. In this sense, the trafficking ring might also be understood as leveling a challenge to the closed-door immigration policies of the French state, engaging with the politics of immigration, not simply with the ethics of humanitarian aid.

In any case, combined with the new focus on national security, the traffic in certificates was enough to effectively shut down the service. When I went back in 2006, the nurses were just closing up shop; they were no longer permitted to receive sans-papiers face-to-face, despite the fact that it was only by receiving them in person that they had detected the trafficking ring. Annette, who was a few years away from retirement, had decided to take early retirement; she was crushed by the closing of their service. She bemoaned the loss of the humanitarian moment that they had lived through and facilitated—it had been a glorious moment for them, and she could not bear to be there anymore, charged to further an agenda based on fear and discrimination.

In fact, the balance had started to tip away from a politics of care toward one of policing and security several years earlier, and it was apparent all over, not just in the state medical office I knew best. From the beginning of Sarkozy's tenure as minister of interior, the right to health for all was challenged; in 2002, he tried to shut out sans-papiers from universal health coverage, or AME (L'Aide Médicale de l'État), by introducing an article into the state budget that proposed to charge all undocumented immigrants fees for medical services and that restricted access to medical care to those who could prove three years of residence.[21] While the desire to stop medical tourism was the justification, humanitarian and public health associations fought this proposed legislation and took it to the level of the International Federation of Human Rights, which chastised France for not respecting the principles of the European Social Charter. But this was just the beginning of the process by which the French state began to enlist the health care system in its desire to control and crack down on immigration. The state came back again in 2003 with new restrictions on AME. As part of this project, the state was determined to undermine the right to protect sick sans-papiers by way of the illness clause, saying that doctors were acting fraudulently. So vehement were the attacks that a group of associations formed the Observatory for Foreigners' Right to Health Care (Observatoire du Droit à la Santé des Étrangers, or ODSE) to monitor the rollback of rights. In 2005, the state tried unsuccessfully to pass a law overturning the illness clause; in 2006, the state tried again by issuing a new circular. And again in 2006, there was an attempt to severely restrict the application of the illness clause by posting country reports online: these listed the so-called available treatments in these countries, so that officials in the Ministry of Health and Ministry of Interior could check. The problem was that these *fiches pays,* or "country reports," did not take into account whether patients had the means to access necessary treatments due to financial or geographic constraints—in fact, their primary purpose was to provide a means of denying illness permits. These country reports were only required to document the existence of *one* hospital or treatment center that purported to dispense the necessary treatment for a certain illness. In 2007, for the first time in ten years—since the illness clause was instituted—this led to the deportation of sick sans-papiers.

The demise of the illness clause was built into its birth; it existed only insofar as it was perceived as outside politics. It was inevitable that, in a historical moment defined by the politics of immigration, the illnesses of undocumented immigrants would be understood as political phenomena and that the sans-papiers would no longer exemplify suffering in what was imagined and desired to be its purest, most innocent, most moral form.

CONCLUDING THOUGHTS

As we have seen, the illness clause was grounded in a universal ethics, one that takes bodily suffering as exemplary of a humanity that transcends partisan political, linguistic, religious, cultural, or other affiliations. Yet while it proposed universality, the illness clause actually produced and protected a very specific, limited category of "humanity": it did so through discretionary political and institutional power and through the highly selective power of compassion. These limitations ultimately forced the sick body to be rendered suspicious, unable to maintain its claim on the humanity protected by humanitarianism.

Insofar as this enactment of universal humanity was located in the medical realm, we must recognize this space as an important site of power, where doctors, nurses, and state officials judge which bodies are worthy of being called human. It is a space for the production of new forms of subjectivity and inequality. Health officials were reconfigured as border guards, and sans-papiers were configured as patients, as ill, as forever marked and interpellated as sick, as already handicapped. The ability of a politics of care to further a more just world must be seriously interrogated when we see how compassion acts as a form of policing, choosing a few exceptional individuals and excluding the rest. That is, while compassion may help to create the sentimental bonds of humanity (Laqueur 2009), it does so using an inherently exclusionary process. Indeed, according to Arendt (1990), by its very definition, compassion is unable to generalize.[22] This politics of care is thus about the exception rather than the rule, about generosity rather than entitlement. It is based on engaging other people in relationships of empathy and in this way *demonstrating* one's common humanity; this is a form of care that, when taken to the extreme, entails *selling* one's suffering, bartering for membership with one's life and body. As the political body loses legitimacy in an increasingly globalized world where national sovereignty is at stake and borders of all kinds are zealously guarded, the illness clause demonstrates that the supposedly apolitical suffering body is becoming the most legitimate vehicle in France with which to do politics. But what kind of politics is this? Next, I turn to an analysis of compassion in a different context, where the focus is more explicitly on the sexually violated body.

FOUR

In the Name of Violence
against Women

In February 2007, three months before the presidential election in France, presidential candidate (now president) Nicolas Sarkozy went to a shelter for battered women in Paris called Coeur de Femmes and listened to the women's stories of violence, humiliation, and rape. The women came from all over—Mali, Morocco, Ivory Coast, China, Poland—and several were *sans-papières,* as undocumented immigrant women have called themselves. According to reports, Sarkozy responded to the stories with compassion. He later publicly offered to rescue them (on April 29, 2007), stating, "To each martyred woman in the world, I want France to offer its protection, by giving her the chance to become French" (Le Monde 2007). When pushed by the Socialist candidate Segolène Royal, in the subsequent presidential debates, to answer if he would really give papers to all women victims of violence *(les femmes martyrisées),* Sarkozy reassured her that he would approach them on a "case by case" basis, as with the politics of immigration more broadly. Yet he explained that he trusted the director of this shelter to bring him the cases that mattered—the "dramatic situations"—what the director herself referred to as "the exceptional cases." Sarkozy continued, "I will hold my promises. . . . These are women who have been chased, raped, beaten and the France I imagine is a generous and welcoming France" (Lerougetel 2007).

I see this as an exemplary moment in the politics of immigration in France, as it reveals how moral and ethical discourses, institutions, and practices have come to play a significant role in the government of immigration and citizenship. Here, sexual violence renders legitimate the claim for papers and basic rights; more precisely, its legitimacy is based on (Sarkozy's) *compassion* for these exceptional, suffering victims. It is all the more striking that violence against women seems to be such an important political issue in France, one so critical that it justifies giving papers to immigrants, particularly in a climate of anti-immigrant sentiment. Sexual violence, like sexuality in general, has tended to fall in the realm of the private, one aspect of a strong distinction made between public and private in French republican discourse and practice—one that has just changed with debates over civil unions *(pacs)*, gender parity in politics *(parité)*, and the sexual lives of major politicians.[1] Nevertheless, Sarkozy's comments reveal a form of moral legitimacy attributed to victims of sexual violence that not only demonstrates but gives France its benevolent status.

This chapter examines how a regime of care that protects women from violence has come to play a role in the politics of immigration. Compassion is not static; its subjects gradually change to fit new contexts and histories even as they appear to be outside of time, outside of history—as universally and timelessly worthy of benevolence. Its signifiers shift. Here, I look at how the victim of gender-based violence gradually replaces the sick body in terms of its ability to generate compassion, yet I argue that the actual subject looks very similar, as do the set of institutions that are used to protect him/her. As in the case of illness, where it is not always clear what qualifies as a humanitarian emergency worthy of exception (see chapter 3), in this case, I am interested in what is understood as violence, worthy of exception. What types of violence get recognized as that which women (and men) must be protected from? What form does the morally legitimate suffering body take?

The transnational movement against violence against women in France was still in its nascent stage during the period of my primary fieldwork, from 1999 to 2001. Domestic violence was rarely spoken about publicly. One of the first doctoral theses on the subject of domestic violence was published in May 2000, by a medical doctor named Cecille Morvant; she told me that when she received funding for this, it was the first of its kind. At the time, I found this quite surprising, particularly since activism in the United States and Canada against violence against women had generated a huge amount of interest and publicity.

So I first encountered the regime of care focused on saving (certain) women from violence in contexts that did not explicitly mention it but that often employed the language of humanitarianism or acted in the name of compassion. Here, as we saw with the illness clause, women victims of violence acted as potent symbols of suffering, even if they were not yet seen through the lens of the newer transnational discourse. Humanitarianism was the guiding logic and legal strategy. But I noticed a significant shift in public interest on the subject of violence against women in France between 2003 and 2004. It is probably impossible to know exactly why, but certainly there were several events that brought it to the fore. First, in August 2003 actress Marie Trintignant was assaulted multiple times and ultimately killed by her boyfriend, Bertrand (Bruno) Cantal—lead singer of the French rock group Noir Désir—during a quarrel in a hotel. Since the two were celebrities, the issue of domestic violence was suddenly all over the French media and entered the national consciousness in a new way. But it entered and was *heard* because a number of initiatives propelled by the transnational campaign were already in motion: For instance, the European Commission's campaign to raise awareness of violence against women—Daphné—was initiated in 2000 as a four-year program "to combat violence against children, young people and women," with an annual budget of five million euros. There was also the French "Enveff" survey undertaken by the French state secretary of women's rights in 2000 in response to the 1995 World Conference on

Women in Beijing; its primary aim was to gauge the frequency of the different types of interpersonal violence directed against adult women in the different areas of their lives (in couples, family, work, and public places).[2] In particular, the idea of "Europe" suddenly had real weight and presence—the European Union, the European Court of Human Rights, and various other initiatives and organizations were finally being understood as important, substantive venues and vehicles for change. People were looking beyond the nation-state; I remarked on this as I listened to the discussions about immigration law and, specifically, about violence against women. Amnesty International launched a ten-year global initiative on violence against women on May 8, 2004, and Amnesty France participated in this, eventually producing a report on violence against women in France in 2006 (Amnesty International 2006). In June 2004, I went to a day-long meeting held by the National Solidarity Network of Women (Réseau National Solidarité Femmes), which focused on violence against women; again, this was striking to me, since when I went to an event on domestic violence at the Paris Women's Center in 2000, only two other people showed up. Just four years later, every women's rights and immigrant rights association working in France was interested in and committed to dealing with the problem.

Violence against women has now become an important language with which to address suffering and injustice in many contexts—from war, to the *banlieue*, to immigration—with all the intended and unintended consequences this might entail.[3] One of my key questions here is how the increasing legitimacy of the discourse works to protect the subjects of gender-based violence and to produce political change. And what role does it play in the politics of immigration? I begin, as I said, in sites that do not purport to deal with the issue of violence against women as it has more recently been defined; rather, I begin with legal contexts that many immigrants come into contact with by virtue of their legal status but where the figure of a particular gendered and racialized subject nonetheless plays an important role. What I encountered in places such as the Refugee Appeals Board or the offices that deal with immigrants (*étrangers*) in the prefecture was the way in which this regime of care could—in the name of a moral imperative—enact exceptions to the law to save particular women "victims" from violence. These were the rare cases granted papers. In a context of "zero illegal immigration" the exceptional cases were what made it through, and a certain racialized, gender-based violence helped to make a case exceptional. My goal here is not to argue for a form of legal formalism, but rather to note that the politics of care—and its protagonist, the morally legitimate suffering body—informs state discourse and practice as well as other realms of expert knowledge, from the medical to the legal. This politics of care stands in contrast to the measure of legal regularity and predictability necessary for autonomous political action in a democratic society. My critique, then, is in the service of a more radical political project of equality, not to call for the lifelessness of legal formalism.

In this sense of tracking a political movement for equality, this chapter outlines the tension in the struggle against violence against women between a case-by-case approach that responds to a moral imperative to rescue and protect women from violence—as exemplified by Sarkozy's statement in 2007, with which I opened the chapter—and one that is grounded in a feminist political struggle for justice. I worked with a number of associations that take the latter approach. They argue, for instance, that immigrant women are disproportionately affected by violence because they are made more vulnerable by state violence—these organizations have dubbed this predicament a "double violence" (see Le Comité d'Action Interassociatif 2004); for instance, immigrant women may be unable to leave violent or abusive marriages because their legal status is contingent upon being married, or they may be unable to escape sexual violence in the workplace because they are in the workplace "illegally" and thereby supposedly forfeit all rights. Yet while they condemn this double violence, the state and its conservative apparatus rally around a regime of care and protection, and its central subject: the morally legitimate suffering body, this time, in the guise of a victim of sexual violence.

I look at this tension around the suffering, gendered body in three different sites: the Refugee Appeals Board; the bilateral accords held with Algeria, Morocco, and Tunisia that protect personal status laws based on shari'a in France; and a later set of humanitarian exceptions to immigration law specifically for victims of violence against women.

THE REFUGEE APPEALS BOARD:
THE LAW OF COMPASSION

I look first to the Refugee Appeals Board (Commission des Recours des Réfugiés, or CRR) as a key location in which decisions about immigrants and refugees are made; where, as one of several important juridical sites, their lives are definitively shaped.[4] The CRR was put in place for those whose requests for asylum had been rejected by OFPRA (the French office for the protection of refugees and stateless people) and falls under administrative jurisdiction, or public law, where the court of last resort is the Conseil d'État (Council of State). I was fortunate to get an "inside" view of the process because I was introduced to one of the judges. François, as I will call him, invited me to sit in on the public part of a session and then said that he would give me a glimpse into the private decision making; without revealing anything confidential, he said he would explain the decisions to me. While my research on this topic included participant observation and interviews with immigration officials, representatives of the UN refugee agency (UNHCR), and NGOs, I draw on this particular process of observing and discussing with this judge because it best encapsulates and illustrates my overall findings. In particular, it illustrates the important place of care in the governance of immigrants and refugees and the focus on subjects of gender-based violence.

The Refugee Appeals Board was located outside Paris in the suburb of Val de Fontenay and included various "judges";[5] when I attended, three judges presided in each session. One judge came from OFPRA, the refugee office; the second judge, who was also chairman of the session, came from the Conseil d'État; and the third was a representative of the UNHCR.[6]

There were several rooms in which appeals were heard each day, and they were each set up identically, with many rows of chairs for people to either observe or wait their turn. In general, the process went as follows: The refugee claimant approached the table and sat opposite the judges; s/he might have a lawyer present, or a translator, and there was a court reporter who sat with the judges. A representative from OFPRA, called the reporter, stood up to relate the details of the case for the judges and the audience, stating why the claimant was initially denied asylum, and ended by suggesting whether or not the decision should be overturned. Then the refugee claimant was given an opportunity to add to his/her story (through the lawyer or translator), and the session concluded with the judges asking the claimant questions. This process went on from Monday to Friday, from 8:45 A.M. until 6:00 P.M. The sessions were open to the public, but the decision making was done in private, with each of the three judges having an equal vote. There is no written report of who disagreed, no "deciding opinion" as in the American or English models. One simply received the answer: yes or no—one has been granted refugee status or not.

This particular session started on time at 8:45 A.M. The room was nearly full, and the audience seemed largely composed of refugee claimants and their families. The refugee claimants were called up in turn. First, there was a Sri Lankan woman who came in with her husband and child. She had been associated with the LTTE (Liberation Tigers of Tamil Eelam), arrested, and tortured. OFPRA's reason for not giving her asylum was that her story was too stereotypical. They argued that her claims of being held and tortured in detention were invented. The judges asked her questions about her involvement with the LTTE, why she was arrested, what the detention center was called, and how she got out. Next a man from the Democratic Republic of the Congo came in, with no lawyer or translator. His brother and sister had both been granted asylum. He explained that he had been active with the Socialist Party and had been arrested and tortured for no apparent reason. The questions posed to him centered largely on the fact that President Mobutu had by this point been deposed, so Mobutu followers were no longer in power. If this man had been arrested because his party was hostile to Mobutu, what would happen if he returned now? Another judge asked if he had medical certificates attesting to the torture. The judges' faces were expressionless, and their tone of voice was hard to decipher. They did not show any overt excitement or engagement, but they asked pointed questions.

The morning continued like this. Among the cases were a man from Sierra Leone; a pregnant woman from the Congo who was part of a Christian evangelist group and who brought her pastor to give evidence; an older Albanian man who said he had been fired from his job, harassed, and attacked because he was not part of the Communist Party; and another Sri Lankan woman with a little baby, also part of the LTTE. While holding and rocking her baby, she described her torture in detail, including being stripped naked and attached to a pole while they stuck needles in her fingers and chest and put her head in a bucket of petrol.

Afterward, I waited eagerly to speak with François to see whom the judges would grant asylum to (i.e., annul the earlier refusal). When I spoke to him later that day, after their afternoon of deliberation, he told me that none of the claimants would receive asylum. I tried to contain my surprise and asked why: how could it be, when the majority of cases seemed—to me at least—to have merit? He explained that the Refugee Appeals Board was not there to admit everyone; they had to follow the stipulations of the 1951 Refugee Convention, which defines a refugee as a person who, "owing to well-founded fear of being persecuted for reasons of race, religion, nationality, membership of a particular social group or political opinion," cannot get protection in the country of his/her nationality and is therefore unable to return to it. That is, not all suffering fits into the convention's strict definitions, even if it is recognizable as suffering elsewhere. In other conversations, he had acknowledged that France followed an extremely limited version of the convention, only recognizing victims of state persecution.

Indeed, it is absolutely crucial to note that the larger context is one in which refugees have been increasingly viewed as suspicious by both the French state and the French public and have been conflated with economic migrants. As discussed in chapter 3, this conflation was made explicit in policies of restricting asylum to control migration flows, joining two processes that should be entirely independent. More broadly, asylum policies must be understood as part of prohibitionist, restrictive immigration policies, where the state seeks to close all doors.[7] In other words, the deliberations in the Refugee Appeals Board might also be understood as part of a process of "renationalization" (Sassen 1996), in which nation-states try to rehabilitate their sovereign power on the backs of immigrants and refugees. An exception to the rule is the only way in.

François then explained to me that the judges from the Refugee Appeals Board did not look for truth. He said that, for his part, he looked for a *good, plausible story.* This need to inhabit a particular subject position in a circumscribed legal narrative resonates with asylum procedures in many Western nation-states. As Susan Coutin (2001) has argued in the case of the United States, there is a narrative incommensurability between victims' experiences of political violence and the legal subject that one must become in order to be granted asylum.[8] Yet François went further than explaining the need to inhabit a legal narrative. He explained that most decisions were made on the basis of emotion; he claimed that the judges all pretend their decisions are grounded in law, but they rarely are, particularly when one is so restricted as to whom one can accept. While law always involves interpretation, and while it is always enacted in specific contexts that help determine its meaning, the difference here is that law's production and execution become indistinguishable. Indeed, this takes on even more significance in the French context, where the civil law tradition involves applying the law, not interpreting or building on it. That is, the law tends to be presented as fixed and uniformly applied, where the focus is on technical competence, not individual discretion. The idea is that the law—as a homogeneous model of French society and values—is there to protect the social order and work in the public interest. Of course, this is not the way it always plays out (Terrio 2009:45–46).

François said that only when he feels he does not know enough about a country or a situation does he turn to the law; otherwise, he relies on his feelings and his intuition, and he assured me that other judges did too. He gave an example of a judge who was not convinced by a Bangladeshi man's asylum claim, stating it was clear that he was an economic immigrant. When François asked his fellow judge how he knew this, the judge simply answered, "It shows." The judge could not explain it, François told me—it was his *feeling.* Once decisions are made, they can always be supported by the law after the fact. François said that each judge had his/her own special priorities, cases that they considered to be the "ultimate injustice" and that they would fight particularly hard for. François's own priorities were, in his words, "women and homosexuals." He said that he went all out for them as exceptional cases, although he did not explain what had led to this emphasis.

When I asked François about the other cases I had witnessed, and why they had not been convincing, he explained that the interesting thing about compassion is that, not only is it evoked differently by certain factors like gender or age, but that the case had to be original—really *exceptional*. He said that the appeals board had heard too many stories of torture from Sri Lankans in the LTTE. There were too many Algerians, too many from the Congo with the same story. He ruled out any truth value in these stories, attributing them to a market in asylum narratives; "people learn what they should say," he explained.[9] "What if they are all similar precisely because they *are* true?" I asked. He was doubtful. "If their stories were true," he said, "they would not get tripped up during questioning." I asked him what kind of story he needed to hear, wondering what made a story different, worthy of exception. The last case for which the judges had reversed the denial of asylum, he explained, was a gay Algerian man who had been gang-raped by five Algerian policemen. It had been an intense case, where François had asked for the session to be closed to the public. He admitted that the decision in this case had been difficult because rape is often used as a strategy to elicit compassion. In other words, this man's rape had to be distinguished from other forms of "banal" rape—presumably, those of women, although, as Inderpal Grewal (1998) notes, ignoring the rape of men as a common but undeclared event in war is part of the upkeep of heterosexual patriarchy.

Then François explained that he did not have sympathy or compassion for people who persecuted others. In other words, he said he did not have sympathy for *persécutés persécuteurs*—the persecuted persecutors—people who are persecuted but have in turn persecuted others. The judges were looking for pure victims, the innocents who were not politically motivated and who, ideally, were passive in the process, their hands not bloodied. Earlier he had given me an example of an Afghani woman doctor, and now, the gay Algerian man. These are both images of innocent, apolitical victims.

In this context, access to the law is determined by the role of compassion and by the exceptional, apolitical, innocent, suffering body. This is a regime of care that resonates with humanitarianism and particularly with the illness clause (see chapter 3), in which the law is applied through exceptional, affective measures. Similar again to the illness clause, the issues that garner the most affective attention—the most moral legitimacy—revolve around sexuality and/or gender-based violence. However, not just any form of gender-based violence—it must be a form of violence that is considered exceptional. "Run-of-the-mill" rape or domestic violence is not sufficient; it must stand out, and cultural Otherness seems to be a critical part of standing out. The gay Algerian who was gang-raped by five policemen is an example of this. In Algeria, homosexuality is illegal, and so it might seem "exceptional" that a man was raped by men as punishment for being gay, by representatives of the state who deem it illegal; although again, this renders invisible the rape of men as a common method of torture or humiliation (Grewal 1998).

But perhaps more importantly, gay rights have become a new form of civilizational marker, deployed in the global North to symbolize modernity, through appeals to liberal principles of tolerance. For instance, the Dutch film *Naar Nederland*, or *Coming to the Netherlands*, is a test required by law for prospective non-Western immigrants.[10] It purposefully shows two men kissing to exemplify how tolerant and liberated the Dutch are, establishing a set of practices that immigrants must be willing to accept. It also explicitly warns that the Dutch do not practice excision or condone honor killings. Muslims are the unnamed audience for this part of the film, marked as unmodern because of their lack of tolerance of homosexuality and their supposed violence toward women. That is, the struggle for sexual freedom here functions as an exclusionary act, enabling anti-immigrant policies. Pim Fortuyn, the Dutch political leader and presidential candidate who was assassinated before the presidential election in 2002, exemplifies this exclusionary freedom—what is, in fact, a form of intolerance justified by the defense of tolerance—with both ruthless anti-immigrant rhetoric and a flamboyant gay style.[11] Returning to the gay Algerian at the Refugee Appeals Board, we see that in this larger European context, where intolerance of homosexuality becomes a form of cultural pathology, granting asylum to a gay man fleeing persecution becomes an act that distinguishes France from Algeria, highlighting France's benevolence and civility.

BILATERAL ACCORDS AND CULTURAL PATHOLOGIES

Even while victims of sexual violence may hold a special place at the Refugee Appeals Board, the board itself is not explicitly concerned with violence against women any more than other types of violence or persecution. Yet elsewhere, associations were fighting for women's rights, particularly for immigrant women's rights—and gender-based violence was a part of this struggle, even if it was only gradually being incorporated into and coordinated with a transnational discourse and set of institutions. For instance, Rajfire, whose mandate is to fight for immigrant women's rights and for equality, had been pushing the French state to accept refugees on the basis of gender persecution, that is, to give asylum to women fleeing gender-specific forms of violence, from domestic violence to excision (or female genital cutting). In particular, they focused on discriminatory state legislation and state violence.

Having examined one situation where, despite this not being the explicit goal, there was a focus on gendered bodies and forms of suffering, I want to turn to a situation where gender-based violence is explicitly used to frame the problem, in order to see how it plays out and what forms of violence are recognized. I refer here to the struggle around what are known as the "bilateral accords." Many immigrant women's associations, particularly those that focus on women of Maghrebi origin, fight against the bilateral accords signed with former North African colonies, which enshrine in the French Civil Code a respect for the *statut personnel,* or "personal status," of those with Algerian, Moroccan, or Tunisian passports, despite their place of residence. In other words, persons with these passports are subject to the legal family code of those countries, largely based on shari'a law. What follows is some general background on these accords, to explain what these women object to and why, and then I will move on to two cases of gender-based violence and what it means for each to be bound by these accords.

With Algerian independence in 1962, France signed a judicial agreement that provides for the application of Algerian laws in France and French laws in Algeria. France made similar agreements with Morocco and Tunisia following independence. These laws, still in effect in contemporary

France, were all designed in the spirit of reciprocity; they were designed to allow French citizens living in these countries to continue to be governed by French law and vice versa. While Article 3 of the French Civil Code already states that all foreigners in France are subject to their own national laws concerning matters of personal status—this is the French interpretation of private international law, which is designed to allow marriages to be respected across borders—the bilateral accords lay out the details of this postcolonial relationship. Of crucial importance here is that these bilateral accords relate to the private sphere; they include the realm of marriage, rights and duties of the husband and wife, custody of children, divorce, inheritance, and division and control of family property.

Many of the sans-papiers women (or *sans-papières*) I worked with fell into the status of undocumented because of these bilateral treaties, or they were unable to obtain papers or to escape from domestic violence because of them. Up until 2004, for instance, French jurisprudence on the application of the personal status laws allowed Moroccan and Algerian women to be repudiated by their husbands despite being residents of France—meaning that they permitted a unilateral divorce on the part of the husband, with or without the wife's knowledge.[12] This usually entailed the husband returning to Morocco or Algeria to enact the repudiation, while at the same time asking the French judge for *exequatur*, or the right to apply a judgment made by an Algerian or Moroccan judge to a French resident. Once the wife was repudiated, she could lose her legal status in France if it was dependent on that of her husband—a very common situation. Immigrant rights associations have recorded hundreds of examples of such discriminations: older women, at sixty-five or seventy, out on the street after being repudiated, with no papers or means of supporting themselves; children taken from women after repudiations, with no chance to fight for custody; and women being repudiated after their husbands get their residency permits.[13]

To understand how this works, it helps to know something about the hierarchies of law, the rules of precedence, and the relationship between international law, the bilateral accords, and the French Civil Code. Basically, the bilateral accords trump the French Civil Code in the hierarchy of French norms—in other words, the bilateral treaties that enshrine respect for shari'a should be respected unless they violate French *ordre public,* or "public order." But international conventions take precedence over bilateral treaties, and hence if the laws enshrined in the bilateral treaties stand in tension with international norms, they must be abrogated. That is, the application of foreign laws in France is valid only insofar as it does not interfere with the public realm or with public order, making this an important concept in deciding what is considered French. Public order is a normative construct that reflects the relationship of law to morality and refers to both social order and basic values. According to John Bowen (2009, 2001), it is an attempt to translate the values of society into law; as the values change, so do the shape and limits of the law.

For instance, in 2001 the Cour de Cassation (the highest court in the French judiciary) ruled that the French conception of public order was not in principle contradicted by a unilateral repudiation.[14] And thus French courts allowed repudiations under certain conditions, finding that they did not necessarily contradict notions of women's rights. But in 2004, when France started to become more receptive to and influenced by the transnational practices against violence against women, the same court ruled against repudiations in France, stating that they go against the principle of equality of husband and wife enshrined in the European Convention on Human Rights.[15]

In addition to repudiation, other practices protected by the bilateral accords have been points of contention for Maghrebi women living in France, who argue that they institute inequality between men and women.[16] But let me be clear: My goal here is not to assess the personal status laws in North Africa, nor to argue that French laws institute equality. What is relevant for my present purposes is what personal status laws do and how they work on French soil, and how the French state reacts to Maghrebi women's complaints about them. An important part of this is to note that the ways in which these laws are enacted in France is different from their practice in North Africa, precisely because the French make judgments about and involving shari'a without actually having shari'a courts. Despite having the right to do so, French judges rarely apply shari'a law in French courtrooms, but they do interpret decisions made in shari'a courts in the Maghreb when deciding whether or not to accept these judgments for French residents. My concern, therefore, is both the particular application and interpretation of these laws in France and the work that these laws do, which has been to leave many women without legal rights.

Women's rights, antidiscrimination, and immigrant women's groups regularly demonstrate against these treaties, calling for equality before the law and denouncing all fundamentalisms, but so far to no avail.[17] When state representatives do respond to these calls for equality, it is to say that these treaties are related to the sovereignty of nation-states and are designed to protect their cultures. Maghrebi women in turn respond by suggesting that this is a racist argument couched as cultural relativism, which assumes that certain people are "programmed to live with injustice" (S., fille de Smaïl et Dahbia, 2004:2). They have stated repeatedly that their nationality is not something they want protected, particularly in this select form.

I want to relate the stories of two women who were subject to gender-based violence but whose ability to escape from it was curtailed by the bilateral accords. I am interested in how the discourse and practice against violence against women comes to make the difference in their cases, and what we can learn therefore about the official framing of gender-based violence and what forms of suffering and inequality it recognizes or incorporates on the ground.

Fadilah

I met Fadilah at the Women's Center in Paris. She had come for help from the feminist network Rajfire. We talked before one of Rajfire's general meetings, during and after. We were the same age, and once, when I accompanied her to court for a proceeding against her husband, we were asked if we were sisters. With Fadilah's consent, I helped Claudie, the driving force of Rajfire, to put together Fadilah's request for papers, learning much about her life in the process. Finding official traces of a person is like detective work, and one must be willing to look in the least likely of places. When Claudie was searching for proof to build Fadilah's case on the basis of having been in France for ten consecutive years—part of the right to private and family life included in Article 12bis of the immigration law—she asked Fadilah how she could prove she had been in France in 1996. Claudie suggested doctor's visits; did Fadilah have receipts, doctors reports? Could they contact a doctor who had seen her, to ask him or her to write a letter attesting to the medical consultation? Fadilah thought for a while and remembered that she had been hospitalized that year after having been severely beaten by her husband. What I present here is based in part on the story that Fadilah constructed for her dossier, but I have filled it out based on our shared time and conversations in the Women's Center, cafés, her home, and my experience accompanying her to family court.

Fadilah was born in Morocco. When I met her, she had been living in France for nine and a half years. Her husband was also of Moroccan origin but grew up in France from the age of eight. She and her husband met in Morocco and married there, but he wanted to return to France to be near his family, so she joined him in a small French village. "Those were good years," she explained to me. She got pregnant, had a little boy. But then he began using drugs, and things deteriorated. He spent all their money on his habit, and he became violent, beating her to the point of hospitalization several times. At some point, he was arrested for petty crimes and lost his residency permit, receiving in its place a request to leave the French territory. Then they were both in France illegally. Without his residency permit, she was not legal either, as her papers were contingent upon her marriage to him. She left him after a bout of violence, which their son witnessed, and went to a social worker. The social worker took the child and put him in a state ward because of the violent environment and because both parents wanted to keep him. By law, he had to stay there for six months, and the social worker then renewed his stay in the state ward for another six months. Fadilah had the right to see him just once a week, and this was almost too hard for her to bear.

She explained to me that the social worker had advised her to get a divorce and begin her life afresh. She was also informed that, to get custody of her child, and perhaps most importantly to get him out of the state ward, she needed to divorce, to distance herself from her husband in order to prove that her son would no longer be exposed to the dangers of a violent home. Fadilah told me that she wanted nothing more than to divorce her husband; however, as a Moroccan citizen, she was still subject to the Moroccan family code, the Moudawana. This is the result of the bilateral accords. Thus, even though she had lived on French soil for close to ten years, she could not appeal to the French Civil Code. Even if she were a *legal* resident, she would not be able to appeal to the Civil Code. Paradoxically, in her case, to become a legal resident she needed to be a subject of the French Civil Code, as it would allow her to divorce her husband and to dissociate herself from him, thereby opening the way for her to submit an independent application for papers. In Fadilah's case, the Moroccan family code active at that time specified that a man could divorce when he wanted, but the wife needed permission from her husband. Her husband said no, he would not grant her a divorce.

Fadilah's dilemma got worse. The state social workers told her that she would need her papers to regain custody of her child; that is, she would need to prove that she had the financial means to support him. While she had a well-paying job as a nanny, and while her employers had supported her application for papers all along, she could not petition for her child without legal employment. Yet she could not hope to obtain legal status while associated with her husband, who was on deportation order. She was paralyzed by the circular nature of her predicament, despite having been extremely resourceful in finding a place to live and work and in otherwise reconstructing her life. Without intervention by the French courts to make an exception to personal status laws, either by ruling that her experience of domestic violence and inability to divorce her husband violated French public order, or that the bilateral accords stood in tension with international norms, she was still subject to the bilateral accords and legally bound to her husband.

Zina

But let's turn now to a very different situation. While an exception was not made for Fadilah, I want to briefly recount the story of a woman for whom an exception was indeed made. I draw on her case in particular because it is one of the rare exceptions that was not about repudiation, in which a judge decided that for reasons of public order, the French Civil Code should take precedence over the bilateral accords. I want to suggest that cultural difference, in a select, exoticized form, is crucial to the exception made; of course, while it is speculative on my part to make this claim without direct access to how or why the decision was made, it nonetheless illustrates the sexually imbued cultural pathology that I am arguing is a necessary (although not sufficient) condition for both talking about sexual violence broadly in France and for being heard.

This story was told to me by Zina herself; the narrative is hers.[18] Before proceeding, I want to draw attention to the way her narrative resonates with Orientalist fantasies that turn on the idea that non-Western and particularly Muslim cultures are more patriarchal than Western ones. These fantasies have clear plotlines, with Muslim men as villains, and they conclude with Westerners coming to the rescue of oppressed, veiled women (Mohanty 1988; Spivak 1988; Razack 2001; Abu-Lughod 2002). Without in any way calling into question Zina's experience of violence, my goal is simply to point out how difficult it is for Muslim women to tell their stories of sexual violence without having them reimagined and translated as Orientalist fantasies. Personal stories are often codified as larger narratives, particularly in the case of traumatic events for which there may be no easy words. In this sense, one might explain Zina's story as drawing on larger narratives simply because the narrative is a familiar way to speak about the violence she endured in such a way that she is able to be heard.

Zina told me that although she was born in Algeria in 1962, right before Algerian independence, she grew up in France and attended French schools. However, at age sixteen, right before completing her *bac*, or "baccalaureate" (the equivalent of a high school diploma), her father took her to Algeria for what she believed to be a family vacation. While there, her papers were confiscated by her father, who arranged for her to marry an Algerian man against her will. She explained that the man she was to marry was an *intégriste*—which translates as an "Islamic fundamentalist" or "Islamic militant."[19] She was kept in her house, confined, without permission to go outside for sixteen years, during which time she had three daughters. She said that these were sixteen years of hell: she was sexually assaulted by both her husband and her husband's brother. Her husband told her he would rather see her dead than anywhere else or with anyone else and that he would kill her if she tried to escape. Eventually, however, after long years of covert planning, she managed to escape back to France.

When Zina was initially taken by her father, she had had a ten-year French residency permit; but because she left the country and did not claim French nationality at age eighteen, she had forfeited her right to it, as one cannot claim it if not resident in France. She was therefore banned from France, unable to continue her studies or to work, despite having been resident there for most of the first sixteen years of her life. In order to return, Zina needed to apply for papers just like any other first-time applicant, which could either be immediately refused or take years to obtain.[20] It was the prerogative of her father and now husband to keep her, as the bilateral accords enshrined male guardianship of wife and children as well as the duty of the wife to obey her husband. Zina was thus still legally bound to her husband while in France, unable to divorce without her husband's permission—and he wanted her back.

Trying first for political asylum and then being rejected, and without any other options, Zina applied for territorial asylum, which was instituted for victims of Islamic groups in Algeria; this was initially a discretionary category used to supplement the French state's narrow interpretation of asylum as only for victims of state persecution. When more formally instituted in 1998, territorial asylum was granted for those "whose life or liberty is threatened in their countries" or "who have been exposed to treatment contrary to article 3 of the European Convention on Human Rights" (which prohibits "inhuman or degrading treatment").[21] However, the minister of interior said that this measure should be applied, "as an emergency humanitarian measure . . . of limited application . . . largely discretionary . . . for exceptional cases . . . and of limited significance."[22] An amendment further specifies that territorial asylum should only be granted "under conditions compatible with the national interest," suggesting that asylum could be granted or denied for reasons other than the individual's protection.[23] When I returned to France in June 2001, Zina had incredible news: she had been granted territorial asylum—one of the lucky few of the tens of thousands who had applied.[24] An exception had been made for her, as her case was deemed in the "national interest" and a violation of French public order—that is, the French Civil Code was allowed to trump the bilateral treaties, as respect for personal status laws in her case was seen as infringing on French legal norms.

Orientalist Exceptions

In order to understand exactly how Zina's case was in the national interest, and why an exception was made for her rather than Fadilah, it is necessary to elaborate on the colonial remnants in contemporary legal and political practices. Indeed, the bilateral accords themselves cannot be understood without looking through the lens of a historically stratified citizenship, in which French citizens with full rights of political participation were distinguished from French nationals, who were subject to French rule but had no political rights. In other words, until 1946 one could be a French national without being a citizen. In the case of the North African colonies, the legal difference between citizens and subjects played out in large part through personal status. For example, from October 1830 until Algerian independence in 1962, France admitted what was called local law—the French recognized various legal codes, courts, and jurists that existed before their arrival in Algeria. These included Koranic and Mosaic laws and institutions as well as Berber and Mozabite customary laws (Shepard 2006). Local law applied only to the arena of civil status—marriage, divorce, filiation, and inheritance—and we see this carried over in the bilateral accords. The goal was to grant citizenship only when people were ready, though colonial subjects were typically seen to be unready and immature. Assimilation policy held that people would be governed by local law until they were ready to assume French law; to this end, clauses of exceptionality were instituted at various points during the colonial regime.[25] In other words, exceptional status was created for exceptionally "civilized" individuals. To qualify as an exceptional individual—a French citizen rather than a national subject—one had to indicate a desire to be French, which involved a performance that proved one could think and act in a French way. One of the best indications of this was renouncing one's legal personal status or local law; that is, personal status was associated with the degree of civilization, and this was about who the person was, not where they lived (Bowen 2009, 2001). This exceptional status, however, was presumed temporary in the process of creating all subjects as equal before the law.

In the colonial era, difference and inequality were thus legally encoded and located in the realm of the private, and this has persisted in the bilateral accords. Similarly, both the colonial era and the contemporary bilateral accords exemplify the idea that the private realm is pivotal in the decision to assimilate or exclude people from the French nation-state. Without denying that the bilateral accords act as both a site of organization of French state power and emancipation from it—allowing certain groups to escape disciplining by the French state—I am concerned with those who want both to follow and to be subject to French laws while they are living in France and who, in having chosen to live in France, would in any other circumstance be entitled to do so. Since one had the choice in the colonial era to renounce local law, at least theoretically, then why not now? Indeed, to put this issue into perspective, it helps to note that Tunisia currently refuses to respect repudiations allowed in other countries, and both Britain and Belgium give immigrants the right to be subject to the laws of the country of residence as opposed to those of the country of origin, preferring not to enact repudiations on their soil. In other words, this is not a simple issue of respecting the sovereignty of other countries or the principles of extraterritoriality; it is about the meaning and enactment of sovereignty itself.

Gender plays a critical role in this system of stratified citizenship. During the colonial regime, women were seen as the embodiment of Algerian life whether in its progressive or regressive guise. As Jane Collier and colleagues (1995) note, by the mid-nineteenth century, Western elites were treating women's status as a key indicator of a people's civilization—and thus women occupied a crucial place in France's civilizing mission. Women's status in local laws was what defined Algerians as uncivilized. Algerian women were seen to be symbols of the colony's cultural identity—that which was "protected" in the local laws. Yet, while maintaining local law, the French attempted to regulate the private life of Algerian "natives" through assistance campaigns aimed at women and children, promoting Algerian women's liberation through education, encouraging them toward Europeanization (Woodhull 1991). Indeed, during the Algerian independence struggle, which was waged from 1954 to 1962, the French defined their fight against the Algerian nationalist group, the FLN (Front de Libération Nationale), as one to liberate Algerian women from Arabo-Islamic obscurantism. Here, as in so many other places, culture and nation were intertwined with gender, coming together to draw both internal frontiers and external boundaries.

If, in colonial Algeria, the French frequently defined their struggle as one to liberate Algerian women, women of Maghrebi origin still play a pivotal role in postcolonial France, marking the interior borders of the nation-state. However, there is a difference in the way that these borders are now drawn: in the colonial era, the French insisted that Algerian Muslims and other native Algerians could become full French citizens if they renounced "local law." Now, the will to give up local law is not enough—in fact, it is not even legally permitted in the bilateral accords. In this regard, Zina's story illustrates both the continuity with the colonial regime and a change in mechanism of exceptional inclusion. Making an exception for her fulfills the original civilizing mission of saving the natives from barbarity—all in the name of care and protection—and it fulfills the well-worn practice of defining Western women as free by representing women elsewhere as enslaved (J. Collier et al. 1995:15). But critically, in order to demonstrate French civility, there must be clearly *recognizable* Otherness, such as forced marriage, a potent signifier of the "backwardness" or otherness of Muslim women (Rytkonen 2002; Volpp 2006). Domestic violence, on the other hand, does not fulfill this requirement of Otherness; the French cannot save women from a practice that also occurs in France with equal frequency. That is, there is no possibility of distinction or hierarchy. In Zina's case, she was familiar to the French officials in that she spoke French like a native and had been schooled in France. As Lawrence Kirmayer (2003) has suggested in the context of refugee claims in Canada, shared cultural background knowledge helps to render stories intelligible and motivations credible in refugee claims. Zina was familiar, and yet they saw a foreign practice imposed on her, one that compromised her freedom and her bodily integrity. She was not simply talking about "common" domestic violence as was Fadilah, but a particular and recognizable culturally marked, exoticized, and patholo-gized form of violence.[26]

If we compare Zina and Fadilah's cases, it seems that women who cannot place their struggles in the discourse of Otherness, those who cannot harness Orientalist tropes or configure themselves as "Third World Women" (Mohanty 1988:51), but who condemn all patriarchies, fundamentalisms, and inequalities full stop, have more trouble mobiliz-ing the attention of the French state. This is why those protesting against the bilateral accords have not been heard: they do not highlight Other-ness but rather similarity and equality. They refuse to call up the colonial specter or harness a neocolonial regime of care that casts Muslim women as victims to be saved; instead, they talk about equality under the law and insist on systematic political and legal reform and inclusion. Yet the French state has trouble engaging in this form of politics when it comes to those of immigrant origin—sexual violence forms a key site for the management of difference precisely because it permits a form of discre-tionary, exceptional power, not a form of politics that addresses either racism or structural inequality; a focus on sexual violence also avoids confronting the colonial history embedded in these contemporary strug-gles. In other words, a discourse against gender-based violence works here only as a form of exceptional care grounded in compassion, not one that helps to further equality through political change; and we see the same types of subjects saved and protected as with the Refugee Appeals Board. While Fadilah was clearly in a terrible situation, unfortunately, her suffering was not seen as exceptional; that is, it could not be distin-guished from the situation of many French women. She did end up get-ting her papers on the basis of ten years of residency, but she had to wait until those ten years had passed to process her claim.

HUMANITARIAN EXCEPTIONS IN THE NAME OF VIOLENCE AGAINST WOMEN

I want to move ahead in time now to a moment when violence against women or gender-based violence is recognized and even used as one of the dominant languages of intervention, invoking an institutionally grounded moral imperative; this moral language, for instance, was used to justify the United States' invasion of both Afghanistan and Iraq for the sake of their women (Abu-Lughod 2002; Volpp 2006). How does this play out in the politics of immigration in France? Does violence against women still work as a regime of exceptional care for immigrants, or has it enabled other forms of political change?

I inquired about this one day in the summer of 2003 when I was back in Paris. Claudie, of Rajfire, was bringing me up to date on the situation with the sans-papiers, explaining that while it was harder and harder to get papers through the illness clause, there was one slight opening in the area of gender-based violence: it seemed that Sarkozy was increasingly focused on this issue. He had commissioned a report, the results of which demanded much stronger action against violence against women. Nevertheless, Claudie bemoaned that one still had to present oneself as a victim to fit these new measures. Rajfire's goal was legal independence and equality for women, and the group fought for this in protest marches, in meetings and conferences with state officials, and through collective tracts written by the sans-papiers women. They held weekly informational sessions to help immigrants with legal or other questions and in general worked with immigrant and refugee women, accompanying them to the prefecture or to court. Yet Claudie had to teach women to play the role of victim for the courts and the prefectures. Furthermore, the state was demanding increased physical proof of violence, such as hospitalization records or police or medical reports.

In practice, then, the increased power and influence of violence against women as a regime of care has translated thus far into more humanitarian and discretionary measures, not other forms of structural change, despite the clear tension between these two approaches. Furthermore, these discretionary measures are coupled with stricter immigration policies that—intentionally or not—actually further entrap women in situations of violence. As in the case of the illness clause, I want to suggest that this exceptional and discretionary power works on the basis of both cultural Otherness and bodily integrity. Claudie and Clara, another Rajfire activist, drew my attention to new measures that illustrate this focus, first elaborated in a 2002 circular and then altered and codified in the subsequent 2003 law on immigration. In the 2002 circular, the 1998 French immigration law is amended to give discretionary power to the *préfet* for "exceptional humanitarian circumstances" linked specifically to individual cases not sufficiently covered by the law.[27] The cases mentioned that might warrant exceptions include women who are victims of violence, forced marriage, or repudiations.[28] These already tend toward "exoticized" forms of violence. But the same circular introduces a clause that if, as a resident foreigner in France, one is the victim of domestic violence and one leaves the conjugal home, one might in exceptional circumstances get papers to stay in France. Yet the circular explicitly refers *only* to those who are married to resident foreigners: "one can consult the commission for residency permits if: . . . there is a rupture of family life when the wife of a foreigner with a residency permit is repudiated by this foreigner, or if, victim of domestic violence from him, she chooses to separate from him." There is no mention of foreign wives of French citizens, whose papers are still contingent upon their marriages. In other words, the underlying assumption is that French men are not violent, or else their violence does not count; this exceptional treatment can only be harnessed as an escape from cultural pathology—from barbaric immigrant men.[29]

This clause was subsequently amended in the 2003 immigration law due to protests by human rights and immigrant women's groups, but the initial impulse is clear. Two paragraphs (or *alinéas*) were added to the 2003 law to allow exceptions to be made for both spouses of foreign residents and those of French citizens, in case of domestic violence, allowing them to renew their permits despite having left the conjugal home (Articles 313-12 and 431-2). Again, of utmost importance is that these measures are wholly discretionary, lending themselves to disparities in application—there is no guarantee of rights. The measures also leave open the question of what domestic violence entails: Is it emotional or just physical? Are threats and blackmail included? The *préfet* has the sole power to decide.

What must be noted here is that, while this law is seemingly progressive in making an exception for immigrants who experience domestic violence, it was passed in the context of increasingly strict legislation that shores up the power of the state and the dependence of immigrants on their spouses—usually that of wives on their husbands. Framed around a suspicion of marriages of convenience, the 2003 law no longer grants foreigners residency permits to join their foreign resident spouses; they must enter through family reunification procedures, which are processed outside of French territory, often with a significant delay. In addition, the granting of the residency permit is contingent on the spouse demonstrating sufficient "republican integration."[30] This means that while the state appears to be newly attentive to domestic violence, in fact, if we look at the law in its overall context, we see that it threatens to trap women in situations of violence for longer, since the length of time required before a spouse can apply for residency or citizenship papers has been extended by one year for both spouses of foreign residents and French citizens. The state solidifies the power of the husband, since the majority of the time it is the wife who joins the husband in France and hence he is the one with papers.[31] This extended legal dependence can leave immigrant women in situations of having to choose between their physical and/or emotional integrity and their legal status—sometimes, their legal status can come at the price of their bodily integrity (see, e.g., Le Comité d'Action Interassociatif 2004:81). Again, this is similar to the situation created by the illness clause, where pathologies are traded in for papers.

Let me return to the question of cultural pathology. I am interested in the cultural signifiers that allow one to qualify as an apolitical suffering body; and in both the medical humanitarian clauses and now the clauses shaped by violence against women, being culturally Other helps someone to be seen as one without agency, without political subjectivity. These signifiers of cultural Otherness also work to determine the content of "Frenchness." This logic underlies the authorization by the French Parliament in July 2004 to expel foreigners who call for discrimination against women—an explicit attack against Imam de Vénissieux and an attempt to get him deported. Whether or not he explicitly called for such discrimination or violence is beside the point: in calling it un-French, in deporting him, it renders invisible similar statements or actions by those deemed French—it uses the language of violence against women to legally police the borders of the nation-state, excluding immigrants and, especially, Muslim men of immigrant origin. It simultaneously produces France as a space of enlightened moral behavior and assumes that violence against women is not practiced on French soil. The 2010 law banning burqas and niqabs is a similar attempt to define the content of Frenchness against the violence of Muslim men; while it only concerns a few hundred women in France, its importance is symbolic. Legislator Bérengère Poletti, of Sarkozy's party, said burqas "are a prison for women, they are the sign of their submission to their husbands, brothers or fathers" (Doland 2010). The bill again aims at husbands and fathers—anyone convicted of forcing someone else to wear the garb risks a year of prison and a €30,000 ($38,000) fine, with both penalties doubled if the victim is a minor.

There are other examples of this logic that imagines foreigners to be more violent than their French counterparts, thereby legitimizing anti-immigrant policies in the name of saving women. This "armed love" is apparent in the case of the struggle against marriages of convenience, which include the June 2004 amendments to the French Civil Code for this purpose. With the explicit goal of "protecting" women from fraudulent marriages, these amendments allow for up to ten years in prison, fines of €75,000, and the denial or removal of papers if a judge doubts the marital intentions. These amendments disproportionately affect immigrants, even if such marriages of convenience happen regularly between French people for financial, administrative, or other reasons, and they encourage false denunciations of marriages in cases of marital conflict. This in turn can lead to papers being withdrawn, or the marriage being annulled, which is a convenient way to get rid of an undesired spouse. Again, this is done in the name of protecting women (see Le Comité d'Action Interassociatif 2004).

CONCLUDING THOUGHTS: A RACIALIZED
POSTCOLONIAL FRANCE

I want to return to Sarkozy's words that began this chapter—and his desire to help all the *femmes martyrisées du monde*—the "martyred" or battered women of the world. It is instructive that the most visible person to respond to Sarkozy's offer to date has been Ayaan Hirsi Ali, the notorious former Dutch parliamentarian of Somali origin. Ali invoked Sarkozy's words to ask for French protection and naturalization.[32] It is not accidental that she has largely made her name critiquing Islam, most notably as the writer of the script for the controversial film *Submission*, for which the director, Theo Van Gogh, was assassinated. The film graphically evokes a connection between Islam and violence against women, picturing a woman in a transparent burqa, with the Qu'ran written on her body, quivering from a beating by her husband that she claims is considered acceptable by the Qu'ran. Ali was primarily elected on an anti-Islam, "pro-woman" platform as member of the conservative Dutch VVD party. *Submission* was only one among her many controversial statements about Islam: in an interview in the Dutch newspaper *Trouw*, she said that, by Western standards, Muhammad would be considered a pedophile, and she has described Islam as a "backward culture." As Peter van der Veer has written with respect to her, "The subaltern can speak, but in order to be heard she has to express the feelings of the dominant community" (2006:121). She received much support from both the French Left and Right for her petition; she offers the perfect symbol of cultural pathology, the right person to rescue—a Muslim woman who rejects Islam and states explicitly that the West is a more *civilized* place.[33] Her request was welcomed in the face of increasingly restrictive immigration and asylum laws, the same type that she herself supported in the Netherlands (E. Fassin 2008); that is, her case was welcomed and understood as the perfect exception to these laws, even if, ultimately, this never actually translated into citizenship for her.

What does it mean to protect and show compassion to victims of exceptional, gendered, largely culturally "alien" forms of violence, to understand these as cultural pathologies? I want to end by suggesting that this set of exceptions helps to create and maintain a racialized postcolonial nation-state, where minorities are named and rendered visible in French society primarily by taking on the form of gendered and racialized victims. Attention is focused on women who are subject to practices such as forced marriage, excision, or modern slavery (see chapter 5), and they are saved by their benevolent French sisters; this shapes the way in which they are understood and received in French society more broadly. When violence against women is represented primarily as the problem of certain neighborhoods (*quartiers*) and certain types of people—as it was starting in 2000 with an explosion of publicity about gang rapes (*les tournantes*) in the *banlieue*, where both parties were of North African origin—this has insidious effects (see, e.g., Hamel 2003; and Mucchielli 2005).

Let me end with an example. In March 2006, during a visit to Paris, I was struck by the array of books in the FNAC—one of the most well-known bookstores in Paris—in the section about women. I remarked on the similarity of images on the covers—they were mostly individual women, covered or veiled, half hidden, eyes often downcast (see figure 5). I noted that the titles and subjects varied from being testimonies about modern slavery, as we will see in chapter 5, to those titled *Married by Force* and *Burned Alive*—again, the covers were similar, showing partially covered brown women, in which the partial covering alternated between a veil or a mask. These testimonies were about gendered and "foreign" or exoticized violence—forced marriages, honor killings. They were on the same display shelf with others titled *Down with the Veil!*—referring to the extremely contentious debate about the headscarf, which was banned in public schools in 2004 as part of a law about ostentatious signs of religious affiliation, but which also insinuated a link between the veil and violence against women;[34] and other titles like *Dans l'enfer dans tournantes* (In gang-rape hell), which is the autobiography of a young French girl of North African origin named Samira Bellil, gang-raped by her male peers in the banlieue of Paris. As several scholars and activists have argued, this particular narrative of gang rape—with which the now well-known group Ni Putes ni Soumises (NPNS, or Neither Whores nor Doormats) originated—repeats the rhetorical strategies of demonizing the Arab boy, casting him as "un-French" while trying to save the poor Arab girl (see Guénif-Souilamas and Macé 2004; Tévanian 2007; and Ticktin et al. 2008). Without going into detail about NPNS, it is worth noting that the group's rhetoric in many ways resembles that of Ayaan Hirsi Ali, hinting at religious and cultural explanations for violence, as in their slogan, *Ni voile, ni viol*—"Neither veil nor rape"—where Islam is turned

Figure 5. Book covers in the FNAC bookstore, women's section, all about a certain kind of violence against women, March 2006.

into a symbol of violence in a seemingly cause-effect relationship.[35] The testimonies about immigrants blend into stories about minority women in contemporary France, emphasizing tropes such as arranged or forced marriage, honor killing, and even the wearing of the veil, and as such work to cast all those with origins in the "third world" and, especially, in former colonies, as the same—not quite civilized, not quite deserving of rights, but in need of help. Indeed, we might say that these images picture women with origins in former colonies as suffering from cultural pathologies that risk spreading and that therefore must be isolated (excluded) or cured (through rescue).

The language and category of "violence against women" was built by feminist political struggles, and it is still carried forth by many of these actors, in more or less powerful forms. However, the struggle against violence against women also inherits the strategies and tensions of the colonial era, which used women as markers of civilizational status. This "imperial debris" (Stoler 2008) is ever present, preceding the discourse of violence against women—as is apparent in the Refugee Appeals Board—and now also contained in it. But as Judith Butler writes, any counterimperialist politics, particularly a feminist or queer one, must oppose "the barbarism of the civilizing mission" (2010:132), which is the real barbarism at issue today. In the context of immigration that I have described, the voice that dominates is based on care and protection, guided by a moral imperative rather than a political language of equality, justice, or anti-imperialism. The operative term here is "violence"—and what is recognized as such. The violence of economic deprivation is excluded, as is state violence, which keeps immigrant women in positions of vulnerability. That not having papers might itself be a form of gendered violence is never broached. This focus not only obscures but forgives the everyday forms of gendered violence that are endemic to much of French society, as they are elsewhere in the world; rather, it isolates violence in certain ethnicized forms. It also sidesteps real political issues such as racism and material inequality by naming the problem in places like the *banlieues* as one of violence against women—and isolating it, as if it could and would stay there. By enforcing narrow definitions of violence against women, the French state can frame itself as benevolent and enlightened; this occurs while other types of violence—state, racist, economic—are allowed to flourish unchecked.

PART THREE Antipolitics

DISEASED CITIZENS AND A RACIALIZED
POSTCOLONIAL STATE

FIVE · Armed Love

AGAINST MODERN SLAVERY, AGAINST IMMIGRANTS

On October 31, 2005, a circular was passed by Nicolas Sarkozy—then the minister of interior—reevaluating the conditions for entry of undocumented immigrants, with a section devoted to "victims of human trafficking." According to the circular, cases that do not strictly fit what the French Penal Code defines as a victim of trafficking "might give proof of the need for [on the part of prefectures] humanitarian and benevolent consideration" (CCEM 2005:12). More simply, these victims should be treated with particular compassion, at the discretion of the prefecture. The circular is too vague to allow for a real right to papers, not least because these ministerial texts are not valid in front of administrative tribunals (CCEM 2005:12). Rather, this is an attempt to institute compassion for certain victims while recognizing that such "true" victims are exceptional.

These terms are familiar: humanitarian and benevolent consideration, exceptional victims . . . but which particular victims are focused on here? Which undocumented immigrants can claim compassionate consideration? This chapter focuses on the struggle around human trafficking and a subset of this—modern slavery—which, as I will argue, take place in many of the same moralizing terms, through similar institutions and logics as other regimes of care such as medical humanitarianism. The discourse around human trafficking produces similar subjects, although in this case explicitly about a gendered form of injustice, and its moralizing impetus comes from gendered and racialized notions of bodily suffering—in particular, a focus on sexual violence among women and children from the global South. A great deal of time, money, and resources have been invested in the struggle against human trafficking globally; it has become a fireball of a topic politically and a media moneymaker.[1] This all happens in the name of the good. Indeed, the strength of the moral rhetoric against trafficking is both illustrated and furthered by the fact that all the major NGOs fighting against violence against women, those for human rights and humanitarianism, and all the governmental and intergovernmental organizations agreed to participate in the struggle against it. Human Rights Watch, Amnesty International, the UN Working Group on Contemporary Forms of Slavery, the UNHCR, the Vatican: no one questioned its implications. Such is the power of claiming the moral high ground: it is hard to argue that trafficking is *good*.

My grounding assumption here is that the exploitative and violent practices associated with trafficking and with modern slavery (which falls under the rubric of trafficking, as I will discuss) are abhorrent; but rather than repeat the rhetoric of horror that is already circulating, I want to approach the questions of violence, suffering, and injustice from a slightly different angle. I am interested in the kinds of responses elicited by a focus on trafficking as the worst possible injustice, and perhaps more importantly, I am concerned by the kinds of responses, injustices, and forms of subjecthood that are rendered unrecognizable or unthinkable by using this particular lens.

My interest in this was initially provoked by an encounter with an organization in Paris fighting against modern slavery. At the time, I knew nothing of its affiliation with the antitrafficking movement, nor did I understand it as humanitarian. All I knew was that they themselves contrasted their work to the sans-papiers movement; and I saw quite quickly that they used a very different logic and practice, one focused on saving others, on care and protection, not on equality. So I begin this chapter with an ethnographic account of the struggle against modern slavery in Paris. I then ask how this struggle links to a transnational set of morally inflected institutions and practices, thinking about how they have come to manage migration in often unintended ways. One of the driving concerns in this book is the effect of "doing good": What is produced by the fight against modern slavery and against human trafficking? How does this regime of care touch other immigrants, what are the effects on the politics of immigration more broadly? How does it actually "help" those designated modern slaves? What does "doing good" end up actually *doing?*

THE CASE OF MODERN SLAVERY

When I first arrived in Paris in 1999, there was much publicity about a young Indian girl who had been kept as a slave by an Indian diplomat. She had been brought by him to France, her papers taken away. She had escaped after eight months, with scars attesting to sexual mutilation and torture. One association, the Comité contre l'Esclavage Moderne (CCEM, or Committee against Modern Slavery) was credited with saving this girl from the Indian diplomat. Articles about her abounded in newspapers of all political bents, including magazines like *Elle,* where the headline in the September 20 issue read, "Lalita, the Martyr: A Slave in Paris," which began, "She doesn't even know her own age. She was exploited, tortured, mutilated. At her wits end, she escaped last week. This is happening in Paris. Her employer risks nothing: he's an Indian diplomat."

As the months went by, CCEM received a lot of media attention that emphasized how the group helped enforce human rights in Paris by saving young girls held as slaves and prosecuting the perpetrators. The story of modern slaves also entered the Paris marketplace, and bookstores

Figure 6. Cover image of *Esclaves en France* (Slaves in France), by Sylvie O'Dy of the Committee against Modern Slavery. Photo courtesy of Albin Michel.

displayed testimonies of former slaves (see figures 6 and 7). Having been in Paris for nearly a year, and having encountered what I considered situations of extreme exploitation, violence, and abuse among the sans-papiers, I went to speak with the Committee against Modern Slavery. I went to ask them how they joined their struggle to the faltering sans-papiers movement.

When I met CCEM representatives at their offices I was taken aback. Not only did CCEM occupy two floors, with computers, a number of paid employees, and ample space—a rarity in Paris—but it was in the center of Paris; in the 1st arrondissement, right near the Louvre.[2] This was surprising, since the sans-papiers movement and all the related associations I had worked with struggled to find space, and rarely had paid employees. This was clearly a professional organization. I spoke with one of the early members—a former journalist. When I asked about the connection to

Figure 7. Cover image of *Une esclave moderne* (A modern slave), by Henriette Akofa. Photo courtesy of Laurent Monlaü.

sans-papiers, he quickly replied that there was no connection, that CCEM was a human rights organization formed to help slaves, not sans-papiers. He stated, "We need to maintain our legitimacy as an organization that fights modern *slavery,* and not simply economic exploitation." He pointed to the fact that the committee had a 100 percent success rate in getting their "girls" *(filles)* papers and explained that those who enslave others do so because they fail to recognize the slaves as human.

His unfriendliness to sans-papiers was echoed by both another employee as well as by CCEM's president and founder. The employee explained to me that CCEM does not deal with sans-papiers, because "sans-papiers will tell any story to get papers." Immediately casting sans-papiers in a criminal light, she regarded them as all equally suspicious, saying that, "after all, CCEM has to remain credible." At a fund-raising event, when asked whether the situations of sans-papiers can gradually deteriorate into those of slavery, the president of CCEM responded with a similarly dismissive gesture by refusing to see any overlap between the two. "Exploitation does not become slavery," she said. "Our modern slaves are not like *travailleurs clandestins*—clandestine workers." Her words revealed an assumption that all those without papers have come to France illegally to work on the black market. This has been proven false many times over; as sans-papiers spokesperson Ababacar Diop stated, "Most of us lived here entirely legally for several years and only became illegal as a result of new legislation" (1997b:2). As I mentioned in chapter 1, the sans-papiers are a remarkably heterogeneous group, brought together only through an administrative category and a label they claimed as a means to emancipation. Indeed, the many histories and trajectories of sans-papiers include asylum claimants denied refugee status, economic immigrants trafficked across borders as cheap labor or as sex workers, wives joining husbands who had long been in France, and students whose visas were not renewed because they failed exams.[3]

With further research, I realized that, in fact, quite a number of the sans-papiers might well qualify under the conditions CCEM had established for modern slavery, which one of the members articulated as (a) threats, such as being sequestered or pressured to stay in the house; (b) confiscation of papers; (c) exploitative working conditions, such as 14–18 hours/day, no rest or vacation, and little or no remuneration; (c) extremely poor living conditions, such as on the floor, in a basement, kitchen, or bathroom, no right to shower or wash; and (d) food scarcity, including not being fed or being fed only one meal per day and therefore being malnourished. CCEM's 2005 report also includes rupturing of family ties and cultural isolation. Yet most of those who came for help were turned away, as CCEM focused on rescuing young girls originally from Africa, Madagascar, or Sri Lanka from employers from these same countries, often diplomats, and only occasionally French.

In the group's offices, I was shown the many binders of newspaper and magazine articles featuring the organization, starting as early as 1996; the committee was founded in 1995 by journalist Dominique Torres. In August 1996, for example, a headline in the conservative newspaper *Le Figaro* read, "Slaves in the Land of Human Rights"; the article discussed

Figure 8. Marianne cover, October 13–19, 1997. "Slavery in France: They are treated like animals, locked away, brutalized. This is happening here, in the home of human rights." Photo courtesy of *Marianne*.

the case of a young Eritrean domestic worker who had been enslaved by a Lebanese diplomat in Paris. An October 1997 story in *Marianne* read, "Slavery still exists in the world, and not only in China, India or the Gulf states; in Europe, they are usually clandestine immigrants. They were hoping to find a better life, they found themselves in hell. In France, three women escaped." This time period overlaps with the height of the sans-papiers movement, in which public sympathy was at its greatest; and interestingly, slaves are not yet fully distinguished from sans-papiers here. Again, on the front cover of the same magazine, we see the caption, "Slavery in France: they are treated like animals, locked away, brutalized. This is happening here, in the home of Human Rights" (see figure 8). In other articles, the national narrative of France as home to human rights is reinforced with a challenge: CCEM's advertising poster says boldly, "Slavery in France is not dead. You are free to do nothing" (see figure 9).

Publicity surrounding CCEM stepped up in 1998, the 150th anniversary of the abolition of slavery in the French colonies. At this point,

Figure 9. "Slavery in France is not dead; you are free to do nothing." Committee against Modern Slavery poster, published in *Citoyens,* 1998. The tag around the ankle reads, "Name: unknown; Age: undetermined; Profession: slave; Place of death: Paris." Photo courtesy of CCEM.

media attention for the sans-papiers cause diminished, as discussed in chapter 1; the 1997 political amnesty for sans-papiers had been enacted and policing of borders increased, labeling those remaining as criminals. And gradually, the narratives that divorce modern slaves from the experience of other sans-papiers became more prevalent, to the point where, when I interviewed people in 1999 and 2000, the link between the two was explicitly denied. The newly constructed distinction between sans-papiers and slaves illustrates the slippery terrain that both—and other marginalized or exploited groups—inhabit between victims and criminals, legal and illegal.

In reading the various newspaper stories and testimonials, and speaking to CCEM members and volunteers, it became clear that certain tropes are crucial to the popularity and success of CCEM in the media and the national imagination, and these tropes relate to the breadth and type of response.[4] They participate in the genre that Carole Vance has called "melomentary"—a splicing of melodrama and documentary—with respect to films about sex trafficking (Adler 2008, interview with Vance). There is constant appeal to emotion—to images of suffering. One member of CCEM was quoted as saying, "Slavery is the highest degree of suffering," and she affirmed that establishing a hierarchy of suffering is necessary to conserve the group's credibility and efficiency (L'Express 2000). There is a certain innocence required of modern slaves, often linked with a trope of childhood; so, nearly all the slaves accepted as such are young girls, who come to France naively, sexually innocent, often without a choice—they are sent by their parents, for instance, casting the state in the role of benevolent patriarch. The motherly and patronizing tone of the CCEM president, as she referred to "her" girls as "adorable," is just one indication of such an infantilizing approach. There is no room for the victim's complicity in wanting a better life—in taking opportunities to leave one's home. The girls are described as vulnerable, defenseless, lost, and excluded. The examples of abuse are related graphically, and while they are undeniably horrible, they are decontextualized. Perhaps most important to the success of CCEM in the French public imagination is the question of *who* the perpetrators are: CCEM literature says that while it is true that 20 percent of those committing crimes of modern slavery are indeed French, 80 percent come from poor, third world countries.

While geographically located in the center of Paris, then, the human rights work of CCEM is necessarily located beyond the national or state realm. Those prosecuted for human rights abuses or being saved from them are already "outside" France: they are imported, never fully part of the French nation-state, and make no pretense to be, unlike the sans-papiers, who are accusing the French state itself and who are an intimate part of the nation-state's economy and identity. While CCEM is based in France, and explicitly draws on what the founders call the French tradition of human rights, it directs its mission outward, working mostly on the European and international levels. Also important to note is that the Committee against Modern Slavery's funding comes from the French government and the European Community, and the group has received money from the European Union to start branches in other European countries—CCEM sees this as France leading the way for the dissemination of human rights practices. In other words, CCEM is less concerned about French missteps than about violations that occur on French soil, by non-French Others, and about exporting what members of the group see as the French principles of human rights.

While CCEM calls itself a human rights organization, and while the executives stressed to me that they are interested in justice, not in "saving people from war-torn zones," I will nevertheless argue that we should understand CCEM as working (at least partly) on the basis of a humanitarian logic, or more broadly, as part of a politics of care. Of course, as Richard Wilson and Richard Brown (2009) point out, there is significant overlap between human rights and humanitarianism that is not always easily (or necessarily) parsed out. The most obvious relation to this history of humanitarianism is through the issue of slavery itself: abolitionism, or the struggle to end the slave trade in the nineteenth century, is taken as one of the first and most exemplary expressions of what we now call humanitarian sentiment (Haskell 1992). But the early struggle against trafficking in women and children, to which I will return, was also understood as a humanitarian one; for instance, the Social and Humanitarian Section took on the issue at the League of Nations, rather than the Political Section, in order to reflect the issue's moral status (Morefield 2009). On a more contemporary note, I attended an evening fund-raiser for CCEM, sponsored by Zonta, "a global organization of executives and professionals working together to advance the status of women worldwide." A representative of Zonta introduced the discussion, calling the struggle against modern slavery "a humanitarian cause"; members of Zonta were interested in the issue because they do service and advocacy work for humanitarian missions.

I place CCEM in this framework, not simply because others do, but because it helps explain the group's actual practice. For instance, CCEM uses a model of emergency response and temporary care, set up for a few exceptional individuals. When it does accept girls, CCEM makes an effort to provide them with social services, yet the committee can only offer exceptional care. CCEM gives "case-by-case" educational support to individuals in CCEM's own locale, and it gives "exceptional" financial aid to certain individuals too, providing that they recognize that it is exceptional (CCEM 2004:9). The organization has one apartment where it can house modern slaves, but as CCEM itself admits, it was designed for those just rescued, not for long-term use. However, it has been stretched beyond its initial allotment as emergency housing to fit girls' needs that last not just for days or months, but years. In other words, the "emergency" is one of *longue durée*—the same dire circumstances faced by all others in France without papers, housing, or jobs—but it must be imagined as an emergency in order for CCEM to engage.

Beyond these few exceptions, CCEM and modern slaves are dependent on the French state's provision of services, such as health care coverage (L'Aide Médicale de l'État, or AME) in the same way as all other sans-papiers. Indeed, in all other instances, they join the sans-papiers, facing the same immigration policies, the same options for legalization. Yet CCEM is careful to set itself apart from the sans-papiers struggle. Clearly, there is a moral economy of suffering at work here; the most horrible form of suffering prevails. This requires distinguishing oneself from all others. Compassion, it seems, is not an egalitarian sentiment; not everyone can reap its benefits.

The result of focusing attention on modern slavery in an exclusive sense is that the reality of migration is rendered immaterial by the language of emergency that accompanies the panic about modern slavery, which focuses on a small slice of the present, paying attention to appalling practices, but without trying to understand or address their causes: caring, not curing. For instance, in all the CCEM publicity, the focus is on the individual, deferring questions of global political economy; there is an erasure of the inequality in resources and power between the global North and South and the resulting issue of migration. What is emphasized besides the immediate horror is the inequality in level of "civilization." CCEM has coauthored several testimonies of modern slaves, and the collective testimony put together and written by then-copresident Sylvie O'Dy, *Esclaves en France,* is revealing in this manner (see figure 6). There is constant reference to the "barbaric" practices that girls are subject to (O'Dy 2001:26), which are said to derive from foreign countries. Thus, the caste system in India is blamed: "it weighs heavily on the mentality (of Indians)" (2001:45); and Madagascar's "ancient tradition" of master and slave families is seen as the culprit (2001:84). Here, if explanations

for violence are given at all, they are found in ahistorical cultural differences and mapped onto a hierarchy of civilizations, but they are rarely
attributed to differences in political, historical, or economic relations
of power. This authorizes a singular form of action: to help save—and
perhaps civilize—others, but not to think about the historical conditions under which these forms of violence come to be, and what role
those in the global North might play in shaping these conditions. Not
surprisingly, then, such approaches do not take into account the many
dimensions of female labor migration, which can often involve the sex
industry as a step in the process of achieving economic independence
(Doezema 2000; Guillemaut 2004; Chapkis 2003; Haynes 2009a, 2009b).
In particular, they do not recognize what the International Organization
for Migration reports as the "feminization" of international labor migration, where nearly half of migrants worldwide are now women (Wijers
and Lap-Chew 1997:44; Parreñas 2001).

In my work with sans-papiers associations, I spoke with several people
who might have qualified as slaves, fulfilling either all or most of the
conditions named by the CCEM—yet they were not young enough, not
women, did not suffer from sexual abuse, or had been "too" strategic
about coming to France, and so complicit in some way in their imprisonment. And, on the whole, their captors were French, and interestingly,
often women. For example, one day I was at one of the women's associations I frequented called Femmes de la Terre (Women of the Earth), reading through legal cases of immigrant women who had lost their papers
due to domestic violence, when one of the employees of the association
called me over to listen as a thirty-seven-year-old Tunisian woman related
her story in her quest for compensation. She was nervous; it was difficult
to tell her age by looking at her—she fluctuated between looking middle-
aged and looking like a young girl. She said she had been imprisoned by
her employer, a female economics teacher, for six years. She was initially
hired to take care of the teacher's daughter in exchange for housing and
pay and was gradually imprisoned, working from 7:00 A.M. to 1:00 A.M.
and sleeping on the couch with no space of her own. She was verbally
abused and said she was paid only three times in six years. However, a
few elements of her story did not fit with the modern slavery narrative:
there was no sexual abuse, and she had initially come to France herself,

in search of a different life, running away from the marriages she claimed her parents kept forcing on her. She had never been forcibly detained in the house—just told not to leave. However, when she did leave once to babysit for a neighbor, her employer/captor was furious and curtailed all future ventures by telling the neighbor that she was a thief and a liar. Finally, she had "escaped" too long ago, a year perhaps; she was not in immediate danger, in need of a savior. In fact, her employer had eventually kicked her out onto the street after a bout of abuse, with nothing but the clothes on her back. Not surprisingly, the CCEM did not take her case.

I came across other cases in my work with sans-papiers; in fact, when I talked with people from associations who worked with sans-papiers, or attended sans-papiers events, I invariably heard about cases of slavery. There was an older woman who came to France as a domestic worker, to take care of her daughter's children, and ended up a slave to the family; she was found in a church after having escaped, and the priest brought her to a sans-papiers association. There was a woman enslaved, not to her employers, but to her husband, and locked in her house for months; she was discovered by someone coming to check the electricity meter, and the police had to break the door down to get her out. Yet these cases do not conform to the stereotypical narrative; as such, they are rendered invisible in a binary world of young sexually abused slaves from the global South versus criminalized sans-papiers.

CCEM certainly banks on its sensationalist appeal. But there is more power to its appeal than that. CCEM does not stand ideologically alone in the spectrum of associations; it belongs in the larger context of transnational antitrafficking groups. And as such, CCEM participates in a politics of care that locates people along a hierarchy of suffering, where only a few are deemed morally legitimate, worthy sufferers.

THE TRANSNATIONAL CONTEXT: HUMAN TRAFFICKING

The international fight against trafficking in human beings is relatively new, dating to the 1990s. In fact, the dramatic surge of publicity for and legal action against trafficking is as recent as the late 1990s and early 2000s, with antitrafficking legislation encoded in UN documents and national laws primarily since 2000, and furthered by the increasingly powerful movement combating violence against women. The most influential laws include the 2000 Trafficking Protocol,[5] which is an optional protocol attached to the UN Convention against Transnational Organized Crime, and the American legislation, the Trafficking Victims' Protection Act (TVPA), which was signed into law two months before the UN convention, on October 16, 2000.[6] Article 3a of the Trafficking Protocol states,

> "Trafficking in persons" shall mean the recruitment, transportation, transfer, harbouring or receipt of persons, by means of the threat or use of force or other forms of coercion, of abduction, of fraud, of deception, of the abuse of power or of a position of vulnerability or of the giving or receiving of payments or benefits to achieve the consent of a person having control over another person, for the purpose of exploitation. Exploitation shall include, at a minimum, the exploitation of the prostitution of others or other forms of sexual exploitation, forced labour or services, slavery or practices similar to slavery, servitude or the removal of organs.

Perhaps most important to note is that this protocol is now embedded in a framework governing organized crime, concerned with criminal activities that cross national borders.

As early as its 2000 report, CCEM defines its struggle as one against trafficking in human beings; it suggests that human trafficking renders the ground fertile for the emergence of modern slavery. While CCEM focuses primarily on "domestic slavery," one aspect of human trafficking, the group is very much a part of the larger antitrafficking movement—rhetorically, financially, legally, and morally. Its triannual newsletters, *Esclaves Encore*, as well as its website and annual activity reports, all connect it to transnational antitrafficking networks. It is part of the European Commission's Daphné program (against violence against children, young people, and women) and its "victims of trafficking" network; it is allied with the British group Anti-Slavery International and a whole series of organizations within and beyond France, in Europe, and in Africa, including in Madagascar, Benin, Ivory Coast, Niger, and so on. Most of CCEM's material speaks about the transnational antitrafficking struggle even as it deals with the legal and social reality on the ground in France: from its 2001 report on trafficking in children in Benin, to the feature in its November 2006 newsletter about a book by Georgina Vaz Cabral on the traffic in human beings. As one example of the larger networks that CCEM is connected to, Cabral was formerly involved with CCEM and subsequently a consultant for international organizations such as the Organisation for Security and Co-operation in Europe (OSCE) and the European Commission. In this sense, CCEM is a local instantiation of a transnational complex of institutions and practices.

I want to turn to think about what makes the antitrafficking movement so powerful; how does it bring disparate sets of organizations together? Here I speak about France but also about the voices dominating the transnational antitrafficking movement, which often come from or are influenced by the United States. The UN Trafficking Protocol, for instance, is often seen as an American policy initiative, following on the heals of the American TVPA (DeStefano 2007; Kempadoo 2005). In this transnational movement, certain types of suffering command more attention, they claim the moral high ground. I want to suggest that there are two key players that help configure the transnational antitrafficking movement's moral bent and its focus on suffering and care: first, the feminist "abolitionists"; and second, religio-moral organizations. The sentiments and institutions these players cultivate—from sexual purity to Christian salvation—also inform the moral legitimacy of other regimes of care, such as medical humanitarianism.

Abolitionism

While there are two major feminist genealogies embedded in this struggle—I will return to the second—the first, abolitionism, dominates in the transnational public imagination, if not in international legal regimes, and is critical in setting the moralistic tone. The term "abolitionism" and the moral crusade it invokes originally arose in response to the Contagious Disease Acts in the United Kingdom, which were passed in 1864, with alterations in 1867 and 1869, the goal of which was to reduce venereal disease in the armed forces by allowing sanitary inspection of prostitutes in military depots (Walkowitz 1980). Josephine Butler and the feminists who followed her fought to repeal the acts, arguing that they gave the state more power to police the lives of women and that they sanctioned a double standard of sexual morality; instead, Butler and others like her placed the blame on male lust and saw prostitutes as victims to be rehabilitated rather than punished. Butler and her followers joined with "social purity" reformers to repeal the laws; and while Butlerites may have initially had a more radical agenda, ultimately it was overtaken by the social purity reformers (which some Butler feminists joined). The latter were more interested in abolishing prostitution and controlling sexual variation through repressive measures, particularly against working-class women (Walkowitz 1980; Doezema 2000).

As scholars and sex workers have noted, the moralizing precursors that began with the social purity reformers really took shape and force in the campaign against "white slavery" in the late nineteenth- and early twentieth-century Europe (Doezema 2000; Levine 2003; Kempadoo 2005; Bernstein 2007). The narrative of white slavery was concerned with the fate of young "white" women and their potential to be abducted for the purposes of prostitution by "foreign" men; it must be remembered, of course, that these racial categories were in flux in the metropole and the colonies. This narrative fed fear in English-speaking nations and some European ones, and central to it was the representation of passive female sexuality and active male sexuality. The "slavers" were represented as foreign, or as a Calcutta police chief stated, "mostly of the lowest class of continental Jew" (Levine 2003:246). The moral panic mixed together a desire to abolish prostitution with a concern about racial mixing and new forms of mobility for women. Sexuality acted as a nodal point for conflicts over various types of boundaries; as Ann Stoler (1989) argues with regard to the colonial context, sexual behavior served to mark race and class in a wider set of relations of power. Indeed, the white slavery narrative did not hold the same power in the colonies, since European women still had to be represented as rational, able to exercise choice; this was in order to distinguish them from the "ignorance" and "passivity" of the indigenous population, especially the indigenous women, who were seen as subject to their "barbaric cultures" (Levine 2003:247).

These same issues—new forms of mobility and mixing—clearly haunt the discussions on trafficking today and activate similar moralizing tendencies. While current antitrafficking laws include trafficking for forced labor as well as for forced sex, trafficking for the purposes of sex still receives the most publicity and emphasis transnationally. For example, as Kara Abramson, legal scholar and advocacy director of the Congressional-Executive Commission on China, writes, "Sex work by women tends to frame the understanding of gender in the context of trafficking, even though women and girls also comprise the bulk of the trafficked non-sex-related labor force. As a result, discourse on trafficking becomes simply another forum for the pro- and anti-prostitution debate" (2003:474). In the United States, the disproportionate focus on sex work was driven by abolitionist forces who thought the White House was "too soft on prostitution," and their position gained traction in the Bush administration, influencing legislation such as the reauthorization of the TVPA in 2003, the HIV/AIDS Act of 2003, and the 2005 revision of the TVPA, which increased the focus on antiprostitution efforts (DeStefano 2007).

From the abolitionist perspective, trafficking is nearly synonymous with prostitution, which in turn is seen as the worst form of patriarchal oppression, a practice inherently violent to women.[7] Abolitionists question the very definition of "voluntary" prostitution;[8] the Coalition against Trafficking in Women (CATW) is the group that perhaps best embodies this point of view. Of course, the term "abolitionism" itself refers back to the nineteenth-century struggle against the slave trade and, in so doing, both claims the moral high ground and renders prostitution and slavery synonymous. This was made explicit by the Bush State Department's top antitrafficking official, Ambassador John Miller, who compared the antitrafficking effort to the work of abolitionists such as Frederick Douglass and Harriet Beecher Stowe (Morse 2006).

Abolitionists have shaped policy in important ways; for instance, the conflation of trafficking with prostitution by the Christian Right in the United States—and by the recent Bush administration—has resulted in restrictions on U.S. aid to foreign NGOs working with prostitutes, who are required to sign an antiprostitution pledge. More specifically, according to this "loyalty oath"—mandated by the U.S. Global AIDS,

Tuberculosis and Malaria Act of 2003, funded through the President's Emergency Plan for AIDS Relief (PEPFAR), and by the 2003 reauthorization of the TVPA—in order to receive U.S. government funding, foreign organizations must sign a pledge saying that they will not promote or advocate the legalization or practice of prostitution or sex trafficking, and that they will demonstrate policies explicitly opposing prostitution and sex trafficking. While this legislation encourages and supports organizations that work with prostitutes to educate and help them "escape," the goal is to eradicate prostitution. Public health researchers and practitioners, among others, have argued that these restrictions have undermined harm-reduction interventions by many NGOs worldwide that work with sex workers in the effort to prevent HIV/AIDS; signing a pledge against prostitution makes it hard to reach these groups and undermines their trust. The government and NGOs of Brazil—well known for their success in reducing HIV/AIDS among sex workers—decided to reject U.S. government money altogether for this reason. More recently, at least two federal courts have ruled this loyalty oath unconstitutional.[9]

Religio-Moral Organizations

Clearly, abolitionist feminists are not the only participants in this struggle either in France or the United States: there are many participants in this transnational care complex, including actors and institutions that would not normally agree with one another or see their struggles as allied. They often make strange bedfellows. For instance, abolitionist feminists have found themselves working on the same side as the U.S. State Department,[10] as well as with the Christian Right, whose motivation comes from the belief that there is a moral crisis in the contemporary world, in which millions of women are being forced into forms of extreme sexual exploitation. Many of the major players in the antitrafficking campaigns are religious organizations. While the TVPA, the American antitrafficking law—probably the most globally influential law passed against trafficking—was passed with significant bipartisan support,[11] one of its key sponsors was a conservative Republican named Christopher Smith, cochair of the House's Pro-Life Caucus (DeStefano 2007; Chuang 2006).

He also authored legislation that prohibited financial support for overseas family-planning clinics that provide abortion services. Like endangered fetuses, Smith sees women and children trafficked into the United States as innocent victims in need of protection—indeed, as victims of sexual slavery (Chapkis 2003).

.   While the "new humanitarianism" has been thought of primarily as a secular movement, the antitrafficking movement makes clear the mix of religious sensibility in many secular, moralist discourses. As already mentioned in chapter 2, humanitarianism appears in both secular and religious forms today; often, this just means that both faith-based and secular organizations are involved. But as we have seen, the history of humanitarianism points to an interesting mix of the two. In particular, as humanitarianism developed in the nineteenth century, rather than focus on otherworldly salvation, religious organizations increasingly focused on improving the conditions of life in *this* world; the guiding principle became a religion of *humanity,* which sought to eradicate human suffering and broaden the scope of moral attention to the secular world, improving the lot of the human race in general (Calhoun 2008). Secular and religious organizations together created what we now identify as a humanitarian focus on suffering, compassion, and human welfare.

This same set of religio-moral principles unites many of the antitrafficking organizations today. Whether they are faith-based, explicitly secular, or a mix of the two, these groups work to address suffering, first and foremost. While the French context is admittedly different in that it is explicitly secular, many of the participants are nevertheless informed by a religious sensibility. France ratified the 1949 UN Convention for the Suppression of the Traffic in Persons in 1960, subsequently adopting an official policy of abolitionism, which meant that state-sponsored brothels were shut down but prostitution itself has remained legal. This despite that other activities around prostitution have been deemed illegal, such as procurement and owning a brothel.[12] The Committee against Modern Slavery is unequivocally secular, a self-declared human rights organization. That said, it too has many religiously inspired and affiliated partners, including the Institut des Soeurs Franciscaines Servantes de Marie; La Cimade, Service Oecuménique d'Entraide; Emmaüs International;

Caritas; and Le Bureau International Catholique pour l'Enfance. These partner associations are influential in shaping the emphasis on suffering and emotion; they are also critical actors for CCEM. For instance, CCEM is dependent on two nuns from the Institut des Soeurs Franciscaines Servantes de Marie to be the primary caretakers of the modern slaves they rescue and house.

In France, religious organizations are often key providers of social services, particularly for immigrants, and yet they do so in keeping with French secular norms—this is a key difference from their American counterparts. For instance, with his organization Emmaüs, the renowned catholic priest Abbé Pierre housed and helped many undocumented immigrants and fought for their mass regularization. As we saw in chapter 2, Emmaüs was a forerunner and inspiration for Médecins sans Frontières. Similarly, La Cimade—a Protestant-based association—is one of the most important defenders of the rights of immigrants and asylum seekers in France; there is always a representative of La Cimade at the sans-papiers meetings and events. The group is important in legal and medical support. The Pastorale des Migrants also provides services to immigrants in France. I met with a priest from the Pastorale who explained that, while part of the mission is to welcome Christian immigrants, the larger evangelical service includes welcoming foreigners.[13] The Pastorale invested significant energy in the sans-papiers movement, something unprecedented for them; but they saw the sans-papiers as "marginalized people" and wanted to raise awareness of their predicament. In particular, they organized meetings for priests whose churches had been occupied by sans-papiers, to think about strategies and mutual support.

While all these organizations work in solidarity with umbrella secular human rights and humanitarian associations, a certain religio-moral set of principles guide most of their work; for instance, Emmaüs has as a fundamental principle to "serve first those who suffer most."[14] La Cimade's mission states that its "goal is to show solidarity with those who suffer, are oppressed and exploited and to defend them, whatever their nationality, political or religious position" (see La Cimade n.d.).

What becomes apparent is that a common set of morally framed affective goals and practices around suffering, innocence, benevolence, and compassion unites these different organizations into a larger complex that cannot be distinguished as either religious or secular—rather, the defining feature is the narrow focus on compassion for certain forms of morally legitimate individual suffering at the expense of all else: past and future.

THE EFFECTS OF ANTITRAFFICKING

The moral imperative of the Committee against Modern Slavery and its antitrafficking sister organizations is central to their appeal; it forces a narrow window of focus, rendering irrelevant or at least secondary the changing geopolitical reality that includes the growing gap in wealth and resources between the global North and global South. The focus on one seemingly unadulterated moral quest does not explicitly mandate a regime of border control; but I want to suggest that, if only as the after-shock of a powerful movement, it does nonetheless further a regime of heightened border security. It functions as a form of what I have called "armed love." If the application of the legal regime against trafficking works to produce and then save exceptional innocent women victims, primarily from the global South, what happens if we widen the lens, if we look beyond those saved to the system by which they are saved? What else do we find? In what follows, I focus on three overlapping effects of this regime of care: a complicity with anti-immigrant politics, an increased regime of policing and security, and the types of victim-subjects produced.

Complicity with Anti-immigrant Politics

When we expand the frame, we see that antitrafficking measures have involved limiting visas to women of so-called trafficking origin countries[15] and levying high penalties on undocumented migrants. In the attempt to stop the "slave trade," then, many scholars and activists argue that anti-trafficking measures have been complicit with anti-immigrant policies. Seeing all forms of migration through this moral lens—which must at all costs "protect" women—allows for a conflation of the types and reasons for migrating: sex work, trafficking, political persecution, slavery, and other forms of economic or social migration. This in turn renders all movement difficult if not illegal, with visas given only under exceptional circumstances to those who are deemed "true" victims of trafficking.

The transnational feminist perspective on trafficking (as opposed to the abolitionist perspective), while made up of many players as well, generally makes visible the types of people who bear the brunt of this regime of care. Broadly put, this feminist perspective understands trafficking as both a discourse and practice that intersects with state, capitalist, patriarchal, and racialized relations of power. Here, patriarchy is only one relation of dominance, but not necessarily the primary one; this means that patriarchal oppression does not always trump other inequalities—they are approached intersectionally.[16] The panic about prostitution, then, is not allowed to justify any and all actions, such as crackdowns on undocumented immigrants, which may either inadvertently or covertly further racist and imperialist agendas. Just as importantly, the transnational feminist stance takes seriously women's desires and strategies to shape their lives in conditions that might involve a complicated mixture of consent and nonconsent (Kempadoo 2005: 36). For this reason, not all prostitution is assumed to be forced; this perspective makes room for the concept of voluntary prostitution. Here, trafficking involves forced prostitution, not *all* prostitution.[17] This position was influenced by the sex-worker rights movement, of which the Global Alliance against Trafficking in Women (GAATW) is an important player.

Françoise Guillemaut, an activist working with a French sex-worker rights association called Cabiria, exemplifies this position in the French context. She argues that women who want to migrate but do not have the legal or financial means to do so often have a choice between working illegally as domestic workers, or working as prostitutes. A woman may have been helped on her journey by networks of traffickers, but Guillemaut (2004) reminds us that these "traffickers" may actually be family and friends, or may be connected to them, and they may be a woman's only hope in reaching her destination. Differently stated, smuggling and trafficking are not necessarily the same thing; many women solicit the help of smugglers. The other end of this continuum, of course, involves the more sensationalized and admittedly horrendous stories of women being kidnapped, raped, or chained to beds in brothels—but it is important to note that there are many situations in between, and that these extreme situations have been rarely documented (Kempadoo 2005). Rather, it is within the labor recruitment process, at the work site itself or on the migratory path, that coercion, physical and sexual violence, and/or deception take place. While many women may not know the full extent of what they have gotten into, they may leave knowing at least part of it, and they may leave willingly even if they are unaware of the nature of the work that awaits them.

The Committee against Modern Slavery's policy of separating itself from the larger sans-papiers struggle plays into the erasure of different migrant trajectories, feeding into exclusionary, anti-immigrant policies. This distance is maintained despite the fact that "modern slaves" experience many of the same dead ends and challenges as do sans-papiers. CCEM has encountered the same difficulties as sans-papiers in getting both longer-term residency papers (beyond three months) and work permits; this leaves modern slaves and sans-papiers in an indistinguishable situation of precariousness. As CCEM's 2005 activity report suggests, the primary way to hold a person accountable for modern slavery is by invoking the law that prohibits helping undocumented immigrants (l'aide au séjour irrégulier). In fact, since the abolition of slavery in 1848, the new French Penal Code only penalizes slavery as a "crime against humanity," which is assumed to be a mass phenomenon (see Article 212–1) and hence is not applicable to individual cases of modern slavery. While a new law against trafficking was introduced in 2003, as I will discuss in the next section, this was primarily a law for security, to safeguard law and order.[18] When I spoke with one of the CCEM representatives, he admitted that they were often obliged to use two other parts of the French Penal Code: Article 225–13 and Article 225–14, which are about, respectively, the abuse of vulnerability to get a service, remunerated or not; and working and living in conditions contrary to human dignity. In other words, slaves and sans-papiers are part of the same category of persons before the law. Again, while this would suggest that a joint struggle might be worth investing in, CCEM, like many of the larger antitrafficking networks, is clear to distinguish its movement from other struggles for immigrant rights, pushing for its "victims" to come out highest on the ladder of suffering; CCEM and its allies thereby denounce sans-papiers as illegitimate. Insofar as the majority of CCEM's clients do not fit the definition of victims of trafficking defined by the Penal Code, short of joining in political struggle, CCEM can only rely on the regime of humanitarian exceptions with which I opened this chapter; as such, it plays into and maintains a logic that depends on discretionary power, hierarchy, and inequality.

Policing and Security: Passive Soliciting

The logic of care and compassion that singles out the exceptional cases has another critical downside. Those who are not worthy of compassion are not simply ignored, but rather they are often criminalized and con-demned: they are perceived as having failed in some important moral way. The response to this is policing. Differently stated, as we just saw, regimes of care are often dependent on humanitarian exceptions and a discretionary practice of both power and the law; they have as their flip side regimes of surveillance and policing, because policing can also be understood as an expression of power with no normative legal con-straints.[19] Like the politics of care, regimes of surveillance and policing work through a logic of exceptions; they are two sides of the same coin. The slippery slope between saving and deporting becomes clear in the words of then–interior minister Nicolas Sarkozy, speaking in the French Senate in 2002: "It seems wise to escort girls who do not speak our lan-guage and who have just arrived in our country back to their country of origin in order to release them from the grasp of their pimps. It is a humanitarian duty!" (Allwood 2004). A humanitarian duty to deport someone—without asking, of course, if this is what these women would want. If one draws on a moralist logic, one is subject to the discretion-ary practices of the state, which may be benevolent and kind, but they may also include deportation, detention, or violence; such is the nature of armed love. Care often goes hand in hand with discipline; the links between social assistance and surveillance have a long history. The Committee against Modern Slavery's work, therefore, is limited in very clear ways; it is limited precisely because it draws on a framework grounded in compassion and benevolence. It matters little whether all parts of this agenda were chosen and agreed to by those who run CCEM.

As just one example of the aftershock of compassion, in the French case, the transnational antitrafficking campaign produced a new law against "passive soliciting" *(racolage passif)*. Specifically, Article 18 of the Internal Security Act of March 18, 2003, criminalizes passive soliciting, giving up to two months in prison and fines of €3,750.[20] In the name of protecting women, the law means that any woman whose dress or attitude gives the impression that she is soliciting money for sex can face both a fine and extended jail time. The dual goals of this law, according to then–interior minister Sarkozy, were to combat human trafficking, and thereby to protect migrant women victims, and to protect public order, could be disrupted by such soliciting (Vernier 2005:131).[21] According to Article 29 of the law, undocumented prostitutes are given a temporary residency permit if they agree to divulge the names of their pimps to the police. Here, the law purports to save the vulnerable by criminalizing the guilty, helping to fight against what has been depicted as a morally repugnant practice—the global trafficking in women.

While the 2003 law on passive soliciting was prompted by this international mandate to fight against human trafficking, it reframed the terms of the debate on prostitution because it was also part of the broadening of state powers in the name of security. Here the intersection between discourses of security and those against human trafficking is rendered explicit.[22] The French state is allowed to act against prostitution if there is active "exhibitionism" that damages public order and security. The law therefore overlays the transnational discourse on protection of women from trafficking with a national rhetoric of law and order. Crucially, the term "passive soliciting" is defined in such a way that the police can act as sovereign—they have the power to determine what behaviors constitute "soliciting" since it is defined as passive, not active. Appearance is what is at stake; and it almost goes without saying that such policing is racially informed. Sarkozy explicitly stated that migrant women are the primary target of this law; in this case, they come primarily from Eastern Europe and sub-Saharan Africa. Indeed, it is estimated that 75 percent of street prostitutes in Paris and 50 percent in France overall are foreign—and are for the most part undocumented.[23] While the law is purportedly about holding mafia and trafficking networks accountable for exploiting women, in practice it encourages policing of undocumented immigrants through scaled-up identity checks and new forms of surveillance of parks and streets. In other words, the fight against soliciting in the name of "security" and to protect women only thinly masks an anti-immigrant politics.

This law gives us insight into how antitrafficking initiatives can facilitate a whole series of projects, from antiprostitution campaigns, to the increased policing of undocumented immigrants, to the global "war on terror".[24] In other words, the larger moralizing tone and approach of armed love that undergirds the antitrafficking discourse opens the door for, and makes it complicit with, various anti-immigrant policies. These antitrafficking policies often end up punishing the women who most need protection from the exploitative conditions they face, both in the process of migrating and as new immigrants. Instead, the enactment of both the French and American laws divide women into those who are helpless, innocent victims who must be saved and those who are seen as responsible for their own predicament and therefore who forfeit their right to state protection. The women who do not come forward to ask for help by denouncing their pimps are often understood as somehow consenting to their conditions—that is, they are *prostitutes* disrupting public order, not victims of trafficking—and hence they are not within the realm of protection. In fact, they are seen as deserving the opposite: rather than being protected, those without papers are deported.

Victims: Subjects of Benevolence

By using a framework where agency and/or complicity in one's migration invalidates one's allegation that one is enslaved or exploited, a very particular, exceptional subject gets produced and protected—one that has no "self-serving" desire to migrate but is instead a passive, "pure," vulnerable victim.

The Campaign against Modern Slavery's literature is centered on this category of victim: its 2000 activity report, for instance, begins with the heading, "Victims: At the Heart of our Initiative." The report goes on to claim that because victims have a central place in CCEM, they are listened to and embraced—a patronizing tone reinforces the notion that this is not a relationship between equals. The 2005 activity report gives a definition of victims of domestic slavery: "in large majority women and young girls, recruited in the poorest countries. Working up to 20 hours per day, with little or no remuneration, they experience psychological violence and physical abuse that can go as far as acts of torture. They are often victims of sexual attacks, or even rape. They do not have any means of defending themselves. Knowing nothing about French law, they do not know that they have rights" (CCEM 2005:5). The victim here is not only without agency, but without knowledge or understanding. This image draws heavily on gendered notions that include sexual purity and passivity and on preconceptions of women as victims, which in turn mark their cultures as "antiwomen" and hence reveal a less civilized status.[25] In other words, modern slaves must be configured as "Third World Women"—Chandra Mohanty's (1988) term connoting the stereotype of suffering victims from oppressive and patriarchal cultures who are saved in the name of a superior moral order.

Is there space to think beyond victimhood in the fight against trafficking and modern slavery, and in the politics of care more broadly? Françoise Guillemaut (2004) takes apart the category of victim, emphasizing that the women she works with have left their countries for all kinds of reasons, including civil war, disastrous economic situations, lack of social mobility, and lack of independence for women. She suggests that while they may not want to be in prostitution, they may also not want to return to their home countries under any circumstances. This is one of the reasons that many migrant women may end up in situations of extreme exploitation, domination, or slavery—they see no possibility of return.

Whether antitrafficking discourses and groups ignore the issue of choice and assume that all women in the sex trade are victims, or whether they use a distinction between voluntary and forced prostitution, most do not allow for the fact that choice is a very limited concept, one in which the "freedom" in choice can mean a situation of prostitution rather than a situation of hopelessness. Even if one assumes that choice is either forced or free, the range of middling experiences are lost, and women in prostitution are labeled either guilty or innocent, agents or victims. In this sense, addressing the violence of trafficking requires questioning the very basis of these classifications, which are grounded in the ideologies of individualism and free choice. It calls for questioning the paradigm of choice that assumes that people always have clear alternatives; and it entails asking if there is an autonomous individual to make such choices, outside of politics, culture, or history. Rather, it is helpful to see that agency is always "contingent" (Sanchez 1997:545), embedded in larger political and structural forms, where its meaning can vary from the liberal idea of resistance to that of a capacity to endure, suffer, and persist (Mahmood 2005). It seems that only a radical change in framing can grasp these varied experiences and dilemmas. That is, a different framing might enable a shift in focus from individuals to the larger structures that help to produce the myriad forms of inequality that many migrants flee, but that also structure their hopes and desires.[26]

Recognizing and penalizing the crime of modern slavery, or of trafficking, therefore, is not simply or obviously an emancipatory framework; winning rights as a subject of modern slavery simultaneously inscribes that subject's life within the state order that recognizes modern slavery as a crime. Michel Foucault calls this the paradox of governmental recognition. Or, in the words of Judith Butler (1997), this is the paradox of "subjectivation" (her translation of Foucault's *assujetissement*), which signifies the process of becoming subordinated by power as well as the process of becoming a subject. The effect of autonomy in this sense is conditioned by subordination. One does become a legal subject, yet always at a cost. In this case, subjectivation means a form of second-class citizenship, and a form of subjectivity where one cannot admit to desires or actions.

The 2000 CCEM activity report mentions that the group's General Assembly approved the idea of electing a "modern slave" representative to CCEM's board of directors. Yet there are no voices of these modern slaves in the reports or in the discussions of the workings of the CCEM— the victims remain silent. They appear only in testimonials written by and with members of CCEM. This is fundamentally different from the sans-papiers movement, which is run by and for sans-papiers them-selves; for CCEM, privileging the victim gives a primary role to those who support and protect them—in other words, it creates and maintains a hierarchy between protector and victim. In this regime of care, modern slaves are governed, therefore, as always lesser, not quite fully formed, political subjects.

CONCLUDING THOUGHTS

Where does the fight against modern slavery and human trafficking fit in the landscape of social and political movements that are trying to change the world? I have been suggesting that the project of fighting modern slavery is appealing precisely because it is about subjects who need to be saved, not primarily political subjects. The slavery narrative—and the larger antitrafficking rhetoric of which it is a part—evokes redress through a rationality of paternal or maternal (as it were) benevolence, by appeal to moral duty rather than a political logic, which, among other things, would suggest that those who seem the least qualified nonethe-less can make claims on the state, and on others; this, according to Jacques Rancière (2004), is the moment of politics par excellence. For volunteers for the Committee against Modern Slavery, this political logic would also mean calling into question their allegiance to a state that turns a blind eye to such exploitation, confronting their own complicity. Instead, as one volunteer—an older French woman—said to me, she came everyday because the work was *passionnant*—"gripping." CCEM addresses excep-tional circumstances and individual crises, and the work is performed by social workers, journalists, lawyers, and volunteers. In contradis-tinction, the sans-papiers movement is about political struggle, about changing the social order; the subjects of the struggle include—first and foremost—sans-papiers themselves, along with those who work in soli-darity with them. It places the suffering endured by sans-papiers in the context of colonialism, contemporary imperialism, and global capitalism and demands redress for these, holding the French state accountable.

People labeled "sans-papiers" and those deemed "modern slaves" often find themselves fighting similar fights, at least on the individual

Esclaves en France

Ils ne portent plus de fers ! Les chaînes de l'esclave d'aujourd'hui sont pourtant tout aussi efficaces: confiscation des papiers, séquestration, travail forcé, absence de salaire et sévices divers...Cent cinquante ans après l'abolition de l'esclavage par Victor Schœlcher, GEO dresse ce terrible constat : des milliers de personnes sont asservies en France.

PAR PHILIPPE BOUDIN | PHOTOS MARIE DORIGNY

Figure 10. Feature article in *GEO,* January 4, 1998. "Slaves in France: They no longer wear irons! The chains of the slave today are, however, just as efficient: confiscation of papers, sequestration, forced labor, no salary, abuse of various kinds. . . . One hundred and fifty years after the abolition of slavery by Victor Schoelcher, *GEO* writes this report: thousands of people are enslaved in France." Photo courtesy of Marie Dorigny/Signatures and *GEO.*

legal level: at the very least, they—and the organizations supporting them—face similar legal challenges in getting papers and legal protection from exploitation and violence. CCEM admittedly works hard to achieve legal redress for the victims of modern slavery; yet it ends up producing subjects not of equal rights, but of pity. This is not necessarily the goal of CCEM members; often, it is incredibly frustrating to them. But CCEM participates in a regime of care larger than itself, one that, as I have been suggesting, is forged by both national and transnational discourses and practices such as humanitarianism and the struggle against violence against women, in conjunction with new regimes of border control, technologies of security, and religio-moral mandates. Together, these work through hierarchy, not equality.

What can we conclude, then? The modern slave story is about victims—characteristically from the global South, or "third world"—who must be saved from instances of particularly "barbaric" violence enacted on them by their own countrymen or women. The images and narratives tell of benevolent French saviors, rescuing their unfortunate sisters; in the images representing modern slaves—from newspapers stories to first-person testimonials (see figures 6, 7, and 10)—we see individual women, partially covered or veiled, submissive, waiting for rescue. The effect of these representations and practices is critical: modern slaves maintain the fiction of the Otherness of the third world. In so doing, they enable a particular postcolonial state that understands its former colonies as utterly different, lesser, not constitutive of its very core. The fleeing slave signals the distinction, civility, and desirability of the French nation-state. As a CCEM-authored collective testimony of modern slaves claims, "It is as if being born outside Europe keeps one in a prolonged state of childhood in what concerns rights" (2001:124). To put this in perspective, again, it helps to recall that the sans-papiers claim both an equal material and symbolic space in the nation-state, blurring boundaries between colony and motherland, center and periphery. And while the modern slave story evokes the desire to help, to protect, to save—the sans-papiers speak back and challenge us all to face our complicity in producing and maintaining situations of injustice and inequality.

six

Biological Involution?

THE PRODUCTION OF DISEASED CITIZENS

In 2001, in a conversation with the former president of Act Up Paris, the gay rights activist group, I learned that Act Up Paris had received calls from people inquiring how they could infect themselves with HIV in order to obtain legal status in France. Although this particular account of HIV self-infection is anecdotal, the rhetoric of willed self-infection can be located in the larger reality I observed during the course of my research: I increasingly saw undocumented immigrants turn to physical injury or infection to claim basic rights supposedly granted to all human beings. As I have been arguing, this tendency occurred in the wake of the limited success of the social movement by and for undocumented immigrants that I discuss in chapter 1, and it is a critical part of what happens with the politics of care, where the morally legitimate suffering body and the notion of emergency ground all political action. In this type of politics, biological integrity holds a sacred place. My goal in this final chapter is to examine the production of the disabled subject in France, at the intersection of the global political economy and universal regimes of care—a counterintuitive subject that is more mobile when disabled, injured, or diseased than when "healthy." In describing these new subject positions, I point to important gaps in bourgeois liberal theory that treat the body as sacrosanct and are unable to explain the *willed* production of disability. I take an approach that questions the relationship between the will to life as biological integrity and the "will to wellness," which embraces an overall well-being, arguing that the will to wellness may not be identical to—and may even be in opposition to—the will to biological integrity. That said, I want to think cautiously about when this will to wellness, which can involve the manipulation of one's biology as a primary resource, may come with limited returns, to the point of death.

I take as my starting point the idea of a willed lethal infection in order to lead a better life. I am interested in this rhetoric of self-infection, because it points to a situation in which biological resources become commensurable with political resources and biological integrity can be traded in for political recognition. The point is certainly not to call into question people's illnesses or disabilities as somehow inauthentic, but rather to understand the effects of a new "biosocial" space, and here I draw on Paul Rabinow's (1996) concept not only to refer to a social community created by shared illness but also to indicate the way that biology is used as a flexible social resource. For instance, once an undocumented immigrant is given papers for illness through the illness clause, as described in chapter 3, s/he might choose to escape this biological community in favor of another political or cultural identity. Biosociality here becomes the socially, politically, and economically framed choice to draw on one's biology.[1] Here, I use "biology" to focus on the materiality of the life processes of human beings, from the molecular to the species level, emphasizing biology as a signifier within the larger fields of biomedicine, biotechnology, and genomics, a signifier that is constantly being negotiated. In other words, this comes from the recognition that bodies are increasingly understood in biological terms, whether through biometrics or genetic testing.

To examine the subject positions produced by the politics of care, the type of society, and the contours of the human, I begin with a discussion of the various subject positions I saw emerge in my ethnographic research, illustrating the production of diseased and disabled subjects who are more mobile than other so-called able-bodied migrants. Second, in an attempt to locate these "diseased" subjects and the notion of willed infection or self-inflicted violence, I turn to other examples of self-mutilation or "willed maiming," such as hunger strikes and organ transplants/ sales, to see if they help explain what is occurring in France. The third section places this discussion in the context of the increasing disincorporation of urban populations in the global South from the supply of formal jobs—a context that helps to produce biology as a primary resource; in this sense, biology comes to be shaped in unexpected ways when it intersects with humanitarianism as a form of government. I end with a discussion of the circumstances under which we need to see a will to wellness as different from a will to biological life or integrity, and when we need to see this as a form of violence embedded in regimes of care, a violence I call "biological involution," drawing on a notion of spiraling self-exploitation with diminishing returns, up to the point of death.

DISEASED AND DISABLED SUBJECTS

In my field research in Paris, I encountered immigrants who inhabited a whole spectrum of unexpected subject positions. In particular, these subject positions emerged in the context of the illness clause, which, as we will recall from chapter 3, states that people living in France with pathologies that entail life-threatening consequences may be granted legal permits to stay and receive treatment in France, if they are declared unable to receive proper treatment in their home countries. Again, as I discussed in chapter 3, what "life" means in the phrase "*life*-threatening" is not always clear, and while the illness clause most explicitly helps people with HIV/AIDS, cancer, tuberculosis, and other serious diseases, it can also refer to something more socially grounded, such as rape or disfigurement, that may be otherwise understood as affecting the *quality* of one's life. I mentioned how legally instituting the illness clause has interpellated state nurses and doctors—and health officials more broadly—into the subject position of gatekeepers of the French nation-state. They inhabit a structural position that allows them to let in certain immigrants for exceptional humanitarian reasons if those immigrants evoke their compassion. Yet this system based on the moral legitimacy of the suffering body creates subject positions on both sides. That is, while interpellating the nurses and doctors into the position of gatekeeper, the structural situation encourages and rewards sans-papiers for configuring themselves as "sick."

If we look at the various subject positions that have emerged in response to this interpellation, we see that on one end of the spectrum is the person I have already mentioned who—at least in theory—infects her- or himself with HIV in order to be treated like a human being, to be granted legal recognition and, hence, to be acknowledged as part of humanity, willfully disabling herself in order to live more fully. My encounter with the idea of willed self-infection with HIV/AIDS came near the end of my fieldwork. I should not have been surprised, because it was the logical end result of the tendency I had been witnessing. A friend involved with Act Up mentioned cases of willed HIV infection to me when I told him about sans-papiers having to manipulate their bodies in order to get papers. When I subsequently interviewed the former Act Up Paris president, he said that they had received calls about how to become infected in the context of obtaining papers, although of course he could not know if anyone had actually done this.

If willed infection is one end of the spectrum, on the other end is the person who refuses the possibility of treatment—purposefully giving up bodily integrity in order to maintain human dignity in the face of the stigma of HIV. Here, bodily integrity and human dignity are decoupled and differently reconfigured. For instance, one day as I sat with the state nurses while they attended to undocumented patients who were requesting papers in order to stay and receive treatment in France, I watched as a woman I call Amina refused to even speak the name of her illness. The nurses questioned her patiently, several times: "What do you have?" they asked. "What are your symptoms?" She shook her head and said nothing. Originally from Mali, Amina had come with her baby strapped onto her back in a colorful wrap, and she spent her time unraveling herself and the baby in order to change his diapers, responding distractedly to their questions. One of the nurses played with the baby, cooing at him and telling him how handsome he was. She was trying to make Amina feel at ease. Amina handed over a slew of documents, both medical and legal—the unruly pile of papers that all those who are "paperless" must carry wherever they go. The nurses seemed bewildered by her lack of response, but they were not ready to give up. After the nurses thumbed through the majority of her documents, their attitude suddenly changed from mild annoyance to care and concern. The one nurse continued to play with the baby, but more tenderly. Again, the second nurse asked, gently, "Do you *really* not know what you have?" This time, Amina responded that yes, yes, of course she did. She left it at that—the illness remained unnamed. They promised her papers and told her to take care of herself and the baby, to be sure to take the medication. When she left, I was told that both Amina and her baby were HIV+.

This different understanding of life—one that values a particular socially embedded life over what is considered an isolated biological life—was explained to me and the nurses by another woman named Fatoumata who was also very hesitant to open up, at first remaining silent and finally breaking into tears. Fatoumata had recently been released from prison. She had been arrested on drug-related charges and infected with HIV through needle use. At the end of her visit, she told us about the many African women in Paris who simply reject the opportunity to obtain a permit by way of the illness clause, which would not only grant them basic rights, such as the right to housing, but would permit and pay for their regimen of triple therapy—a permit that would literally provide them with both the right to live and life itself. The stigma of AIDS was great enough in their communities that they would rather compromise their bodily integrity than live ostracized and without dignity. This ostracized life, then, is not considered "life"; it is life without dignity, without respect, disincorporated from all sociality. Fatoumata had a tough exterior, but when she mentioned her inability to trust her closest family or friends with the news that she was HIV+, she began to cry softly. The nurse on duty crossed over to where she was sitting to touch her shoulder and then to hug her. Fatoumata would have to hide her diagnosis from her roommate and from her son. After hugging her and giving her a tissue to wipe away her tears, the nurses told her about an association for women of African origin with HIV/AIDS called Ikambere. The association acted as both family and community for women who no longer had their own. While Fatoumata had decided to take advantage of the opportunity to get papers for treatment, her situation was such that she would be living a dual life in the future, with two separate identities.[2]

In talking to Fatoumata, I became aware of the gendered nature of the stigma of HIV/AIDS in African communities in France and how this in turn helped to create new subject positions on the spectrum of the politics of care. All pregnant women in France must by law be tested for HIV, whereas men are never forced to get tested. Thus, more women find out about their illness than do men, leading to an unequal gender dynamic. This stigma was central to what one young woman from Ivory Coast experienced, which the state nurses told me about. This woman was brought in to marry a man already living in France. Once she arrived, the man insisted she be tested for HIV, and she turned out to be positive. The husband-to-be abandoned her, leaving her alone in France. She received papers through the illness clause, and Ikambere became her new family. Indeed, this gender dynamic has the consequence of increasing the numbers of women granted papers through the illness clause; it also results in more women than men having to lead double lives, hiding their diagnosis from their loved ones or leading lives that define them solely in terms of their illness, existing outside all community affiliation except for the patient groups they may belong to. In other words, this stigma creates a subject position for women in particular, where their reason for living becomes their illness—it becomes their only source of social recognition—yet it was also, until the relatively recent development of antiretroviral drugs, their death sentence.

Further illuminating the various subject positions created by the structural situation that favors suffering and sick bodies, the nurses told me about cases where people would purposefully not treat their illnesses in order to prolong them, and thereby keep their legal status. Legal papers are initially granted as temporary permits, which can be renewed. Even something as simple as a cataract can serve the purpose of prolonging one's stay. Of course, this means the advantages of legality are exchanged for the difficulties of living one's life through partially blind eyes. I say this with an added caveat, in that those who do not treat themselves often have good structural reasons for not doing so, such as not having sufficient money to cover the costs, or the time, or the means to get to and from the hospital. The nurses themselves agreed that a patient's reasons for not pursuing treatment were not always clear. The point here is still valid, however; one must *remain* diseased to stay in France and to eventually claim citizenship. Both the medical officials and sans-papiers realize this.

Each of the cases I have mentioned plays on different configurations of bodily integrity, human dignity, and life. Along this spectrum are other unanticipated subject positions. For instance, one of the doctors I worked with treated a patient who took on the identity of someone who had AIDS, including taking the medication. In fact, he literally stole the identity of a friend who died of AIDS. He did this to get French papers—to obtain legal recognition that enabled him to live a life free from daily violence and to enjoy a modicum of human dignity. Paradoxically, *his* dignity was not recognized, in the sense of his unique, individual self. He preferred to give up his own identity in order to get legal recognition as someone else, again complicating theories of the liberal individual that ground French citizenship.

Finally, the case of a Senegalese woman named Aicha illustrates the results of a politics of care that creates political subjects who are forced to highlight their biological injuries and conceal their political selves. Aicha had a thyroid tumor and a serious skin condition aggravated by heat. I first met her at a hospital clinic and then followed her case to the state medical office. She had left her family in Senegal, including her five children, in order to live in France and eventually obtain treatment for her conditions. Aicha had previously lived in France with her husband for many years, so she knew the French system. He had married her when she was sixteen and brought her to France, but she had subsequently divorced him and returned to Senegal. Because her illnesses were chronic, she needed both the thyroid medication and the skin creams on a constant basis, and neither medication was readily available in Senegal. She left her life and family, ironically, in order to protect what the French law calls her right to "private and family life," the legal category under which the illness clause is inserted. Not only was she not legally permitted to bring her children to France, she was not given papers to work, transforming her life into a monotony of nights in shelters and days in cafés and parks—shelters force people out at 8:00 A.M.

It was in these parks and cafés that she told me about her life. She had been a hairdresser and had opened her own salon in Senegal; she had always been independent. It made her situation of dependence in France all the more difficult—particularly dependence on the French state. Aicha was always well dressed, often in bright colors, and nearly each time I saw her she had a different hairstyle. She had no home and no money, so to keep well groomed must have taken enormous effort, but she said she did it to maintain her dignity. She volunteered occasionally in a hair salon to help a friend of hers, but she did not work under the table—I do not know if this was by choice or if she could not find a job. Aicha was therefore dependent on friends and cousins to invite her to dinner or to give her a little extra cash so she could telephone her children. Her hope was that her eldest son would join the French military and come to Paris and that she could then live with him.

The nurses and doctors at the hospital clinic for the disenfranchised where Aicha received treatment were her main source of community— and even their friendship and support were contingent. One day as she sat in the waiting room of the clinic, they complained to me that they did not need to see her anymore and wished she would leave space for other patients. In their understandable desire to give others a chance at health and bodily integrity, the larger structural reality of which they are a part dictated that they deprive Aicha of one of her only sources of humanity that went beyond a minimal, biological life. Occasionally, Aicha wondered aloud to me whether her life was worth living—what kind of life was it, she asked, no family, no work, no money, no fulfillment, nothing to wake up to each morning except one's illnesses, the simultaneously driving and disabling force of her life. She cannot escape her state of injury, which is not only named as such but is embodied. She is just one of the new subjects given life by the consequences of regimes of care that are both created and circumscribed by transnational capitalism.

In the face of this new space in which biology is remodeled not only on culture but also on structural need—where biological compromises are made as a primary form of political action—the subjects that I have just described are not easily explained by liberal notions of the self, the good life, or of human flourishing. In this emergent ethics where biology is central, those with cancer, HIV, polio, or tuberculosis, and those who have physical evidence of gendered violence, become the most mobile, the most able to travel without hiding themselves in the cold-storage containers of trucks[3] or making mad dashes through the Channel Tunnel, risking their lives in the process.

One moment during my fieldwork struck me as particularly illustrative of this new space where biology is a central field of action: the European Commission made a statement chastising France for not taking necessary measures to ensure the "free circulation of goods" by stopping asylum seekers who were attempting to cross into Britain through the Channel Tunnel. The British blamed the Sangatte refugee detention center just out-side Calais in France for the fact that freight traffic was halted, once for up to three days, to deal with the problem of immigrants and refugees. These immigrants and refugees gambled with their lives by hanging under-neath the high-speed trains or lying on top and risking electrocution; they had also tried to simply walk across, through the tunnel (Landes-man 2002). In response, Sangatte—which was originally opened in 1999 by the French Red Cross—was closed in 2002 (see La Libération 2002). Goods were unashamedly identified as more important than people; this exemplified the devaluation of the subjects of both labor and politics, and a shift in the hierarchy between subjects and objects deserving protection.

Notions of the mobility of the diseased or injured—indeed, the emer-gence of the disabled as the modal subject of political economy—forces us to confront our ideas of *who* is "able-bodied" and *what* "able-bodied-ness" actually signifies; and even more broadly, what "good health" or "well-being" signify. The standard of able-bodiedness as the norm and the ideal is herein exposed as fictional, constructed and normativized for certain types of economic and civic functionality. Indeed, the assumption that the normative human is able-bodied begs us to redefine notions of the "human."

WILLED MUTILATIONS
AND SELF-INFLICTED VIOLENCE

I want to turn to think about how we understand this "new human." Liberal social and political theory comes to an aporia of sorts in the face of this realm of biosociality. This set of theories limits our understanding of what is happening and why: the range of subject positions I have just mentioned challenge us to reevaluate liberal meanings of bodily integrity, agency, and human dignity. Most strands of liberal social and political theory find the idea of willed maiming abhorrent or aberrant. Indeed, practices such as the mutilation of children by beggar gangs are interpreted as the result of "native" forms of violence, barbaric cultural practices and uncivilized ethical systems (Breckenridge and Vogler 2001). As Talal Asad (2003) recounts, ritualized practices of self-harm, such as the practice of hookswinging in late nineteenth-century British India,[4] or the annual practice of self-flagellation by Shi'a Muslims mourning the martyrdom of the Prophet's grandson Hussain, are qualified by liberals as nonmodern, as irrational, and often, as inhumane. How do the subject positions of the sans-papiers compare with other examples of self-harm or violence, particularly those not simply dismissed by the liberal state, such as self-mutilation in the case of war, hunger strikes, and the global traffic in organs? Can these help us understand the subjects produced by the politics of care?

Self-mutilation in the case of avoiding the military draft, including practices such as cutting off one's fingers or knocking out teeth are by no means new: they were strategies as early as the 1800s and have been documented in World War I, the Vietnam War, the Gulf War, and most recently by American soldiers trying to avoid multiple deployments to Iraq after the U.S. invasion in 2003. During World War I, *The American Journal of Psychiatry* reported "epidemics of self-inflicted injuries," including slashed Achilles heels and punctured eardrums. Self-inflicted injuries are not easy to document or identify; they become visible as part of larger protests against war or militarism. One report suggests that there were three hundred cases of self-mutilation among U.S. soldiers who did not want to go to the Gulf (Practical History 1998). In the case of American soldiers deployed to Iraq post-2003, cases of self-harm seem to be on the rise, particularly since soldiers are doing multiple rounds of service: new military technologies have meant that fewer soldiers die, even if more are disabled. There were reports of an Iraq-bound soldier swallowing, not one pen, but two; a soldier from the Bronx getting a hit man to shoot him in the knee the day he was scheduled to return to Iraq; and a soldier escaping a second tour of duty by strapping on a backpack full of tools and leaping off the roof of his house, injuring his spine (Dokoupil 2008).

In many ways, draft-resisting self-mutilation is similar to that inflicted by the sans-papiers who may explicitly harm themselves, reframe their injuries, or else refrain from treatment; they, like the soldiers, aim for a recognizably injured body. In the case of self-harm by soldiers or draftees, however, it may not matter, ultimately, whether the injury occurred intentionally or not; they have debilitated themselves enough not to be sent (back) to war. While they may be reprimanded if their intentions are discovered, they have nevertheless achieved their goal. In the case of the sans-papiers, to reiterate, if their intentions are discovered, they will not only lose the chance to get papers, but they risk being deported, imprisoned, or being put in a detention center; the humanitarian mandate is to save (morally legitimate) suffering bodies and innocent victims, not political actors.

Hunger strikes are another strategy of biological manipulation that have a long history, and yet they are particularly important for this context because they have been frequently used by sans-papiers. Johanna Siméant (1993) traces the emergence of hunger strikes as an explicit strategy of sans-papiers in France, starting as early as 1972. She describes them as a violent means of conducting nonviolence; here, of course, the violence is self-inflicted. Sans-papiers' hunger strikes are distinct in their mass character; there have been fifty and sixty people conducting hunger strikes at once. In fact, the exact numbers are never known, nor people's names, which distinguishes them from other hunger strikes that name individuals. The strikes are always conducted with the underlying threat of death. Indeed, the threat of death or irreversible physical damage must be present for the strike to be effective. Siméant argues that one reason for this is that few democratic governments are willing to take responsibility for the death of a person who did not him/herself use violence. But she suggests that the driving force of the hunger strike lies in the challenge posed to the state's monopoly on the legitimate use of violence. In contemporary biopolitical modernity, one does not have the *right* to kill oneself—the state has a monopoly over both life and death. As Michel Foucault (1978) notes, sovereign power fosters life or disallows it to the point of death. Taking one's own life interferes with the sovereign power to administer and manage life. This logic has led to hunger strikers being force-fed or forcibly taken to the hospital, which was what occurred at Saint Bernard Church in 1996 when the police broke down the doors and violently evicted all the sans-papiers, taking hunger strikers to the hospital against their will. Indeed, the mission of hunger strikes is to call attention to the state's violence. In the case of sans-papiers, this state violence has taken many forms, including imprisonment, deportation, police violence, and harassment. The hunger strikers attempt to make the state take responsibility for their suffering bodies. As a result, suffering must be exhibited in great detail. The goal is to show how one is a victim of violence (Siméant 1993).

In many ways, the self-inflicted violence of the hunger strike is similar to the violence of self-inflicted illness or of altered bodily integrity. In both cases, the mutilations reappropriate a body that has already experienced violence through imprisonment or deportation or the everyday practices of social erasure or nonrecognition. Both are ways to reclaim a body that has been reduced by the state to precisely that—a biological body, devoid of political, civil, or legal subjectivity. Carrying out hunger strikes, the sans-papiers were responding to being reduced to laboring bodies. The strikes enabled them to reclaim political subjectivity while explicitly denouncing the violence of the state. But this is where the hunger strikes differ from the self-inflicted violence used to access humanitarian exceptions. In the case of self-infection or nontreatment, the goal is not to expose the state, to make the state accountable for its violence, and in so doing to become a political subject. In fact, quite the opposite is true. In order to be successful, the suffering, injured or sick body must remain precisely that: apolitical, suffering, and in need of aid that only the French state can provide—aid the French state can give *without* being held accountable for the person's suffering. In addition, while the hunger strikes are mass political actions (for the sans-papiers in particular), self-infection only works if it is individualized, atomized. If there is any hint of political strategy, of collective action, the game is over—no papers are granted. Here, the distinction between "politics" and "the political" is instructive; that is, self-infection may be a type of politics in that it engages with power, but it is not political—it is unable to further radical collective change.

In contrast to the previous two examples, which employ strategies with a long history, the global trade in organs is a recently available form of biological manipulation; it is enabled by new forms of medicine and technology, such as immunosuppressants that have evolved with transplant technology (Cohen 2002), and provoked by conditions that often do not allow one to formally sell one's labor power. Here, biology becomes an ever more important potential commodity. *Dirty Pretty Things*, director Stephen Frears's 2002 film, tells us this story vividly through Okwe, a Nigerian in exile in London who drives a cab during the day and works as a hotel clerk at night. Working to survive, and negotiating life as an immigrant without papers in England, he never sleeps; he manages only by chewing on a mysterious medicinal root. Okwe is in London illegally, like many of those around him. The film's plot comes to a climax with Okwe's discovery of an illegal trade in vital organs, taking place in the hotel in which he works. After finding a human heart clogging a toilet in a hotel room—a botched transplant that killed the donor—he gradually realizes that immigrants like him are selling their kidneys or other organs in exchange for forged passports.

Not long after the release of the film, a *New York Times* (2003) article reported that in Durban, South Africa, at least thirty people were believed to have sold their kidneys in exchange for money and passports. Thus, while *Dirty Pretty Things* is itself fictional, it works on the terrain of reality, as chronicled by organizations such as Organs Watch and by anthropologists Nancy Scheper-Hughes and Lawrence Cohen.[5]

Organ donation as self-inflicted violence involves some level of commodification of the body, meaning that body parts are fungible and gain value on the market as objects. Many people assume that money is the only reason to have an operation to remove a healthy kidney for someone else's use, when the donor does not know the recipient. Yet as Lawrence Cohen (1999, 2002, 2004) suggests in his work on the subject, the rhetoric around kidney transplants takes on the form of "life for life," blurring the distinction between gift and commodity.[6] It is the exchange of one person's "surplus money" for another person's "surplus kidney." "Life for life" is also understood as money that gives life to the poor, the real wound being poverty and the gift being the ability to sell a kidney. Cohen (1999) writes that, in a Chennai slum, just outside the real "kidney belts" of southern India, kidneys have become a "normal" way for the poor to pay off their debts. However, he makes clear that kidney zones are not simply the result of a naturalized state of poverty. Rather, they emerge at the intersection of poverty and established networks for trafficking in kidneys—moneylenders lend more to those who live near kidney zones, creating greater debt crises than might have otherwise occurred. Yet kidney donation/selling is spoken of in missionary terms, stressing an ethics of care over commerce. It is, again, the rhetoric of the gift. In this sense, a kidney "donation" becomes more than selling one's body, more than simply prostitution—it becomes the ground of agency, the proof that one *does* have choices. In this rhetoric, the vendors define themselves through the gift, and the clients are beneficiaries. A couple who insisted that all their wedding guests sign up to donate something are one example of this strange blend of commodification and "Christian love" (Cohen 1999).

Both the traffic in human organs and the situation of willed self-infection among sans-papiers is about capital. The people who find themselves in situations where willed infection or prolonging an illness becomes an option move with the same global flows of capital as those looking to sell organs: from the South to the North, third world to first. They are poor, black, or brown and often women (Scheper-Hughes 2000:193). They want to be in France to work as well as to live. They

come to make money, which is often sent home in the form of remit-
tances.[7] Viewing organ selling and willed infection in the same frame
draws attention to the fact that the markets for humanitarianism and
capital often either run parallel or directly intersect: as Yves Dezalay
and Bryant Garth (1998) have pointed out, there is a market in civic virtue, and capital from one market (venture capital, for instance) can be
converted into capital (or advantage) in another. They directly intersect
when humanitarian exceptions try to stem the tide of the effects of capitalism. While the markets for organs and sickness are not exactly the
same, they run in similar directions, each based on missionary rhetoric
stressing the ethics of care and the structure of clients and benefactors.
Those who sell their kidneys and those who compromise their bodily
integrity for access to humanitarian exceptions do so in such a way that
makes others feel good about themselves: they do not condemn exploitation, poverty, inequality. All that said, while there may be a similar quest
for papers or money in both cases, for the sans-papiers who get access
to papers through humanitarian clauses, the exchange is not a directly
commodified one; and just as importantly, they can never be known to
be actively working on their biology.

Of course, there are many other practices of self-harm. Without delv-
ing into them all here, we can say that, in very general terms, liberalism dismisses these in one of two ways: religious rituals of self-harm
are discounted as nonmodern or even potentially "barbaric," while other
practices of self-harm or body modification are medicalized, that is, identified as deviant, and then treated with medical technologies to bring the
person back in the range considered "normal." For instance, these latter
include "amputees" (or "apotemnophiles") who may choose to cut off
one (or more) of their own limbs that they feel do not fit with their bodies (Elliot 2003), or those with anorexia nervosa. Yet, as Talal Asad (2003)
points out, there are practices of self-harm that are nevertheless incorporated and accepted by liberalism: these include sadomasochism and
competitive sports, which engage directly with discipline, suffering, and
pain and sometimes with technologies—such as steroid use—that cause
direct bodily harm. Contemporary performance art also occasionally
engages with self-harm, from sticking needles through one's eyebrows

to piercing one's body parts, including one's genitals;[8] as Asad suggests, these practices are accepted because they are seen through the lens of the autonomy of individual choice and the right to self-fashioning. Yet taken together, these various practices point to the fact that the difference between the real and the theatrical, and between pain and pleasure, is more difficult to discern than we may think and that it needs to be continually produced and reproduced.

Does pleasure figure in the practices of self-infection by the sans-papiers? It is worth considering that those who infect themselves to get papers, or who purposefully alter or leave their bodies untreated, find some form of pleasure in working to achieve a particular goal; that is, we might understand the engagement with self-infection as part of the goal of action and the pleasure of recognition. But the discourse of pleasure becomes more relevant insofar as the sans-papiers are always also engaged in performance. All along the route to papers, as discussed in chapter 3, the illness clause requires performances, both by the medical and immigration officials and by the sans-papiers; that is, the difference between "real" and "theatrical" pain and suffering—and between pain and pleasure—can collapse here for all concerned. Nevertheless, the performances required by the sans-papiers exceed explanations grounded in pleasure, insofar as their raison d'être is inequality: the sans-papiers' self-harm is not a performance to achieve or reiterate group belonging, faith, individual identity, or to engage in competition, artistic expression, or sexual pleasure. The situation of the sans-papiers is defined by a form of structural violence that *requires* this exchange, precisely because they are not granted the right to self-fashion or to choose where and how they live; pathologies are required for the papers that allow these actions and choices.

A SURPLUS HUMANITY: BIOLOGY AS RESOURCE

The cases of willed infection just discussed, while helpful in drawing out the specificity of the situation of sans-papiers, stop short of giving us an understanding of why subjects are produced in this way, at this time.

The increasingly important role that biology plays both politically and economically gives us another perspective on what is happening. In "Biological Citizenship," Nikolas Rose and Carlos Novas (2005) adapt Adriana Petryna's concept of the same name to describe a system in which biology has become manipulable, creating what they call a "political economy of hope" (see also Rose 2007). In this logic, life is open to shaping and reshaping, even at the molecular level. As Rose (2001, 2007) writes, "natural" life is no longer the ground or norm against which a politics of life may be judged: the "natural" must be produced through labor on the self. In this neoliberal logic, bodies are all open to alteration and modification: it is not the exception to be treated with Prozac, Viagra, and plastic surgery, but the routine—it is almost expected. Indeed, in this moral economy, ignorance and resignation in the face of the future are denigrated.

The idea of biology as manipulable is useful in helping to explain the subjects produced by the politics of care. However, it needs some critical qualification to make sense in the context of immigrants coming largely from the global South, into a situation governed primarily by regimes of care such as humanitarianism. That is, one's corporeality is subject to different types of manipulation and choice depending on one's positioning in relation to the circuits of capital and governance. The first part of this claim means that, insofar as we draw on the notions of biology shaped by biotechnology and biomedicine, these cannot be divorced from systems of capitalism and from the different ways that capital circulates and produces subjects. Kaushik Sunder Rajan (2006) calls this link "biocapital," but it has a particular and perhaps unexpected valence in the field of immigration. The second part of the claim suggests that biology intersects with forms of governance and takes on meaning in these contexts; in particular, humanitarianism as a form of government works with an understanding of biology as immutable, so that biological-based suffering can be legible and treatable wherever it is found. These two factors lead us to a different notion of hope, an understanding of the limits and costs of the malleability of biology, and to a different understanding of well-being. Ultimately, I suggest that the question of violence haunts situations where biology is a primary resource; here I ask whether the hope connected to it might need to be qualified by what I call "biological involution"—the way that the manipulation of one's biology can come with limited returns.

First, then, to examine the links between biology and capital, I turn to the context of the global political economy and the conditions under which many from the global South turn to migration. Even as we all become potential sources of "biovalue" (Rose and Novas 2005:454),[9] and part of a market economy of health more broadly, this market is by no means the same for everyone. Mike Davis calls those produced by the changes in the global political economy "the New Wretched of the Earth" (2004b:11). He describes a situation where the developing world is increasingly a universe of urban slums and shantytowns, and where 90 percent of the increase in world population over the next generation will be accommodated in urban areas of the developing world (2004b:11). This has resulted in people fitting themselves into further subdivided economic niches such as casual labor, street vending, begging, and crime and existing outside formal relations of production.

There are different ways of naming and thus thinking about the people engaged in temporary, physically dangerous and socially degrading forms of work, whose everyday life is dominated by risk; for instance, Sandeep Pendse (1995) calls the poorest of the poor in Mumbai "toilers," distinguishing them from the working or laboring classes. Zygmunt Bauman speaks of the production of "wasted humans," or those he defines as "excessive" or "redundant," as an inevitable outcome of modernization and now globalization, where the modern form of life creates greater and greater numbers of "human beings bereaved of their heretofore adequate ways and means of survival in both the biological and social/cultural sense of that notion" (2004:7). He likens a state of redundancy to that of being disposable, like a plastic bottle or syringe, the destination of which is the garbage heap; he is careful to distinguish this state from what it meant earlier to be unemployed, that is, part of the reserve army of labor (2004:12). A critical difference here is that this redundant or excess group is excluded from the realm of social communication—they are unable to speak and be heard. Perhaps most damningly, Bauman reminds us that, to be modern, each of us requires the production of excess, the production of human waste and wasted humans—we need them to become our modern selves. This is because modernity is about "order building," which casts out some parts of the population as undesirable; but perhaps more importantly, it is also about "economic progress," which creates overpopulation and larger and larger amounts of waste—requiring new geographies in which to dispose of them.

Whether we call this group "wasted humans," or as Davis does, the "outcast proletariat," scholars such as Davis argue that it is both the fastest growing social class on the planet and yet also the most novel, in the sense that this urban informal working class is not a more traditional labor reserve army with the strategic economic power of socialized labor, but is rather "a mass of humanity structurally and biologically redundant to global accumulation and the corporate matrix" (Davis 2004b:11). For this "surplus humanity," informal survivalism is the new primary mode of livelihood in a majority of third world cities (2004a:26). Ultimately, Davis is interested in the sorts of historical subjects that emerge from these circumstances; he does not assume that this "surplus humanity" is passive, and he points to the way they tap into historical and cultural traditions of resistance. However, as part of this process, he nevertheless argues that there are vicious networks of microexploitation, with poor exploiting the poor and, indeed, "ever more heroic feats of self-exploitation," what Davis, adapting Clifford Geertz, calls "involution": "a spiraling labour self-exploitation . . . which continues, despite rapidly diminishing returns, as long as any return or increment is produced" (2004a:27).[10]

This condition of a "redundant" portion of humanity, existing outside formal relations of production and channels of social communication, must be placed alongside the "biological citizenship" Rose and Novas speak of, where biology is no longer seen as destiny. Biology becomes one of the few sources of value for the "new wretched of the earth," who exist outside the socialized collectivity of labor and lack significant power to disrupt the means of production. I do not mean to suggest that biology is the *only* resource available to the poorest of the poor; as Arjun Appadurai (2002) suggests in his essay "Deep Democracy," there are those who engage in what he calls "the politics of patience," by opting for various sorts of partnerships with other, more powerful actors, including the state, to achieve their goals. What I am arguing is that for those moving from the South into the North, or from what Bauman calls the "social homelessness" of the redundant into social recognition, biology is clearly a *central* field of action, as it is for those designated "modern."

My point here is that this choice about biology must be placed in a context in which those migrating—to France, Western Europe, North America, or elsewhere in the global North—may be part of networks that make biological trades more thinkable than selling one's labor power, which has become difficult in any formal manner. Here, we must ask whether "involution"—a spiraling labor self-exploitation—can also become *biological involution*—a spiraling biological self-exploitation, which continues despite diminishing returns. In other words, we must ask how and under what conditions the exploitation of one's biology can potentially become a losing proposition, the biggest risk of course being death.

HUMANITARIAN GOVERNANCE: WHEN BIOLOGY IS IMMUTABLE

While biology may be the domain of action and self-labor for those considered in Rose and Novas's notion of biological citizenship, to understand the case of the sans-papiers, we must ask not only about whether everyone has access to the various means of bodily alteration—about the relation to regimes of capital and what people might want to do with their biology—but also about regimes of governance that help to determine who is *allowed* to work on their biology. Here, regimes of care are critical, as they play a central role in governing *how* people can leverage their biology. What limits does a humanitarian regime of government place on those it governs? How does it alter people's relationship to their biology?

My claim is that there are limits to who is allowed to work on their biology, and how, and these limits take shape at several junctions related to governance. Most importantly, biology as hope must be qualified by the epistemology integral to humanitarianism, where biology is understood as immutable, fixed, so that it can remain legible. The mediating influence of humanitarianism in the politics of immigration, and the fact that regimes of care have become significant as means of entry for immigrants and refugees, means that certain types of subjects become intelligible in France through their biology, but only when their biology is read as pure, untouched. Biology is seen as their essence.

As I have argued throughout this book, the legitimacy of the suffering body is predicated on the desire to recognize the universality of biological life above all else. That is, suffering bodies are understood as the manifestation of a universal humanity, a humanity that exists beyond the specificities of political and social life—the belief is that we can recognize people as *humans* in this guise. Liisa Malkki has illustrated the tendency of humanitarian practices to make refugees into "universal man"—how they set up a "bare, naked or minimal humanity" (1996:390). This is achieved by letting the refugee's corporeal wounds speak louder than words; for this universal humanity, political history is rendered irrelevant (Malkki 1996). In this sense, we see that humanitarian clauses presume that biology is the domain of the incontestable; they derive legitimacy from the belief in biology's fixity. Biological bodies tell the truth; biology cannot dupe the system. Scars in the right place attest to torture, and immunity levels cannot lie about one's HIV status. This reveals that a *dual regime of truth* is at work. For the modern liberal subject, biology is fluid, open to choice; biological norms can be created and manipulated. In fact, they must be, according to Rose and Novas, for the modern liberal subject to be a responsible citizen. Yet for immigrants, particularly those from former colonies or from the global South, biology is seen as their very essence. While biology may be one of their only resources, they are seen, ironically, as unable to work on themselves, to be subjects or agents: they are perceived as victims of their environment, of war, of larger struggles.

Paradoxically, this goal of recognizing universality through biology has produced two different populations: those who are seen as able to work on their biology and those who cannot. The latter are the subjects of humanitarian regimes and other regimes of care, who must be recognizable in their suffering and whose suffering must have universal solutions, treatable by the one-size-fits-all humanitarian kit (Feldman 2010; Redfield 2008). In this sense, biology as hope works at the intersection of acts and identities; it is not just about manipulating bodies and body parts, but about who the person is perceived to be and whether that person can be seen to be working with/on their biology. This depends both on the act of biological manipulation, what it entails—a tummy tuck, a genetic test, an organ transplant, or an act that purposefully lowers immunity levels—as well as the identity of the person performing the act. Not everyone who works on their biology is perceived as an enterprising, liberal subject, and not every act of body modification is designated as productive labor on the self. Thus, while biology is rendered a central field of action, for many migrants it is unable to *appear* as such.

While in Western liberal democracies—or rather, in a privileged sector of these societies—biology may no longer be imagined as destiny, in that it is newly bound up with general norms of enterprising, self-actualizing, and responsible personhood, now those who belong are distinguished from those who do not by a different imagined relationship to their biology. As I have suggested, the illness clause is based on an imagined notion of the biological fixity of immigrants. And this takes on added significance as a postcolonial condition when we are reminded that those who come in for papers are primarily from former French colonies (see chapter 4, table 3). In the time I was doing research, over 80 percent of claimants came from former French colonies. Yet, rather than the French state grappling with its colonial history, racial, political, and economic inequalities are mapped onto the body in new ways, stratifying and classifying bodies and populations. Indeed, because many immigrants confront a regime of truth that understands them as simply immutable biological bodies, they enter into the strange situation of being exemplary liberal individuals but with essentially illiberal choices. Insofar as modern liberal sensibilities still recoil from willing engagement with suffering, as Talal Asad (2003:121) has noted, examples such as willed infection, which take advantage of biology as a resource to be manipulated, are labeled "uncivilized" rather than being seen as enterprising. And in this manner, immigrants are categorized as Other.

THE "NEW HUMANITY"

We have seen that for the sans-papiers biological integrity may be traded in for political recognition: political action is constituted as a series of biological compromises. If we now understand that biology is a central modality of action in the world, produced and circumscribed both by the inequalities of global capital and regimes of care, what more can we say about this type of action? What can we say about the subjects produced by these trades?

In trying to make sense of such biological compromises, I want to propose an approach that distinguishes the will to wellness in the sans-papiers from the will to biological life, understood as biological integrity; the will to wellness embraces an overall flourishing or well-being that may not be identical with—and may even be in opposition to—the will to biological integrity. I have chosen this framing to expand our understanding of action and personhood beyond that of a liberal, autonomous self, to avoid paradigms that cast the sans-papiers as desperate or as victims, as nonmoderns or as deviant, even as I am attentive to the context of material inequality. As one doctor said to me as she waited for an undocumented patient to enter her office, "No one gives these immigrants credit for their strength in pursuing things we all want, such as hip new clothes, new technology, modern lives. Sans-papiers are not just people fleeing; they are not just passive, suffering bodies." She continued, "They are heroes; they are people with extreme courage, in search of better and more exciting lives. They leave everything to pursue their dreams and desires!"

In order to attend to both the will to wellness and its larger context, I want to expand the transactional frame beyond the ideas of hope or agency provided by biology to include what Lawrence Cohen (1999:148) calls the "secondary order phenomena." In the case of the kidney trade that Cohen writes about, this means looking beyond the dyadic relationship between buyer-seller, or donor-recipient, to look at everyday phenomena such as the debt bondage of those who decide to sell their organs, which does not go away with the sale of the organ. Those who sell do get money. However, it rarely lifts them out from their situation of poverty. This is not always part of discussions of organ sales. With this in mind, I turn to look more closely at two cases of sans-papiers that I already mentioned—Boris and Aicha—to understand how the will to wellness plays out. As you will recall, Boris—the young man from Eastern Europe discussed in chapter 3—was forced into a prostitution ring linked to drug smuggling, and he escaped to France where he requested asylum. While his request was not granted, an immigration official took pity on him and referred him to the state medical officials to judge whether he was eligible for papers by way of the illness clause, since he had hepatitis B and possibly HIV/AIDS.

Like many sans-papiers, Boris experienced his illness as a *political condition.*[11] In other words, for him, he experienced his illness first and foremost as a way to get papers, establishing his relationship to the French state. He seemed less concerned with treating his illness—it was incidental, in some sense, that he had hepatitis, and likely other illnesses. He had fallen ill through his forced participation in a prostitution ring—for him, *that* was the problem. His condition was at once political, social, and biological, but he understood it primarily through a political and social lens—he wanted to escape the prostitution ring. Yet he was granted papers for "humanitarian reasons," that is, on the basis of the illness clause. Ultimately, his biological condition determined his social condition—that is, insofar as he proved he was life-threateningly sick, he was granted social and legal status in France. Of course, because the illness clause requires a life-threatening condition, it is in fact his biological life that Boris trades in for social recognition—the prospect of his death is what ensures his social life. He has to remain ill. While he has papers, belonging is limited by the fact that he needs to be officially recognized as sick or disabled; this usually precludes a work permit. Being part of the formal economy of illness requires that he remain part of the informal labor economy. In this sense, biology both allows for the political claim, but it also reveals the impossibility of a more comprehensive form of recognition or belonging. This forces us to face how biology can offer hope while also keeping strict limits on its actualization; the danger is that it could leave him even worse off. Here, the agency linked to biology—his will to wellness—can slip quietly into biological involution; the hope offered by biology can translate into an unequal and minimal social and political recognition, at the potential cost of one's biological life.

I return also to the story of Aicha, whom I discussed earlier in this chapter, the Senegalese woman with a thyroid tumor and a serious skin condition aggravated by heat. I kept in touch with Aicha over the years that I went back to Paris. Did her illness permits lead her to citizenship papers, as they had promised to do? Could illness be translated into a permanent political status? In 2006, when I spoke to Aicha, she still had not received her citizenship papers—this was six years after she initially got her illness permit, and it was despite the fact that her illness permit had been granted for an indeterminate amount of time, to allow her treatment for chronic, life-threatening illnesses. After five years, when she could have applied for a ten-year residency permit (which in turn finally opens the door to apply for citizenship), the doctor in charge of her case was dismissed. In her stead, a new doctor judged Aicha well enough to leave France; this new doctor told her that she could get her thyroid medications in Senegal and that her skin condition was much improved. She withdrew Aicha's illness permit—and her hope for papers. Aicha surmised to me that the doctor who had given her the illness permit had been removed because she was perceived as too sympathetic to sans-papiers like herself; the clinic, which had primarily helped those in precarious situations, was also subsequently shut down. So when I spoke to Aicha, she was living in a shelter run by Emmaüs—the movement created by the Catholic priest Abbé Pierre to help the homeless and the poor and, in more recent years, refugees (see chapters 2 and 3). She worked for her keep, delivering meals to those admitted and helping to clean the shelter. While she was still fighting for her papers with the help of Emmaüs, it was not clear on what grounds or when—if ever—she would get them; she still lived a precarious life, not knowing from one day to the next what could happen to her, still dependent on the benevolence of others. And as the history of welfare has revealed, subjects dependent on public provision for basic needs are marked as particular types of subjects, not quite equal, not quite able to take care of themselves.

These cases make us look more closely at both the effects and consequences of the politics of care. While the hope might remain the same, there is nonetheless a distinction between those who have their biology as a primary resource, and those for whom biology is still one of *many* potential arenas in which one's recognition—as a legal, moral, cultural, social, and economic actor—can be enacted and claimed. Or, in Lawrence Cohen's (2004) terms, people must be understood as differently "bioavailable," a term he uses to describe the likelihood that a person's or a population's tissues may be disaggregated and transferred to some other entity or process. If we revisit situations where the will to wellness is distinguished from the will to biological life, this time we can include the secondary-order phenomena in our frame, such as the costs of modern forms of life; that is, while taking seriously the idea of a will to wellness that is distinct from an often fetishized notion of biological integrity, we can nonetheless see that such pursuits of wellness take shape in larger contexts of inequality. If we follow Zygmunt Bauman (2004), modern life requires the production of excess, surplus, "wasted humans." In this logic, well-being for one inevitably circumscribes the well-being of the other. While a few sans-papiers might succeed in getting papers and changing their lives in this system—while the hope offered by biology might be realized in some limited sense, albeit requiring the maintenance of one's status as sick—this will inevitably be on the backs of others.

Circuits of migration from the global South to the global North—or from the underclass to positions of privilege—might predictably involve biology, seeing as it may be one of the few resources available; yet insofar as regimes of care increasingly perform the techniques of government, targeting certain disenfranchised populations including immigrants, these manage the ways that biology is leveraged. As humanitarian subjects, immigrants' biology only has value when it is perceived as pure, untouched; it gives them access to the circuits of wealth and privilege only insofar as it does not reveal them as modern, political subjects. Biology therefore plays a fundamentally different role in their relationship to the nation-state, due to the mediating influence of regimes of care. And here, I think biological involution could take on a different, more powerful meaning, related not only to the individual physical returns, but to the spiraling effect on the host societies of the global North; while biology provides hope for a better life, this politics of care refuses inclusion or recognition under conditions of equality, which in this case would mean recognizing that all people can be self-enterprising subjects, able to engage and fashion themselves and to actualize their aspirations and desires. Recognition is given instead to subjects of regimes of care as victims, as nonmoderns. This can only have diminishing returns, both in terms of future possibilities and sense of self for those trying to make their way, and for a society built on the principles of equality for all. Biological involution, then, will haunt us, not only because of the threat of biological death for some, but because of the death of an egalitarian vision of society that it ensures for all. Here, recognition for sans-papiers only comes as the necessary Other against which the privileged of the West, or the global North, may continue to define themselves.

.   .   .   .   .

We can draw some conclusions, then. The subjects produced by the anti-politics of care have inequality literally inscribed on their bodies. They are forever marked and interpellated as sick, as already handicapped—they are unable to realize equality. Regimes of care are grounded in a politics of universality, but they produce a stratified, anti-Enlightenment universality—one that sets suffering bodies against explicitly rational, enterprising, political beings. Immigrants are stripped of their legal personas when identified solely as suffering bodies, and, as such, they cannot be protected by law; they are rendered politically irrelevant. And although they may be liberated from a certain form of suffering, as Aicha's case reveals, they are not liberated into full citizenship.

To understand the nature of their particular status, Hannah Arendt's ideas are instructive. In her famous passage in *The Origins of Totalitarianism*, she argues that being thrown out of one's national community means being thrown out of humanity altogether—being stateless deprives one of the essence of humanity: its political character. Conversely, she suggests that citizenship, as membership in a polity, conveys full belonging in the category "humanity" (Arendt 1951). In what I have described, the antipolitics of care does not allow undocumented immigrants to be expelled from humanity altogether, as Arendt believes, because regimes of care are now institutionalized and operative in a supranational political framework; but it does create and sustain a new humanity that is forced to make new forms of biological compromise as their main source of action in the world—one that must barter with biology for belonging. Ultimately, it sustains a more powerful distinction between citizen and human while impoverishing both: one can be either a citizen or human but not both—once one is affirmed as part of humanity and protected by a regimes of care, one loses one's political and social rights.[12] Since the people entering France through humanitarian clauses generally come from already marginalized backgrounds, primarily from former colonies, this process reinforces racial hierarchies while casting France as benevolent. Indeed, the postcolonial space created through this anti-politics of care continues in the manner of its colonial predecessors—it is reconfigured for ever-greater forms of exclusion that take place in the name of a universal humanity.

Conclusion

While France has served as my focus, the "new humanity" produced and protected by regimes of care is not limited to the French context. Increasingly, pathologies serve as global strategies for crossing borders, whether across national, class, or geopolitical borders: from South Africa, where unemployed and poverty-stricken South Africans use the language of CD4 counts and viral loads to gain access to government disability grants given to HIV+ citizens with CD4 counts below 200 (Robins 2009), to Gaza, where those trying to escape conditions of poverty and misery may pay for one of the only escape routes—medical reports that allow a limited number of Gazans out for treatment of serious illnesses like cancer (Ha'aretz 2009). In the United States, Johanna Crane and colleagues (2002) discuss how, for low-income, marginally housed, and former or active substance users, a diagnosis of HIV+ status or AIDS can result in improved quality of life by allowing access to subsidized housing, food, and services. In this case, Crane and her coauthors argue that an HIV/AIDS diagnosis operates as a commodity. Of course, what counts as "morally legitimate" suffering differs in each context: in the United States, for instance, low-income, unemployed, or marginally housed citizens who are HIV+ cannot get assistance with housing or social services unless their T-cell count goes below 200, which means five to ten years after infection—significantly different from the French illness clause.

Gendered violence, too, travels across borders well beyond France, but again, largely in the form of cultural pathology. As I write, there is much discussion of an eighteen-year-old Afghan featured on the cover of *Time* magazine (2010), whose nose and ears were cut off as punishment by the Taliban for fleeing her abusive husband. She has been offered entry to the United States, for surgery to reconstruct her nose and ears, which will be paid for by an American-based humanitarian foundation.[1] Of course, I do not wish her fate of violent disfigurement on anyone. I draw attention to her simply as an example of a suffering body allowed to travel across borders, one whose moral legitimacy is inseparable from the way it condemns the Taliban as barbaric, at a time when the United States is at war in Afghanistan. The problem, of course, is not that she will get care, but rather that one would need to undergo what she did *in order* to get care, and in order to travel. How about the many other women—the many other people—who live in violent conditions and yet are blocked at every turn from moving, crossing borders, making their lives better? I say this because, as I hope to have shown, responding to the suffering individual can work to preclude responses to and by the suffering (and often angry) masses.

Does this mean we must dismiss care and compassion in political life? It is worth recalling that there is an impressive history of revolutionaries—Frantz Fanon and Che Guevara to name only two—who started out as doctors and care workers. This is not accidental; they went down political paths *precisely* because their medical practices brought them face to face with the intimate, daily sufferings caused by much larger systems of inequality. They exemplify the politicization of medicine, rather than what we have seen in the preceding pages, which is largely about the medicalization of politics. Even a contemporary figure like Paul Farmer—medical doctor and anthropologist—who cofounded the NGO Partners in Health to provide basic health care in impoverished areas of the world, is committed to longer-term structural change, to fighting "structural violence," to curing, not simply to caring. While he draws on the languages of human rights and liberation theology that each play a part in the regimes of care and compassion discussed in this book, he nevertheless combines these with an analysis of political economy, insisting on meeting social and economic needs as part of the delivery of health care. He is a complex figure, interpellated as hero and savior in ways that threaten to make his quest into a form of armed love, but he nevertheless evokes the potential of those who provide care to engage "the political."[2]

This book is not about getting rid of care, then; it is about opening the way to think about how we might care differently, that is, in ways that are not about saving racialized and gendered individuals deemed "exceptional" and hence morally legitimate, but about *not* making exceptions when it comes to questions of inequality, suffering, and violence or when it comes to the possibility of human flourishing. Of course, this has its own challenges: not making exceptions involves being able to apprehend different forms of life as *life*, to expand what Judith Butler (2009:5) calls the field of "recognizability," a task that is inherently incomplete, but one that a political project committed to equality must nevertheless take on. But perhaps more immediately, this ethnography demonstrates that humanity as universal solidarity—that is, as shared community, which means recognizing and respecting the "ecology of relations" (Benjamin 2010) of life in the world—is hard to even imagine without first broaching the current unequal access to the means of existence. In making clear how contemporary regimes of care are complicit in furthering the structural inequalities forged by capitalism, my hope is to breathe new life and legitimacy into political struggles that look beyond the immediate present and that dare to confront the limits of this order. By focusing on the time of emergency, regimes of care render invisible other forms of suffering and violence that extend beyond the immediate present. As such, poverty and other forms of inequality and

oppression that are long-term, chronic conditions are not always understood as morally legitimate suffering, worthy of care—and therefore not
worthy of political action or redress.

In their current, institutionalized, and discursive forms, care and compassion do not suffice to address unequal access to the means of existence, insofar as they themselves are grounded in structural relations of
inequality. In this context, some people are consistently understood as
active, others as passive: there are those who are able to feel and act on
their compassion, and those who can only be the subjects (or objects) of
compassion. This is not a temporary condition, as it might otherwise be,
responding to momentary misfortune; when these sentiments are institutionalized in regimes of care and imbricated with transnational regimes
of capital and labor, this distinction—as we have seen—is embodied,
serving to separate out two, unequal populations. Such inequalities
between populations, created and maintained by geopolitical borders,
have been denounced as forms of "apartheid" (Balibar 2004; Richmond
1995); these types of segregation increasingly have life-or-death consequences. In this sense, even while this book may serve to undermine one
of the few openings to legality that the sans-papiers have by exposing the
way regimes of care function, allowing people to make claims with their
morally relevant suffering bodies—I take political responsibility insofar
as to protect this form of action would serve to reproduce the violent
structural inequalities from which it derives in the first place. It would
mean allowing a few to be recognized—and even then, only as disabled
or diseased—while excluding the rest. I hope this book has made clear
that these exceptions do not serve to alleviate the forms of violence or
suffering that they purport to address—gendered or otherwise.

In direct contradistinction to this antipolitics, then, the political must
be a shared act, a "common operation" (Balibar 2004:77); this involves
rethinking and rearticulating what political action means for everyone—
not just for those who are understood as unable to act, as needing help
or care. Political engagement, compellingly articulated by Jacques Rancière (2004) as the participation of those least likely to be political actors,
necessarily changes the meaning of political action for everyone. We all
must think beyond care, beyond help, to forge a shared engagement.

Migrants and others are leading the way on this, claiming their rights based on residence, including the right to labor where one lives; this type of action sidesteps borders as we know them and instead prioritizes negotiations by the people living there, recognizing all those concerned as political actors and participants—all of whom can contribute to shaping their own reality. This opens up flexible political communities, not those fixed in blood. This is not about suddenly erasing all borders, nor about turning to the state for accountability—both of which would involve their own forms of violence—but about recognizing a radically different political landscape that is already taking shape among people on the ground, with migrants who are often, by necessity, at the forefront. The sans-papiers are helping to forge these changes, whether or not they have been formally recognized.

I want to end by saying that it has not escaped my attention that anti-immigrant proponents could try to use the ethnography of this book to play into the rhetoric of immigrants as "liars" who manipulate the system in order to take advantage of state benefits—in other words, they could try to use what I show are the multifaceted ways in which sans-papiers have responded to restrictive and exploitative French legislation in order to have a chance at better lives. While I think it would be difficult even for anti-immigrant proponents to hide the violence of a system that makes infecting oneself with HIV a viable option for a *better* life, my broader response is to remind readers of the ethnographic example I wrote about in the introduction to this book: the case of HIV+ sans-papiers who chose to stop their medication once they received papers. While this is a complex, multilayered example that raises a host of questions, one thing is clear: even when given the option, they preferred not to take advantage of the system of health benefits. They simply wanted to be able to live and work freely. The policies grounded in a politics of care are what make it more legitimate to be sick than to be a worker. Every sans-papiers I met preferred to work than to be sick, but they were not always given that choice.

Notes

INTRODUCTION

1. See Feldman and Ticktin 2010 for a discussion of different understandings of the category "humanity" and claims to act "in the name of humanity."

2. See Siméant 1998 for a full account of the sans-papiers struggle.

3. For instance, while France could not curtail practices of family reunification and asylum without contravening Article 8 of the European Convention for the Protection of Human Rights and Fundamental Freedoms (also called the European Convention on Human Rights, or ECHR), or the 1951 Refugee Convention to which it is signatory, it nevertheless worked to limit these forms of entry to the very bare minimum.

4. For the way in which the state has allowed corporate entities to increasingly regulate certain "zones," see Aihwa Ong (1999) and her discussion of what she calls "graduated sovereignty."

5. On methods of transnational feminism and solidarity, see, for instance, Mohanty 1988, 2003; Visweswaran 1994; Smith 2005, 2006; and Tuhiwai Smith 1999. My particular situation rendered this type of solidarity particularly complicated: I was identified as North African—meaning of Algerian, Moroccan, or

Tunisian origin—by nearly everybody I met. That is, by those who identified as of North African origin and by other French people—by activists, immigrants, doctors, policemen, border officials, even shopkeepers (although I am of mixed Jewish, Indian, and Anglo background, and raised in French Canada by a South African father and Indian/Australian mother). While this clearly denied me access to certain realms, it also allowed me to walk into activist meetings and not be questioned; people assumed I belonged and spoke to me with more familiarity. This familiarity raises ethical questions. While the goal may be solidarity and common cause, this methodology is highly attentive to power differences and histories of domination, and clearly I came in with the power of a researcher, the power of legal papers; while I may have looked the part, I did not come from that community. I was careful to be honest and transparent about who I was, and in the case of my interactions with activists and other immigrants, solidarity meant supporting their actions however I could, not trying to lead. As Linda Tuhiwai Smith (1999) writes, such "decolonizing methodologies" involve power sharing and addressing the sorts of questions that (in this case) immigrants want to know about.

6. Rajfire is a network that stands at the intersection of activist groups that work for women's rights, the rights of immigrants, the rights of minority groups, and local community groups. Many of the activists were longtime Marxists; others had been undocumented immigrants but stayed involved after they received their papers. At the time I began my research, Rajfire was not an association; in other words, it lacked funding and official status. Those who participated did so on their own time; they were all volunteers in the struggle for justice. They had opted not to apply for associational status partly because they wanted to remain independent and not beholden to funding agencies or the state. This had both benefits and drawbacks—obviously one drawback was that they did not have money for services.

7. I am grateful to Didier Fassin for making me aware of the illness clause and for helping to open the way for me to do ethnographic research on this issue.

8. See Kristin Ross's (2002) discussion of the role of these two figures in May '68 and their subsequent disappearance in our contemporary world.

9. There are various insightful and distinctive approaches to the relationship between biology and citizenship: Nikolas Rose and Carlos Novas (2005) take Petryna's term "biological citizenship" to discuss a political economy of hope based on biological manipulation; Vinh-Kim Nguyen describes what he calls "therapeutic citizenship," which he defines as "claims made on global social order on the basis of a therapeutic predicament" (2005:126); Deborah Heath, Rayna Rapp, and Karen Sue Taussig (2007) describe "genetic citizenship"—a new form of technosocial engagement where emergent forms of public discourse take place related to identities and subjectivities inscribed at the molecular level. Nancy Scheper-Hughes and Loïc Wacquant (2002) have talked about "medical

citizenship," while João Biehl has written about "biomedical citizenship" (2004) and "patient citizenship" (2007) in the context of AIDS in Brazil. Didier Fassin (2001b) provides an analysis of the links between biology and citizenship in France using a slightly different concept, "biolegitimacy." Finally, Stephen Collier and Andy Lakoff (2005) describe the relationship between citizenship and biology as "a counter politics of sheer life."

10. *Jus soli* is a nineteenth-century term that describes a model of citizenship based on territory, giving citizenship to anyone born on that territory, while *jus sanguinis*, exemplified by the German model, is based on passing on citizenship through blood, that is, ancestry or race. However, much scholarship has since shown that these models are not as starkly opposed as they were presumed to be.

11. See Mehta (1990) on the idea of "anthropological minimum" that is required for people to be recognized as liberal individuals.

12. For comparisons of human rights and humanitarianism, see Wilson and Brown 2009; Moyn 2007; Ticktin 2006; and Feldman and Ticktin 2010. See Merry 2006 for a reading of gender-based violence and human rights together. See also, among many others, Grewal 2005; and Kapur 2002.

13. For more on this perspective, see Boltanski 1999 and Haskell 1985. See also Wilson and Brown 2009 for a map of different perspectives on humanitarianism.

14. See Janet Halley's (2009) discussion of "governance feminism," which she argues has made radical feminism into a powerful form of top-down governance that fights against a "global war against women." See also Elizabeth Bernstein's (2007) discussion of "carceral feminism."

15. Rome Statute of the International Criminal Court, UN Doc. a/CONF.183/9, July 17 1998. This UN statute includes "rape, sexual slavery, enforced prostitution, forced pregnancy, enforced sterilization, or any other form of sexual violence of comparable gravity" when these crimes are "committed as part of a widespread or systematic attack directed against any civilian population" (MacKinnon 2006:345). The *Akayesu* decision of the International Criminal Tribunal for Rwanda expressly defined rape under international law for the first time in 1998, charging it as a crime against humanity.

16. Chantal Mouffe (2005) also uses this distinction, but for her the political is the dimension of antagonism that is constitutive of human societies. Jacques Rancière's (2004, 2010) idea of "dissensus" offers one interpretation of the political—that is, the opposite of consensus, a process where an interval opens up. See Michel Agier's (2008) discussion of *le politique* and *la politique* where he draws on Rancière.

17. See Wendy Brown's (2001) distinction between "morality in politics" and "moralisms"; the moral order I am speaking of generally corresponds to her idea of moralisms, although in what I saw on the ground there was always a tension between morality in politics and moralisms.

18. For critiques of humanitarianism as apolitical, see, for instance, Malkki 1996; de Waal 1997; Teitel 2004; D. Fassin 2005; Pandolfi 2008; Fadlalla 2008; and Mamdani 2009. For critiques of human rights as preserving the status quo, see Wilson 1997, 2005; Mutua 2002; Collier 2002; Žižek 2004; Brown 2004; Englund 2006; and Slaughter 2007. For critiques of feminism as moralism/antipolitics, see Brown 1995; Grewal 1998; Kapur 2002; and Halley 2006, 2009.

19. See Ross 2002 for an insightful discussion of this moment.

20. These included Pascale Bruckner, Bernard Henri-Lévy, and Andre Glucksmann. They confessed their errors; for instance, in his book, "Tears of the White Man," Bruckner decried European guilt in the face of the suffering poor and called for a return to European values, such as democracy and especially human rights.

21. See Calhoun 2008 for a discussion of how taking hold of events as emergencies accompanies the growth of humanitarian intervention.

22. Jean-Hervé Bradol, the president of the French section of Médecins sans Frontières, states that the appeal to law "must remain purely opportunistic" (2004:7), suggesting that law can also mean violence.

CHAPTER ONE

1. As Susan Terrio (2009:66) writes, it is instructive to compare the coverage of the 2005 riots to those in Paris by middle-class "French" youth during March 2006, who were fighting for labor contracts—journalists recognized these youth as legitimate political actors, while denying the status of autonomous political actors to the rioters in the banlieues, rendering visible only violent forms of protest.

2. For analyses of the movement, see D. Fassin et al. 1997; and Balibar et al. 1999. In addition, there are a number of books written as witness accounts; for instance, the leaders of this movement, Madiguène Cissé and Ababacar Diop, have each written books (Cissé 1999; Diop 1997a).

3. The first big mobilizations of undocumented immigrants occurred in 1972. Protests have been ongoing in different forms ever since. In 1980 there were important hunger strikes; in 1991–92 the issue flared up again with protests by refugees whose claims had been denied. However, the current movement by and for sans-papiers began with the occupation of Saint Ambroise Church in 1996. For a detailed account of the sans-papiers movement, see Siméant 1998.

4. There were local sans-papiers collectives—every region in France had its own; these were grouped under the rubric of the national coordination of sans-papiers, located in Paris. There were special collectives for women without papers, or sans-papières; there were human rights organizations whose primary activities were to fight for the basic human rights of sans-papiers. There were labor unions, which also focused their fight on the exploitation of migrant

workers; in addition, community groups, those committed to democratic rights, artists, and others fill out the range. To name but a few: ASFAD, Collectif National Droits des Femmes (CNDF), Marche Mondiale des Femmes (CNDF), Alliance des Femmes pour la Démocratie, Cadac, Collectif Féministe Ruptures, FDIF, Femmes de la Terre, Femmes contre les Intégrismes, Maison des Femmes de Paris, Mix'Cité, Rajfire, SOS Sexisme, SOS Racisme, Toutes Ensemble (CNDF), Alternative Libertaire, AMF, ATTAC, CGT, Confédération Paysanne, Génération Écologie, FCPE, FSU, Groupe Femmes et Mondialisation d'ATTAC, LCR, LDH, Les Humains Associés, Les Verts, MNCP, MODEF, Mouvement de la Paix, MRAP, PRG, PCF, PS, Ras l'Front, Union Syndicale-G10-Solidaires, Association des Marocains de France, Association pour l'Égalité devant la Loi (Femmes Algériennes), Association des Tunisiens en France, Association de Solidarité avec les Femmes Algériennes Démocrates, Association des Travailleurs de Turquie en France (Groupe Femmes), ARDHIS, Coordination Nationale des Sans-Papiers, Citoyennes des Deux Rives, Droits devant!!, FASTI, Fédération IFAFE (Initiative des Femmes Africaines en France et en Europe), Groupe du 6 Novembre, LDH Commission Femmes, Pluri'elles Algérie, GISTI, La Cimade, MSF, Médecins du Monde, MIB, Les Nanas Beurs.

5. Paradoxically, this arbitrariness was exaggerated by the new law that went into effect in 1998 in the name of respecting human rights, which added Article 12bis, the right to "private and family life," to the two previously existing conditions for legal immigration—family reunification and asylum. Article 12bis was instituted partly to address the sanctioning of the French state by both French tribunals and the European Court of Human Rights for not protecting the right to private and family life.

6. In the absence of a spouse or children in France, which would allow one to enter under the family reunification clause, this law is the next best option, giving those who have lived in France for ten consecutive years or more the right to papers.

7. There is a large and still growing literature on the *banlieues,* or what have come to be known as *les quartiers sensibles* (vulnerable neighborhoods). For an example this literature, see Silverstein 2004; and Tissot 2007, 2008.

8. RER stands for Réseau Express Régional, or Regional Express Network.

9. For instance, on immigrant detention in the United States, see Simon 1998; and De Genova 2007. More broadly, see work on the prison industrial complex, which includes the growth of immigration prisons.

10. The European directive 2008/115/EC brings the practices of EU-member states into line by prescribing a two-step process: third-country nationals are given up to thirty days to leave voluntarily; failing departure, detention to help facilitate departure may last six months and can be extended an additional twelve months. In addition to these three types of detention, there are two other types

of "centers to detain foreigners": prisons, for those condemned for the criminal infraction of being without papers or not following a deportation order; and a camp like Sangatte, outside all legal regulation. See Claire Rodier (1997), who lists four models of "camps" for foreigners. Sangatte was the refugee center in Pas de Calais, which received 1,800 asylum seekers outside all regulation. It was initially erected by the Red Cross in 1999 to help undocumented foreigners who hoped to cross the English Channel and claim asylum in the United Kingdom but whom legal barriers stopped. It functioned without any legal basis for three years. For a comprehensive analysis and portrayal of Sangatte, see Laacher 2002.

11. The category of *zones d'attentes* was introduced in July 1992 under the Quilès law. This consisted of a new article added to the Edict of November 2, 1945, on Conditions of Entry and Residence of Foreigners in France.

12. *Zones d'attentes* are regulated by CESEDA (Code de l'Entrée et du Séjour des Étrangers et du Droit d'Asile; in English, Code for Entry and Residence of Foreigners and Asylum Seekers), specifically Articles L221 and L222.

13. In French, "prestations de type hôtelier." See the website and regular reports of ANAFE (Association Nationale d'Assistance aux Frontières pour les Étrangers), www.anafe.org.

14. See also the reports by ANAFE (such as ANAFE 2003, 2004) and by GISTI (GISTI 1994 and others); and *Bienvenue en France! Six mois d'enquête clandestine dans la zone d'attente de Roissy* by an undercover journalist (de Loisy 2005). ANAFE's 2003 report stated that the conditions in the *zones d'attentes* were "contrary to human dignity."

15. This was changed in 2005 when the decree of May 2, 1995, was modified by the decree of May 31, 2005, which allows certain member associations of ANAFE to visit (ten people per association). This was adapted again with the decree of May 30, 2006, which extended the list of associations allowed to visit to ten, plus three non-ANAFE members: Médecins sans Frontières, Médecins du Monde, and the French Red Cross.

16. A convention was signed in October 2003 allowing the Red Cross to be present in Roissy's *zone d'attente* (zpajol e-mail list, October 6, 2003, http://archives.rezo.net/archives/zpajol.mbox; see also de Loisy 2005). (The French zpajol e-mail list discusses the struggle of undocumented people in Europe and elsewhere—it began soon after the occupation of Saint Bernard Church; see also http://pajol.eu.org.) The convention allows "mediators" a permanent presence in the *zone d'attente* to inform immigrants of their rights, give psychological counseling, and help mediate between different interned groups. This agreement still does not allow regular access by lawyers, doctors, or other types of associations. The Red Cross is allowed in because of its neutral status.

17. After two years of further negotiations with the Ministry of Interior that drew on these reports of abuse, ANAFE signed a convention on March 5, 2004,

allowing it six months of access, helping it to provide legal assistance to detainees, which was extended to permanent access to zapi 3.

18.   For a full report on the increasing occurrence of minors in *zones d'attentes*,
see ANAFE 2004.

19.   The original French reads: "Je m'étais préparée aux violences décrites
régulièrement par les associations. Malheureusement, les faits que j'ai constaté
sont pires que tout ce que j'aurais pu imaginer."

20.   See zpajol e-mail list, January 24, 2003, http://archives.rezo.net/
archives/zpajol.mbox. See also de Loisy 2005:15.

21.   These increased powers included people being put in prison for acts
such as the failure to produce metro tickets; but more significantly, they included
a plan to construct twenty-eight new prisons, including eight for minors.

22.   Raymond Carré de Malberg's writings about the police state, from 1920,
are relevant here; see chapter 5, note 19.

23.   As Akhil Gupta (1997) notes, Ernest Mandel predicted many years ago
that the growing centralization and concentration of capital was likely to lead
to the reterritorialization of space as ever larger capitalist conglomerates ran up
against the limits of specially protected segmented national markets. He envisaged the creation of three regionally based capitals, one of which was centered
in a united Europe. Yet this alternate production of Europe, while not national, is
still built on the violence and exclusion of others.

24.   There are several ways in which the French state is complicit in keeping undocumented immigrants as readily exploitable illegal labor. For instance,
when the pseudo-amnesty was enacted in 1997, hundreds of thousands of sans-
papiers applied; the government made a promise, however, that it would not
use the information given in the applications to deport the sans-papiers if their
requests were denied. Yet the government refused to grant papers to all the
sans-papiers who applied, thereby condoning their illegal presence in France.
Similarly, the European Court of Human Rights dictates that one cannot deport a
person with close family ties to a territory, and thus mothers of children born in
France cannot be legally deported, but they do not necessarily qualify for regularization either.

25.   In March 2000, the Populations Division of the United Nations published
Replacement Migration: A Solution to an Aging and Declining Population, which
states that industrialized countries, particularly European Union members, need
immigrants to maintain their standard of living (as measured by active working
members of society versus those retired) as the populations age and birthrates
continue to decline. The report suggests that Europe needs to admit 12.7 million immigrants per year—1.7 million in France per year—to offset these trends
and maintain the necessary labor. Other studies contest or revise this notion;
for instance, an article by Jakub Bijak and colleagues (2005) suggests that, while

replacement migrants would be needed in a number of EU countries, such as Germany, Romania and Poland, many EU countries, including France, would not require additional migrants from "outside Europe" apart from the ones "scheduled under the base assumptions."

26. See Bertaux 2009 for an analysis of the formation of the category "third world" at that time.

27. The term "Beurs" appeared in the 1970s, initiated by Maghrebi youth living in the *banlieues*. It was created from *verlan*—a type of slang that inverts the syllables of words—in this case, the word "Arabe" was inversed to make "Beur." It had the advantage of not being pejorative like "Arabe" and offered young Maghrebis a way out of labels based on national or ethnic identity (i.e., French, Algerian, Arab). However, in the 1980s the mass media popularized it, and now it has been largely rejected by those who first coined it. Women or girls were called "Beurettes" with the same end result (Hargreaves and McKinney 1997:20).

28. The cultural associations of the 1980s still exist and still function at the community level, providing social services—but they have largely disappeared from the larger French political scene. Of course, since September 11, 2001, Islam has become the most contentious issue not only in France but in Europe more broadly, and the government has focused on creating links with mosques and with the various Muslim communities, and developing a French Islam (see Bowen 2009). However, at the time I was there, the sans-papiers issue dominated in the public imagination.

29. On the relationship between Senegalese *tirailleurs* (soldiers) and the sans-papiers, see Mann 2005, 2006. The controversial 2006 French film directed by French Algerian Rachid Bouchareb, *Days of Glory,* or *Les indigènes,* also took on this subject.

30. One might include the ban on the veil (which is officially about ostentatious religious symbols) as part of this. See Bowen 2004, 2007; Scott 2005; Tévanian 2004, 2005; Asad 2005; Geisser 2003; and Ticktin 2008.

31. Anglophone postcolonial theory has argued this point for some time. Some examples of the more recent French scholarship include Ferro 2003, Liauzu 2004, Bancel and Blanchard 1998, Bancel et al. 2006, and Bancel et al. 2010.

32. This echoes the law of February 23, 2005 (no. 158), of which Article 4 originally stipulated that historians in publicly funded schools should be forced to teach about "the positive role of the French presence" in France's colonies. There were vehement protests about how this infringed upon academic freedom, and also about how it played down the violence of colonialism, but ultimately it was overturned due to the argument about academic freedom. See Ticktin et al.2008.

33. See Bryant 2006.

34. As one publication by the European Commission stated, "With free circulation of goods, services and capital now a reality, people are still subject to

identity controls when crossing certain borders. The problem consists, in this case, of reconciling the exigencies of the mobility of people with the necessity to control international crime and reduce illegal immigration" (Rodier 1997:224, my translation).

35. The commission was called Direction Centrale contre l'Immigration et pour la Lutte contre l'Emploi des Clandestins.

36. Indeed, these issues played no small part in the "no" votes on the European constitution in both France and the Netherlands in 2005.

37. Transnational legal regimes have moved to fill some of these voids, including private systems of commercial arbitration and public regimes of international human rights, such as the European Court of Human Rights, yet these remain fragmentary. See Yves Dezalay and Bryant Garth (1995), who earlier described international commercial arbitration as a delocalized and decentralized system of justice, based not on a global system of law but rather on a system of competing national approaches. For a good discussion of the crisis of sovereignty, see Aihwa Ong's (1999) discussion of graduated sovereignty.

38. Sarkozy began a second term as interior minister in June 2005 after a brief hiatus during which Dominique de Villepin took over the position.

CHAPTER TWO

1. In French, RESO is Réseau d'Accès aux Soins pour Personnes en Situation de Précarité.

2. SAMU stands for Service d'Aide Médicale d'Urgence, or Emergency Medical Assistance Service. This is the French EMS.

3. See Craig Calhoun (2008) for a description of the tension between these two approaches to humanitarianism, which he labels "consequentialist" versus "minimalist" and which are embodied by Michael Ignatieff in the first case David Rieff in the second. It should be noted that, according to Calhoun, the International Committee for the Red Cross paved the way for Médecins sans Frontières in opposing the consequentialist version of humanitarianism.

4. See Bertrand Taithe's (2004) discussion of the place of religion in French humanitarianism.

5. See Anne Vallaeys's (2004) biography of MSF.

6. Liisa Malkki (2007) makes the point that the ICRC should not just be seen as a precursor, but as an important contemporary player in the humanitarian field.

7. See Vallaeys's (2004:117–18) discussion of the founding of MSF, where she recounts *Tonus* journalist Raymond Borel's initial reaction to the "Biafra" doctors.

8. See Allen and Styan 2000:825–42. While a heroic achievement at the time, later the broader intervention was recognized as "an act of unfortunate and

profound folly" in that it prolonged the war for a year and a half and contributed to the deaths of 180,000 people (Smillie 1995:104, cited from Allen and Styan 2000:830).

9. Emmanuelli wrote a letter to the press in 1979 denouncing Kouchner's idea to charter a ship called *Île de la Lumière* to rescue Vietnamese refugees, or "boat people," who were fleeing Cambodia's regime. This ultimately led to the splitting of MSF, with Kouchner and many of the original founders in the minority. They subsequently left to start Médecins du Monde. See Vallaeys 2004.

10. See SAMU's website, www.samu-social-international.com (accessed June 23, 2010).

11. MSF emphasizes a universalistic conception of human worth, and the unity of the human condition, downplaying different social and cultural attributes of both the doctors and those whom they assist. Renée Fox (1995) writes that, early on, the U.S. branch of MSF paid more attention to cooperation with indigenous medical organizations and to learning about the history and cultural background of the places in which it intervened; the French branch (and the headquarters) was less inclined to learn about cultural differences because it worked with a notion of universality that it believed rose above cultural particularities.

12. The original French reads: "Il faut être du côté de la victime, c'est clair, et qu'importe son identité politique."

13. The original French reads: "Enfin, nous n'allions plus nous poser ces questions. Mais tendre simplement la main à ceux qui se noyaient, c'était ça, l'extrême urgence."

14. See, for instance, *Condemned to Repeat? The Paradox of Humanitarian Action* for what Fiona Terry (2002) calls the "paradox of humanitarian action": that humanitarianism can contradict its fundamental purpose by prolonging the suffering it intends to alleviate. See also Weissman 2004 and Rieff 2002.

15. For more on Kouchner, see Traub 2008; and Péan 2009.

16. As Anne Vallaeys (2004) notes in her biography of MSF, in actual fact, the first MSF charter was a lot less radical than it later claimed to be; not only was it not written by Kouchner, it followed the ICRC's principles of neutrality and confidentiality.

17. Kouchner (1986) discussed the complex relationship between NGOs, the media, and policy makers in his book *Charité business*.

18. For how such mediatization of suffering must be harnessed in self-interest, to push certain causes and to compete for funds, recognition, and prestige, see Bob 2002.

19. There is clearly another important debate here about how mediatization runs the risk of dehumanizing and numbing both the victims and spectators, rather than creating a sense of empathy for a common humanity. For insightful discussions of the role of media in producing suffering as a distant spectacle

upon which one feels no compunction to act, see Boltanski 1999 and Keenan 2004.

20. Kouchner, interviewed by Tim Allen, April 1999 (Allen and Styan 2000:839).

21. For a detailed discussion of the place of *témoignage,* see Redfield 2006.

22. Of course, the provision of antiretrovirals (ARVs) to poorer populations who do not have access to them—by MSF or other NGOs like Partners in Health or Oxfam—responds to a different sort of two-tiered system, where rich people receive ARVs and the poor do not.

23. See Blanchet and Martin 2005 and, in particular, the essay by Egbert Sondorp comparing the different ethical approaches taken by French and "Anglo-Saxon" humanitarian organizations, as well as Rony Brauman's preface. A debate between the U.S. head of MSF, Nicolas de Torrente, and CARE's advocacy coordinator in Afghanistan, Paul O'Brien, illustrates this difference, with O'Brien (2004) arguing that other international aid agencies have multiple mandates—not just to save lives through health mandates, but to rebuild after crises and to help people feed and educate themselves.

24. Since the Rwandan genocide, the United Nations has been engaged in a program to develop the "coherence" of peacekeeping and peace building, human rights, and humanitarianism, where "the political effort to bring peace, the human rights attempt to prevent impunity and the humanitarian effort to save lives are managed in harmony" (Henry Dunant Centre for Humanitarian Dialogue 2003:4). The objective of this integrated approach is to bring all forms of doing good under one umbrella, from emergency humanitarian response to sustainable development; that is, to combine the goals of peace, justice, security, and assistance.

CHAPTER THREE

Some material in chapters 3 and 6 was published in significantly different and condensed form in my *American Ethnologist* article (Ticktin 2006).

1. When I refer to "universal medical coverage," I mean *couverture médicale universelle,* or CMU, which is a particular system of health insurance in France.

2. I am referring to the 1998 amendment to the Edict (Ordonnance) of November 2, 1945, no. 45–2658, on Conditions of Entry and Residence of Foreigners. Article 12bis is the right to "private and family life," which is itself a direct reference to Article 8 of the European Convention on Human Rights. There are eleven categories, of which the *autorisation provisoire pour soins* (APS, or temporary authorization for medical care) is the eleventh.

3. The law states, "Une carte de séjour temporaire est délivrée de plein droit à l'étranger résidant habituellement en France dont l'état de santé nécessite

une prise en charge médicale dont le défaut pourrait entrainer pour lui des con-
séquences d'une exceptionnelle gravité, sous réserve qu'il ne puisse effective-
ment bénéficier d'un traitement approprié dans le pays dont il est originaire" (A
temporary residency permit is granted to the resident foreigner in France, whose
state of health requires medical treatment in the absence of which there would
be consequences of extreme gravity; this is subject to the foreigner's inability to
obtain appropriate treatment in his/her country of origin; my translation).

4. The collective included associations for sick people, doctors' organizations, trade unions, and associations for immigrant rights.

5. DDASS in French stands for Direction Départemental des Affaires Sani-
taires et Sociales, which in English is Departmental Directorate of Health and
Social Affairs.

6. A *département* is a unit of government, the seat of which is the prefecture.

7. These figures come from the *banlieue* that has given illness permits since
1990.

8. See chapter 1 for a more detailed discussion of the criminalization of
immigrants and sans-papiers. Also see Delouvin 2000.

9. By restrictive legislation, I am referring to the Sarkozy law of 2003.
Interior Minister Nicolas Sarkozy proposed changes, voted in by parliament
in December 2002, to the finance bill of 2002 (Loi de Finances Rectificative of
December 30, 2002, no. 2002–1576), which began the dismemberment of access
to state-subsidized health care—L'Aide Médical de l'État (AME)—for those most
disenfranchised in France. As of January 1, 2004, sans-papiers no longer benefit
from immediate and free access to health care; they have to first put together a
file proving their presence in France for a period of three months. Vociferous
protests met the 2004 proposal to limit free health care and to require proof of
three-month residency. See also D. Fassin 2001b for an earlier discussion of the
right to health versus other rights.

10. A circular originates from a ministry as an interpretation of a legal text
or regulation, with the aim of applying the regulation consistently. The circular
of June 24, 1997, which reexamines the situation of certain categories of undocumented immigrants, states in Section 1.7 that an APS, or temporary permit,
granted to *étrangers malades* (sick foreigners) can include a work permit if the foreigner asks for it and if the *médecin inspecteur de santé publique* (state public health
doctor) suggests that the person's health is compatible with a professional activity: "Celle-ci portera la mention 'salarié' si l'étranger le demande et si le médecin
inspecteur départmental de la santé estime que l'état de santé de l'intéressé est
compatible avec une activité professionnelle."

11. On moral economy, see also D. Fassin 2005; and Redfield 2008. Both
works build on the term used by E. P. Thompson (1971).

12. For a discussion of the role of humanitarianism in this process, see
Lochak 2001; and D. Fassin 2001a, 2001b.

13.   One of the state nurses explained to me that the informal process was initiated by the head of the prefecture in the suburb where I worked. The state public health doctor at the time was enlisted to help with corruption in the prefecture by reviewing files; and through his involvement, a pilot program was launched that involved the DDASS (i.e., the state medical office) in the regularization of undocumented immigrants.

14.   Legalizing this process was an attempt by the new Socialist government to change the arbitrary treatment of sans-papiers. Before the 1998 legal provision, people who were gravely ill were still being deported, but in quite a few cases administrative judges intervened to comply with Article 8 of the European Convention on Human Rights, which protects people's fundamental liberty to private and family life. There is actually significant jurisprudence on the matter; see for example Dominique Delettre's (1999) dissertation.

15.   I tried to get access to the state medical office in the Préfecture de Police in Paris, as did Didier Fassin. We wrote numerous letters and I called several times, but on each occasion I was rebuffed and told that these were confidential matters.

16.   See Liisa Malkki's (2007) argument about the difference between the International Committee of the Red Cross and Médecins sans Frontières—she argues that those working for the ICRC are driven by an ethic of professionalism, not by a desire to save the world.

17.   People started lining up at the prefecture at 2:00 A.M. or 3:00 A.M. or 4:00 A.M.—in the middle of winter, in the rain, or in the hot sun. They stood and waited, because that was the only way to get an appointment, in this case, at the state medical office. People may have had to do this several days in a row in order to actually get an appointment. It was a demoralizing, dehumanizing process. There were stories of the prefecture seeing only ten people per day. When I left, there were changes proposed to the system for those applying on the grounds of illness, such that they would be able to send in their applications by mail rather than waiting in line at the prefecture to present themselves in person.

18.   Adriana Petryna's (2002:3) work points to the dangers of leaving the value of a person undefined: she demonstrates that physical risks, abuses, and uncertainties escalate when the value of life is undefined.

19.   See Jain 2007 on sentimental empathy and the "ideal" subject of breast cancer.

20.   For more on sexual politics and racial regimes, see Stoler 2010; on vulnerability, see Butler 2004, 2009.

21.   This is Article 57 of the Loi de Finances Rectificative of December 30, 2002, no. 2002–1576. See the zpajol e-mail list, http://archives.rezo.net/archives/zpajol.mbox.

22.   Arendt's exception to this rule is Jesus Christ, as portrayed by Fyodor Dostoevski; the sign of Jesus's divinity was his ability to have compassion for

all men in their singularity, without lumping them together into one suffering mankind (Arendt 1990:85).

CHAPTER FOUR

Parts of this chapter were published in an essay in *Signs* (Ticktin 2008), and I thank *Signs* for letting me revise and publish them here. Similarly, the subsection on the Refugee Appeals Board was published in a different form in *Interventions: A Journal of Postcolonial Studies* (Ticktin 2005).

1. See Eric Fassin's discussion of the politicization of sexuality in France (2006) as well as his work on sexual democracy (2010); and Christophe Deloire and Christophe Dubois's *Sexus politicus* (2006) on sex and French politicians. See also my "Sexual Violence as the Language of Border Control: Where French Feminist and Anti-Immigrant Sentiment Meet" (Ticktin 2008).

2. See E. Fassin 2007 on the controversy caused by the Enveff study, which demonstrated that violence against women was not just a problem of the "dangerous classes"—it crossed class, race, ethnic, and religious borders, and this was a disturbing revelation to some.

3. To demonstrate how violence against women has been defined as a problem at the highest level, on September 30, 2009, the UN Security Council unanimously adopted a resolution that addresses the need to end sexual violence against women in conflict-affected countries. Introduced by the U.S. government at a session chaired by Secretary of State Hillary Clinton, the resolution builds on Security Council Resolutions 1325 and 1820, both of which helped to put the issue of sexual violence on the Security Council's agenda.

4. Since 2008, the CRR has been replaced by the Cour Nationale du Droit d'Asile (National Court of Asylum).

5. In France they use the term *juge assesseur,* which can also be translated as "magistrate's assistant."

6. France is the only country to have a mandatory representative from the United Nations on its Refugee Appeals Board. As one of the main representatives for the UNHCR in France explained to me, this procedure was instituted post–World War II, in light of the French (Vichy) government's participation in the Nazi regime, as a measure of caution. The understanding was that an outside member would keep things from getting out of hand, as they had during the Nazi/Vichy period.

7. The one exception here is for immigrants with high-tech skills. To see how policies that restrict immigration lead to a perversion of the rule of law, see Lochak 2001.

8. Sherene Razack (1995) has made a similar point with respect to the Canadian context of asylum for gender persecution; the subject must present herself

through a particular narrative, in this case, as a victim of a dysfunctional and patriarchal culture or state. If one cannot configure oneself in such a way, one is not granted asylum—and there are many factors that inhibit the ability of claimants from becoming subjects of such liberal legal narratives.

9.   The 2001 French film *La faute à Voltaire* depicts the process of "learning what to say" in an opening scene, where a Tunisian stowaway is instructed on how to present his claim as an Algerian refugee.

10.   Those exempt from taking the test include immigrants from the European Union, United States, Canada, New Zealand, Australia, Japan, and the Vatican (see E. Fassin 2010). There are now two versions of this film, one "edited" for countries where certain images are prohibited; yet, as Eric Fassin points out, positing an edited version already demarcates two populations, one that censors and the other that is free.

11.   For an analysis of the Dutch situation, see van der Veer 2006. For a discussion of sexual politics in Europe, including the Dutch situation, see Butler 2009; and E. Fassin 2010. Eric Fassin describes a similar, discriminatory 2006 "loyalty test" for foreigners applying for citizenship in Germany.

12.   While the bilateral accords themselves remain unchanged, reforms of the personal status laws in the Maghreb, along with French jurisprudence on the matter and the fluctuating influence of international legislation, together shape the effect of these accords on Maghrebis living in France.

13.   See S. (fille de Smaïl et Dahbia) 2004. See also Le Comité d'Action Interassociatif 2004.

14.   See Bowen 2001 for an analysis of the different approaches to the issue of repudiation in France.

15.   In particular, the court found that repudiations are in tension with international public order. The legal records from the Cour de Cassation reflect this change, with a series of cases brought in 2004 by women of Algerian or Moroccan nationality who are French residents, appealing to French judges to overturn the repudiations pronounced by their husbands in Algeria or Morocco. The French judges responded by making exceptions to the bilateral accords, justified by the European Convention on Human Rights as well as by the protection of international public order. In other words, while French judges may not have always agreed with the application of all elements of the bilateral accords, it is largely through the intervention of international norms that a change has been made to their application.

16.   See, for example, Duchemin and Si Mohamed 2005. The family code was reformed in Algeria in 2005, and the Moudawana, the family code of Morocco, in February 2004, but many of the provisions in both codes remain objectionable to Maghrebi women in France and in the Maghreb. For instance, in Algeria women still require the permission of a guardian to marry, they only receive half of what men receive in matters of inheritance, and repudiation and polygamy are still legal. In Morocco, polygamy and repudiation are both still legal, even while the

law of obeying one's husband has been abolished. See, for example, S. (fille de Smaïl et Dahbia) 2004.

17.   There are many associations of Maghrebi and other women who are fighting to abolish the institution of the personal status laws in France, such as Femmes contre Intégrismes (Women against Fundamentalisms), which, while based in France, now has a transnational presence. Others include FIJI (Femmes Informations Juridiques Internationals) in Lyon, BRRJI (Bureau Régional de Resources Juridiques Internationals) in Marseille, and CICADE (Centre pour l'Initiative Citoyenne et l'Accès au Droit des Exclus) in Montpellier.

18.   I met Zina (a pseudonym) during my fieldwork in Paris during 1999–2001, and the story I present here is drawn from our many conversations as well as from her presentation of her story to an immigrant rights group in her quest for papers.

19.   As Minoo Moallem (2001) has pointed out, the demonizing representation of fundamentalism has led many scholars to avoid the term altogether or to use the alternative terms "political Islam," "Islamic militancy," "communalism," or "orthodoxy." I use "fundamentalism" here as what I understand to be the closest translation for *intégriste,* which was the word Zina herself used.

20.   See Le Comité d'Action Interassociatif 2004, where this is called "double violence" against women of immigrant origin.

21.   Law no. 98–349 of May 11, 1998, on the Entry and Residence of Foreigners in France and the Right to Asylum.

22.   National Assembly, December 15, 1997, Paris, cited from Delouvin 2000:67, my emphasis.

23.   Law no. 98–349 of May 11, 1998.

24.   See the description of different types of asylum in France, with statistics showing gradual degradation of the category, at Le BIP 40 website, www.bip40. org/immigration/degradation-asile (accessed January 5, 2011). There were a total of 1,058 people accepted out of nearly 90,000.

25.   Of course, most subjects could never be quite civilized *enough*—see Colonna 1997 and Stoler 1997.

26.   For more on the role of the exotic Other in women's rights discourses, see Grewal 1998, 2005; and Engle 1995.

27.   I refer to the December 19, 2002, circular, and the November 26, 2003, law on immigration. Article 2-2-5 gives discretionary power to the *préfet.*

28.   The other situations that might warrant exceptional consideration, mentioned in Article 2-2-5 of the December 19, 2002, circular, include foreigners who are severely disabled and foreigners who accompany sick people.

29.   More specifically, Article 1-5 of this circular purports to make an exception for foreigners who are the subject of domestic violence, but who entered through family reunification to join their husbands and were given temporary resident permits contingent upon marriage. In this situation, if one leaves the

conjugal home within two years of the temporary residency permit being issued, one loses one's papers.

30. Foreign spouses of foreign residents receive a one-year temporary residency permit that must be renewed once in order to qualify to apply for a residency permit after two years; however, again, it may not be renewed if conjugal life ceases before these two years are over. According to Article 12 bis°4 of the Edict of 1945 on Conditions of Entry and Residence of Foreigners in France, adapted by the law of November 26, 2003, foreign spouses of French citizens also receive a one-year temporary permit initially, and only after two years can they apply for French citizenship or residency, as opposed to the one year they had to wait previously.

31. Gay unions are legal in France with the PACS (Pacte Civile de Solidarité). This enables a foreigner to receive a residency permit after one year if the union is with a French or EU citizen; if with a foreign resident, one must apply under the title of "private and family life," and the PACS is just one factor that will be taken into account. In other words, it does not guarantee residency papers. See Rajfire 2007.

32. See Amal Fadlalla's (in press) more recent discussion of how the Sudanese journalist Lubna Hussein also began discussions with Sarkozy about French protection after she was convicted for public indecency in Khartoum for wearing trousers in public.

33. I went to a debate at NYU's Remarque Institute in October 2006, moderated by Tony Judt and titled "Religion and the Limits of Tolerance: Dutch Multiculturalism in Question." Ayaan Hirsi Ali spoke and explicitly said that the West is more civilized and that colonialism had been a good thing for Muslims. She was in conversation with Frits Bolkestein, former president of the conservative VVD party in the Dutch Parliament, and Bas Heijne, Dutch journalist and author of *Hollandse toestanden* (The state of the Netherlands).

34. For a sampling of the literature on the debate on the veil, see Bowen 2007; Tévanian 2005; Scott 2005; and Asad 2005.

35. NPNS combines its struggle against violence against women in the *banlieues* with a struggle against violence in places like Saudi Arabia. In so doing, its discourse contributes to naturalizing a relationship between Islam and violence: it does not ask why such violence is occurring now in the banlieues and why it did not take place ten years ago, or how violence in these housing estates (*cités*) compares to violence in other disenfranchised areas.

CHAPTER FIVE

1. One example is journalist Nicholas Kristof of the *New York Times*, who consistently writes sensationalist stories about trafficking. See, for instance, Volpp 2006.

2. CCEM has subsequently moved locations, to the 11th arrondissement.

3. See Didier Fassin and Alain Morice (2000), who demonstrate the state's complicity in creating the category of "undocumented" and unpack the variegated histories and trajectories of sans-papiers.

4. I am grateful to Carole Vance (2001) for stimulating me to think about the tropes active in the modern slavery narrative.

5. The full name of the Trafficking Protocol is the Protocol to Prevent, Suppress and Punish Trafficking in Persons, Especially Women and Children, supplementing the UN Convention against Transnational Organized Crime. It entered into force December 25, 2003.

6. The TVPA has subsequently been rendered "stronger" in its reauthorizations in 2003 and 2005 (Gozdziak and Bump 2008:4).

7. The linking of prostitution and trafficking was embodied in a U.S. Department of State fact sheet (November 24, 2004) titled, "The Link between Prostitution and Sex Trafficking," which stated that "where prostitution is legalized or tolerated, there is greater demand for human trafficking victims and nearly always an increase in the number of women and children trafficked into commercial sex slavery" (cited from DeStefano 2007:112). This document was challenged by a group of activists, lawyers, and researchers, who argued that it was not supported by valid research or data. They challenged the numbers given and the assertion that "where prostitution is legal or tolerated, there is a greater demand for human trafficking victims."

8. This abolitionist perspective is encoded in the 1949 UN Convention for the Suppression of the Traffic in Persons and of the Exploitation of the Prostitution of Others (www2.ohchr.org/english/law/trafficpersons.htm, accessed July 2010). This convention understood prostitution as being "incompatible with the dignity and worth of the human person" and required states to penalize those who make a profit from prostitution. Perhaps most important for the abolitionist genealogy, it rendered consent irrelevant to the definition of prostitution itself. That is, one could never voluntarily choose prostitution.

9. On the Open Society Institute lawsuit against the loyalty oath in the United States, see www.soros.org/initiatives/health/focus/sharp/events/pledge_2007 (accessed December 22, 2010). See also Masenior and Beyrer 2007 and Elizabeth Bernstein's (2007) discussion of "carceral feminism" in the context of "the new abolitionists," who fight trafficking and prostitution in the United States.

10. For instance, the U.S. president's cabinet-level Interagency Task Force on Trafficking in Persons included, among others, Secretary of State Colin Powell, National Security Advisor Condoleezza Rice, and CIA director George Tenet (Kempadoo 2005:55).

11. Paul Wellstone, a former Democratic senator from Wisconsin, was the other sponsor, and he proposed antitrafficking legislation in the Senate. See DeStefano 2007.

12. See the French Penal Code, Article 2–2–5.

13. Interestingly, this same service was initially founded for priests to accompany Christians going to the colonies. When the direction of migration changed, so did their service, and now they work in solidarity with a far-reaching collective for human rights.

14. "Universal Manifesto of the Emmaus Movement, Adopted in Bern, on May 24th, 1969, by the 1st International Assembly of the Emmaus Movement, www.emmaus-europe.org/IMG/pdf/EN_Universal_Manifesto_of_the_Emmaus_Movement.pdf (accessed January 1, 2011).

15. Using the issue of trafficking, the United States has assumed the mantle of imposing a form of global discipline: it measures compliance according to its TIP (trafficking in persons) reports and sanctions or embarrasses those countries that do not comply, ranking them as Tier 1, Tier 2, Tier 2 Watch List, and Tier 3. Those with a ranking of Tier 3 may be subject to the withdrawal of nonhumanitarian aid. See Warren 2010.

16. For more on the idea of intersectionality, see Crenshaw 1995; and Smith 2005.

17. In 2000, the UN special rapporteur on violence against women, Radhika Coomaraswamy, put out a report suggesting a central consideration in deciding whether or not women are victims of trafficking is whether prostitution is forced or free. "It is the non-consensual nature of trafficking that distinguishes it from other forms of migration" (Coomaraswamy 2000:8, cited from Jeffreys 2006:198). This went against the earlier 1949 UN Convention for the Suppression of the Traffic in Persons and parted ways with the contemporary UN Working Group on Contemporary Forms of Slavery.

18. The Internal Security Act of March 18, 2003 (Project de Loi pour la Sécurité Intérieure, or LSI) introduced the criminalization of "trafficking in human beings" into French law. Article 225-4-1 of the Penal Code states: "Trafficking in persons is the act, in exchange of payment or any kind of benefit or promise of benefit, to recruit, transport, transfer, host or accommodate a person, to put him or her at the service of a third party, even unknown, in order either to facilitate against this person infractions of procurement, sexual aggression or harm, begging exploitation, working or living conditions contrary to human dignity, or to coerce this person to commit any crime or offence."

19. As Raymond Carré de Malberg states, "L'état de police est celui dans lequel l'autorité administrative peut, d'une façon discrétionnaire et avec une liberté de décision plus ou moins complète, appliquer aux citoyens toutes les mesures dont elle juge utile de prendre par elle-même l'initiative, en vue de faire face aux circonstances et d'atteindre à chaque moment les fins qu'elle se propose" (L'état de police is that in which the administrative authority can, in a discretionary manner and with complete freedom, initiate and apply to citizens all measures it deems useful to address the circumstances, and at each moment,

achieve the ends it proposes). Carré de Malberg 1920, cited from Chevallier 1994:16, my translation. In a similar manner, Michel Agier (2010:29, 30) calls humanitarian intervention "the left hand of empire" that is in "secret solidarity" with a police order.

20. In addition, Article 28 of this law withdraws the residency permit of anyone arrested for passive soliciting—a direct attack against immigrants.

21. Again, the debate on prostitution in France was initially spurred on by the need to bring French laws into conformity with international and European laws, specifically those on trafficking in human beings (Vernier 2005:128). To this end, there was an intense debate in France between the official state policy of abolitionism and prostitutes' rights advocates and health associations, who insisted on a distinction between forced and voluntary sex work. The whole debate was part of a larger discussion on the newly legitimated category of violence against women, raised in part at the UN Beijing+5 Conference in New York in 2000.

22. This connection is made clear in Article 32 of the March 2003 Internal Security Act, where a definition of human trafficking was introduced into the Penal Code (see CCEM 2004:4).

23. These are estimates from the French Senate, Europol, and French research institutes. See New York Times 2002.

24. In a similar manner, on December 16, 2002, President George W. Bush signed into law the National Security Directive 22, which also linked human trafficking to "terrorism and public health concerns." See Haynes 2009a.

25. Much literature attests to how women's status has been used as an indicator of level of civilization. See, for instance, Jane Collier et al., 1995.

26. See also Mahmood 2005 for a challenge to liberal understandings of agency and the contingency of the desire for freedom.

CHAPTER SIX

Some material in chapters 3 and 6 was published in significantly different and condensed form in my *American Ethnologist* article (Ticktin 2006).

1. Although I use the term "biosociality" somewhat differently than Rabinow does, I still focus on practices of life as important sites of new knowledges and powers and employ the term to indicate the ways that nature is known and remade through technique. Instead of the techniques of scientists, however, I refer to the techniques of "ordinary" lay people—such as undocumented immigrants—who manipulate their biology to the extent that they overcome the nature-culture split.

2. Fatoumata was lucky in some ways to get papers despite her situation, and this was probably aided by the fact that she was a woman. That is, the illness clause cannot be accessed by those considered a "threat to public order" (D. Fassin 2001c); Fatoumata could have been disqualified because of her prison sentence. But young men (often of Maghrebi origin) are more often considered a threat to public order than are women—criminality is gendered.

3. I refer here to the fifty-eight undocumented Chinese immigrants who were found dead in Dover (Britain) on June 19, 2000, in the back of a cold-storage container of a Dutch truck, mentioned in the introduction.

4. Talal Asad draws on unpublished work by Nicholas Dirks to discuss the late nineteenth-century British views of hookswinging, which involves a person swinging from a crossbeam, suspended by two steel hooks thrust into the small of his back. This is part of a ceremony (Asad 2003:111).

5. Organs Watch was founded by Nancy Scheper-Hughes and Lawrence Cohen in 1999 and was originally funded by the Open Society Institute. See Scheper-Hughes 2000, 2002, 2006; and Cohen 1999, 2002, 2004.

6. See also MacFarquhar 2009 on those who choose to give away their kidneys to people they do not know.

7. For example, villages in Senegal send rotating representatives to work in France, with the agreement that they will send back their earnings—this is money on which the whole village then subsists. The French state is complicit in this arrangement—while not legalizing such immigrants, one state official explained to me that the French state could not deport them without causing greater problems for itself. In other words, the spaces of development are no longer geographically circumscribed but bridge the North and South, working through informal means.

8. The needle performance took place at the Institute of Contemporary Arts in London, by Ron Athey, who, by the end of the performance, was "encrusted with needles, garlanded with wire and oozing blood" (Armistead 1994:26, cited from Asad 2003:120). The genital piercing I refer to was performed and filmed by performance artist Bob Flanagan.

9. Nikolas Rose and Carlos Novas take this term from Catherine Waldby (2000:30) in her study of the Visible Human Project, where it refers to the ways that bodies and tissues derived from the dead are redeployed for the preservation and enhancement of the health of the living.

10. Geertz's original notion of involution referred to "an overdriving of an established form in such a way that it becomes rigid through an inward over-elaboration of detail" (1963:82).

11. See Didier Fassin's (2001c) article about immigrants with HIV/AIDS, in which he describes how HIV/AIDS can function as a political condition before it is experienced as an illness.

12. See Agier 2004, which elaborates on the incompatibility between citizen and human in the context of refugees in Africa.

CONCLUSION

1. The foundation is the Grossman Burn Foundation.

2. In addition to reading his many books, for more on Farmer, see Tracy Kidder's *Mountain beyond Mountains: The Quest of Dr. Paul Farmer, a Man Who Would Cure the World* (2003).

Bibliography

Abramson, Kara
  2003   Beyond Consent, Toward Safeguarding Human Rights: Implement-
          ing the United Nations Trafficking Protocol. Harvard International
          Law Journal 44(2):473–502.
Abu-Lughod, Lila
  2002   Do Muslim Women Really Need Saving? Anthropological Reflec-
          tions on Cultural Relativism and Its Others. American Anthropolo-
          gist 104(3):783–790.
Adler, Jessica
  2008   "Juanita/Svetlana/Geeta" is Crying: Melodrama, Human Rights and
          Anti-trafficking Interventions: Carole Vance. Feminist News 26:6.
Agamben, Giorgio
  1998   Homo Sacer: Sovereign Power and Bare Life. D. Heller-Roazen,
          trans. Stanford: Stanford University Press.
Agier, Michel
  2004   Le camp des vulnérables: Les réfugiés face à leur citoyenneté niée.
          Les Temps Modernes (Dossier sur l'humanitaire) (627):120–137.

2008   Gérer les indésirables: Des camps de refugiés au gouvernement
          humanitaire. Paris: Flammarion.
2010   Humanity as an Identity and Its Political Effects (A Note on Camps
          and Humanitarian Government). Humanity 1(1):29–45.
Akofa, Henriette
2000   Une esclave moderne. Paris: Editions Michel Lafon.
Allen, Tim, and David Styan
2000   A Right to Interfere? Bernard Kouchner and the New Humanitari-
          anism. Journal of International Development 12:825–842.
Allwood, Gill
2004   Prostitution Debates in France. Contemporary Politics
          10(2):145–157.
Amnesty International
2006   Les violences faites aux femmes en France: Une affaire d'état. Paris:
          Editions Autrement.
ANAFE (Association Nationale d'Assistance aux Frontières pour les Étrangers)
2003   Violences policières en zone d'attente. March. www.anafe.org
          (accessed August 1, 2008).
2004   La zone des enfants perdus: Mineurs isolés en zone d'attente de
          Roissy. November. www.anafe.org (accessed August 1, 2008).
Appadurai, Arjun
2002   Deep Democracy: Urban Governmentality and the Horizon of Poli-
          tics. Public Culture 12(1):21–47.
Arendt, Hannah
1951   Origins of Totalitarianism. New York: Meridian Books.
1990   On Revolution. Harmondsworth: Penguin Books.
[1963]
Armistead, Claire
1994   Piercing Thoughts. Guardian Weekly, July 17.
Asad, Talal
1999   Agency, the Body, and Pain. Paper presented on the panel "Moral
          Reasoning and Embodiment: Queries into Notions of Human
          Agency" at the Doreen B. Townsend Center for the Humanities,
          University of California, Berkeley. February 5.
2003   Formations of the Secular. Stanford: Stanford University Press.
2005   Reflections on Laicité and the Public Sphere. Items and Issues
          5(3):1–5.
Associated Press
2000   Une Sierra-Léonaise porte plainte après la mort de l'enfant qu'elle
          portait lors de sa rétention à Roissy. October 3.

Badiou, Alain
    2008   The Communist Hypothesis. New Left Review 49 (January–February): 29–42.
Balibar, Etienne
    2004   We, the People of Europe? Reflections on Transnational Citizenship. J. Swenson, trans. Princeton: Princeton University Press.
Balibar, Etienne, Monique Chemillier-Gendreau, Jacqueline Costa-Lasoux, and Emmanuel Terray, eds.
    1999   Sans-papiers: L'archaisme fatal. Paris: La Découverte.
Bancel, Nicolas, and Pascal Blanchard
    1998   De l'indigène à l'immigré. Paris: Gallimard.
Bancel, Nicolas, Pascal Blanchard, and Françoise Vergès
    2006   La république coloniale: Essai sur une utopie. Paris: Hachette Littératures.
Bancel, Nicolas, Florence Bernault, Pascal Blanchard, Ahmed Boubeker, Achille Mbembe, and Françoise Vergès, eds.
    2010   Ruptures postcoloniales. Paris: La Découverte.
Baubock, Rainier
    1994   Transnational Citizenship: Membership and Rights in International Migration. Aldershot, UK: Edward Elgar.
Bauman, Zygmunt
    2004   Wasted Lives: Modernity and Its Outcasts. Cambridge, UK: Polity Press.
Bénévise, Jean-François, and Alain Lopez
    2006   Avis rendu par les médecins inspecteurs de la santé publique (MISP) sur le maintien des étrangers malades sur le territoire. Rapport no. RM2006–139A. September.
Benjamin, Andrew
    2010   Tranforming Intellectuals: Walter Benjamin, Foucault, and the Question of Europe. Conference paper, University of Colorado, Boulder, April 8.
Berlant, Lauren Gail
    2004   Compassion: The Culture and Politics of an Emotion. New York: Routledge.
Bernstein, Elizabeth
    2007   The Sexual Politics of the New Abolitionism. Differences 18(5):128–143.
Bertaux, Sandrine
    2009   Recasting "Third World" in the First World: Alfred Sauvy, Fascist Legacies, Colonial Domination, and the Rise of American Social

Demography. Paper presented at the workshop A World of Popula-
tions: Twentieth-Century Demographic Discourses and Practices in
Global Perspective, German Historical Institute, Washington, D.C.
May 29–30, 2009.

Biehl, João

2004   The Activist State: Global Pharmaceuticals, AIDS and Citizenship in
Brazil. Social Text 22(3):105–132.

2005   Vita: Life in a Zone of Social Abandonment. Berkeley: University of
California Press.

2007   Will to Live: AIDS Therapies and the Politics of Survival. Princeton:
Princeton University Press.

Bijak, Jakub, Dorota Kupiszewska, Marek Kupiszewski, and Katarzyna Saczuk

2005   Replacement Migration Revisited: Migratory Flows, Population
and Labour Force in Europe, 2002–2052. UN ECE Work Session on
Demographic Projections, Vienna, September 21–23. http://circa.
europa.eu/irc/dsis/jointestatunece/info/data/paper_Bijak.pdf
(accessed July 10, 2010).

Blanchet, Karl, and Boris Martin, eds.

2005   Critique de la raison humanitaire: Dialogue entre l'humanitaire
français et anglo-saxon. Paris: Le Cavalier Bleu.

Blatt, David

1997   Immigrant Politics in a Republican Nation. *In* Postcolonial Cultures
in France. Alec Hargreaves and Mark McKinney, eds. Pp. 40–55.
London: Routledge.

Bob, Clifford

2002   Merchants of Morality. Foreign Policy. April.

Boltanski, Luc

1999   Distant Suffering: Morality, Media and Politics. G. Burchell, trans.
Cambridge: Cambridge University Press.

Bourdieu, Pierre, ed.

1993   La misère du monde. Paris: Editions du Seuil.

1999   The Weight of the World: Social Suffering in Contemporary Society.
Priscilla Parkhurst Ferguson, Susan Emanuel, Joe Johnson, and
Shoggy T. Waryn, trans. Stanford: Stanford University Press.

Bourgois, Philippe, and Jeff Schonberg

2009   Righteous Dopefiend. Berkeley: University of California Press.

Bowen, John R.

2001   Shari'a, State, and Social Norms in France and Indonesia. Leiden,
Netherlands: ISIM.

2004   Muslims and Citizens: France's Headscarf Controversy. Boston
Review, February–March: 31–35.

2007   Why the French Don't Like Headscarves: Islam, the State, and Public Space. Princeton: Princeton University Press.

2009   Can Islam be French? Pluralism and Pragmatism in a Secular State. Princeton: Princeton University Press.

Bradol, Jean-Hervé

2004   Introduction: The Sacrificial International Order and Humanitarian Action. *In* In the Shadow of "Just Wars": Violence, Politics and Humanitarian Action. F. Weissman, ed. Pp. 1–24. Ithaca: Cornell University Press.

Brauman, Rony

2004   From Philanthropy to Humanitarianism: Remarks and an Interview. South Atlantic Quarterly 103(2–3):397–417.

Breckenridge, Carol A., and Candace Vogler

2001   The Critical Limits of Embodiment: Disability's Criticism. Public Culture 13(3):349–357.

Brown, Wendy

1995   States of Injury: Power and Freedom in Late Modernity. Princeton: Princeton University Press.

2001   Politics Out of History. Princeton: Princeton University Press.

2004   The Most We Can Hope For . . . ? Human Rights and the Politics of Fatalism. South Atlantic Quarterly 103(2–3):451–463.

Bryant, Lisa

2006   French Official's Visit to Africa Sparks Protests. Voice of America. May 18. www.voanews.com/english/archive/2006–05/2006–05–18-voa36.cfm?CFID=242571202&CFTOKEN=14911456 (accessed July 10, 2010).

Butler, Judith

1997   The Psychic Life of Power: Theories in Subjection. Stanford: Stanford University Press.

2000   Antigone's Claim: Kinship between Life and Death. New York: Columbia University Press.

2004   Precarious Life: The Powers of Mourning and Violence. London: Verso Books.

2009   Frames of War: When Is Life Grievable? London: Verso Books.

Caldwell, Christopher

2009   Communiste et Rastignac. *Review of* Le Monde Selon K by Pierre Péan. London Review of Books 31(13):7–10.

Calhoun, Craig

2008   The Imperative to Reduce Suffering: Charity, Progress and Emergencies in the Field of Humanitarian Action. *In* Humanitarianism in Question: Politics, Power, Ethics. M. Barnett and T. Weiss, eds. Pp. 73–97. Ithaca: Cornell University Press.

Carré de Malberg, Raymond
1920   Contributions à la théorie générale de l'état. Paris: Sirey.

CCEM (Comité contre l'Esclavage Moderne)
2000   Rapport d'activité. Paris: Comité contre l'Esclavage Moderne.
2001   Rapport d'activité. Paris: Comité contre l'Esclavage Moderne.
2004   Rapport d'activité. Paris: Comité contre l'Esclavage Moderne.
2005   Rapport d'activité. Paris: Comité contre l'Esclavage Moderne.

Chapkis, Wendy
2003   Trafficking, Migration and the Law: Protecting Innocents, Punishing Immigrants. Gender and Society 17(6):923–937.

Chevallier, Jacques
1994   L'état de droit. Paris: Montchrestien.

Christelow, Allan
1985   Muslim Law Courts and the French Algerian Colonial State in Algeria. Princeton: Princeton University Press.

Chuang, Janie
2006   The United States as Global Sheriff: Using Unilateral Sanctions to Combat Human Trafficking. Michigan Journal of International Law 27:437–494.

Cissé, Madiguène
1997   The Sans-Papiers: A Woman Draws the First Lessons. London: Crossroads Books.
1999   Parole de sans-papiers. Paris: La Dispute.

Cohen, Lawrence
1999   Where It Hurts: Indian Material for an Ethics of Organ Transplantation. Theme issue, "Bioethics and Beyond," Daedalus 128(4):135–166.
2002   The Other Kidney: Biopolitics Beyond Recognition. In Commodifying Bodies. Nancy Scheper-Hughes and Loïc J. D. Wacquant, eds. Pp. 9–30. London: Sage Publications.
2004   Operability: Surgery at the Margins of the State. In Anthropology at the Margins of the State. Veena Das and Deborah Poole, eds. Pp. 165–190. Santa Fe: SAR Press.

Cole, Joshua
2003   Remembering the Battle of Paris: 17 October 1961 in French and Algerian Memory. French Politics, Culture, and Society 21(3): 21–50.

Collier, Jane
  2002   Durkheim Revisited: Human Rights as the Moral Discourse for the
            Postcolonial, Post-Cold War World. *In* Human Rights: Concepts,
            Contests, Contingencies. A. Sarat and T. R. Kearns, eds. Pp. 63–88.
            Ann Arbor: University of Michigan Press.
Collier, Jane, Liliana Suarez-Navaz, and Bill Maurer
  1995   Sanctioned Identities: Legal Constructions of "Modern" Person-
            hood. Identities 1(1–2):1–27.
Collier, Stephen J., and Andrew Lakoff
  2005   On Regimes of Living. *In* Global Assemblages: Technology, Politics,
            and Ethics as Anthropological Problems. Aihwa Ong and Stephen J.
            Collier, eds. Pp. 22–39. Oxford: Blackwell Publishing.
  2008a   Distributed Preparedness: The Spatial Logic of Domestic Security in
            the United States. Environment and Planning D: Society and Space
            26(1):7–28.
  2008b   The Vulnerability of Vital Systems: How "Critical Infrastructure"
            Became a Security Problem. *In* Securing "the Homeland": Critical
            Infrastructure, Risk and (In)Security. M. A. Dunn Cavelty and K. S.
            Kristensen, eds. Pp. 17–39. London: Routledge.
Collier, Stephen J., Andrew Lakoff, and Paul Rabinow
  2004   Biosecurity: Proposal for an Anthropology of the Contemporary.
            Anthropology Today 20(5):3–7.
Colonna, Fanny
  1997   Educating Conformity in French Colonial Algeria. *In* Tensions of
            Empire. Frederick Cooper and Ann Laura Stoler, eds. Pp. 346–370.
            Berkeley: University of California Press.
Le Comité d'Action Interassociatif, Droits des Femmes, Droit au Séjour: Contre
            la Double Violence
  2004   Femmes et étrangères: Contre la double violence; témoignages et
            analyses. November. http://doubleviolence.free.fr (accessed June
            30 2010).
Conklin, Alice L.
  1997   A Mission to Civilize: The Republican Idea of Empire in France and
            West Africa. Stanford: Stanford University Press.
  2000   Boundaries Unbound: Teaching French History as Colonial History
            and Colonial History as French History. French Historical Studies
            23(2):215–238.
Coomaraswamy, Radhika
  2000   Report of the Special Rapporteur on Violence against Women, Its
            Causes and Consequences, on Trafficking in Women, Women's

Migration and Violence against Women, submitted in accordance with Commission on Human Rights resolution 1997/44. E/CN.4/2000/68. Geneva: United Nations.

Cooper, Frederick, and Ann Laura Stoler, eds.
1997   Tensions of Empire: Colonial Cultures in a Bourgeois World. Berkeley: University of California Press.

Coutin, Susan B.
1994   Enacting Law through Social Practice: Sanctuary as a Form of Resistance. *In* Contested States: Law, Hegemony and Resistance (After the Law). Mindie Lazarus-Black and Susan Hirsch, eds. Pp. 282–303. New York: Routledge.
2001   The Oppressed, the Suspect, and the Citizen: Subjectivity in Competing Accounts of Political Violence. Law and Social Inquiry 26(1):63–94.

Crane, Johanna, Kathleen Quirk, and Ariane van der Straten
2002   "Come Back When You're Dying": The Commodification of AIDS Among California's Urban Poor. Social Science and Medicine 55(7):1115–1127.

Crenshaw, Kimberle
1995   Mapping the Margins: Intersectionality, Identity Politics, and Violence against Women of Color. *In* After Identity: A Reader in Law and Culture. Dan Danielson and Karen Engle, eds. Pp. 332–355. New York: Routledge.

Dale, Gareth
1999   Capitalism and Migrant Labour. *In* The European Union and Migrant Labour. Gareth Dale and Mike Cole, eds. Pp. 281–314. Oxford: Berg.

Dale, Gareth, and Mike Cole, eds.
1999   The European Union and Migrant Labour. Oxford: Berg.

Das, Veena, Arthur Kleinman, Margaret Lock, Mamphela Ramphele, and Pamela Reynolds, eds.
2001   Remaking the World: Violence, Social Suffering and Recovery. Berkeley: University of California Press.

Das, Veena, Arthur Kleinman, Mamphela Ramphele, and Pamela Reynolds, eds.
1997   Violence and Subjectivity. Berkeley: University of California Press.

Davis, Mike
2004a   Planet of Slums: Urban Involution and the Informal Proletariat. New Left Review 26 (March–April): 5–34.
2004b   The Urbanization of Empire: Megacities and the Laws of Chaos. Social Text 22(4):9–15.

De Genova, Nicholas
  2007   The Production of Culprits: From Deportability to Detainability
          in the Aftermath of "Homeland Security." Citizenship Studies
          11(5):421–448.
de Loisy, Anne
  2005   Bienvenue en France! Six mois d'enquête clandestine dans la zone
          d'attente de Roissy [Welcome to France! Six-months undercover at
          the Roissy holding center]. Paris: Le Cherche Midi.
de Torrente, Nicolas
  2004   Humanitarian Action Under Attack: Reflections on the Iraq War.
          Harvard Human Rights Journal 17:1–29.
de Waal, Alex
  1997   Famine Crimes: Politics and the Disaster Relief Industry in Africa.
          Oxford: James Currey, in association with Africa Rights and the
          International African Institute.
  2007   Humanitarianism Reconfigured: Philanthropic Globalization and
          the New Solidarity. In Nongovernmental Politics. M. Feher, ed.
          Pp. 183–195. Boston: MIT Press.
Delettre, Dominique
  1999   Le maintien des étrangers pour raisons médicale sur le territoire
          français: Le rôle du médecin inspecteur de santé publique dans
          la procédure. Rennes: École Nationale de la Santé Publique
          (ENSP).
Deloire, Christophe, and Christophe Dubois
  2006   Sexus politicus. Paris: Albin Michel.
Delouvin, Patrick
  2000   The Evolution of Asylum in France. Journal of Refugee Studies
          13(1):61–73.
DeStefano, Anthony M.
  2007   The War on Trafficking: U.S. Policy Assessed. Piscataway: Rutgers
          University Press.
Dezalay, Yves, and Bryant Garth
  1995   Merchants of Law as Moral Entrepreneurs: Constructing Interna-
          tional Justice from the Competition for Transnational Business Dis-
          putes. Law and Society Review 29(1):27–64.
  1996   Dealing in Virtue: International Commercial Arbitration and the
          Construction of a Transnational Legal Order. Chicago: University of
          Chicago Press.
  1998   Droits de l'homme et philanthropique hégémonique. Actes de la
          Recherche en Sciences Sociales (March):121–122.

Diop, Ababacar
    1997a   Dans la peau d'un sans-papiers. Paris: Editions du Seuil.
    1997b   The Struggle of the "Sans Papiers": Realities and Perspectives.
             www.bok.net/pajol/sanspap/sptextes/ababacar2.en.html
             (accessed December 22, 2010).
Doezema, Jo
    1998   Forced to Choose: Beyond the Voluntary v. Forced Prostitution
             Dichotomy. *In* Global Sex Workers: Rights, Resistance, and Redefi-
             nition. Kamala Kempadoo and Jo Doezema, eds. Pp. 34–50. Lon-
             don: Routledge.
    2000   Loose Women or Lost Women? The Re-emergence of the Myth
             of White Slavery in Contemporary Discourses of Trafficking in
             Women. Gender Issues 18(1):23–50.
Doland, Angela
    2010   French Parliament Approves Ban on Face Veils. Associated Press.
             July 13. http://news.yahoo.com/s/ap/20100713/ap_on_re_eu/
             eu_france_forbidding_the_veil_9 (accessed July 21, 2010).
Dokoupil, Tony
    2008   Anything Not to Go Back. Newsweek. June 7.
Donzelot, Jacques
    1991   The Mobilization of Society. *In* The Foucault Effect: Studies in Gov-
             ernmentality. Graham Burchell, Colin Gordon, and Peter Miller,
             eds. Pp. 169–180. Chicago: Chicago University Press.
Dubois, Laurent
    2000   La République Métissée: Citizenship, Colonialism, and the Borders
             of French History. Cultural Studies 14(1):15–34.
duBois, Page
    1991   Torture and Truth. New York: Routledge.
Duchemin, Nathalie, and Nasséra Si Mohamed
    2005   Le code de la famille: Au centre de la problématique démocratique
             Algérienne. *In* Femmes d'ici et de là-bas de l'Association Culturel
             Berbère. www.acbparis.org/index.php?option=com_content&task=
             view&id=48&Itemid=58 (accessed August 15, 2010).
Dunant, Henry
    2003   Politics and Humanitarianism: Coherence in Crisis? Centre for
             Humanitarian Dialogue (February): 4.
Eisenstein, Zillah R.
    2007   Sexual Decoys: Gender, Race and War in Imperial Democracy. Lon-
             don: Zed Books.
Elliott, Carl
    2003   Better than Well: American Medicine Meets the American Dream.
             New York: W. W. Norton and Company.

Emmanuelli, Xavier
    2005   L'homme en état d'urgence. Paris: Hachette Littératures.
Engle, Karen
    1995   Female Subjects of Public International Law: Human Rights and the
              Exotic Other Female. *In* After Identity: A Reader in Law and Cul-
              ture. Dan Danielsen and Karen Engle, eds. Pp. 210–228. New York:
              Routledge.
Englund, Harri
    2006   Prisoners of Freedom: Human Rights and the African Poor. Berke-
              ley: University of California Press.
Escobar, Arturo
    1995   Encountering Development: The Making and Unmaking of the
              Third World. Princeton: Princeton University Press.
Fadlalla, Amal
    2008   The Neoliberalization of Compassion: Darfur and the Mediation
              of American Faith, Fear, and Terror. *In* New Landscape of Global
              Inequalities: The Erosion of Citizenship in a Neoliberal Era. M. D.
              Leonardo, J. Colins, and B. Williams, eds. Pp. 209–228. Santa Fe:
              SAR Press.
    In press State of vulnerability and humanitarian visibility: Lubna's pants
              and Sudanese trans-politics of rights and dissent. Signs.
Fassin, Didier
    2001a   The Biopolitics of Otherness: Undocumented Foreigners and Racial
              Discrimination in French Public Debate. Anthropology Today
              17(1):3–7.
    2001b   Quand le corps fait loi: La raison humanitaire dans les procé-
              dures de régularisation des étrangers. Sciences Sociales et Santé
              19(4):5–34.
    2001c   Une double peine: La condition sociales des immigrés malades du
              sida. L'Homme 160:137–162.
    2005   Compassion and Repression: The Moral Economy of Immigration
              Policies in France. Cultural Anthropology 20(3):362–387.
    2007a   Humanitarianism as Politics of Life. Public Culture 19(3):499–520.
    2007b   Humanitarianism: A Nongovernmental Government. *In* Nongov-
              ernmental Politics. M. Feher, ed. Pp. 149–159. Boston: MIT Press.
Fassin, Didier, and Alain Morice
    2000   Les épreuves de l'irrégularité: Les sans-papiers, entre déni
              d'existence et reconquête d'un statut. *In* Exlusions au coeur de la
              cité. D. Schnapper, ed. Pp. 261–309. Paris: Anthropos.
Fassin, Didier, Alain Morice, and Catherine Quiminal, eds.
    1997   Les lois d'inhospitalité: La société française à l'épreuve des sans-
              papiers. Paris: La Découverte.

Fassin, Eric

　　2006　　The Rise and Fall of Sexual Politics in the Public Sphere: A Transatlantic Contrast. Public Culture 18(1):79–92.

　　2007　　Sexual Violence at the Border. Differences: A Journal of Feminist Cultural Studies 18(2):1–23.

　　2008　　Ayaan Hirsi Ali, Voltaire des temps modernes? Regards. March 1. www.regards.fr/article/?id=3056&q=Voltaire%20des%20temps%20modernes? (accessed August 9, 2010).

　　2010　　National Identities and Transnational Intimacies: Sexual Democracy and the Politics of Immigration in Europe. Public Culture 22(3):507–529.

Feldman, Allen

　　2004　　Memory Theatres, Virtual Witnessing, and the Trauma-Aesthetic. Biography 27(1):163–202.

Feldman, Ilana

　　2007a　　Difficult Distinctions: Refugee Law, Humanitarian Practice, and the Identification of People in Gaza. Cultural Anthropology 22(1):129–169.

　　2007b　　The Quaker Way: Ethical Labor and Humanitarian Relief. American Ethnologist 34(4):689–705.

　　2011　　The Humanitarian Circuit: Relief Work, Development Assistance, and CARE in Gaza, 1955–67. In Forces of Compassion: Humanitarianism between Ethics and Politics. Peter Redfield and E. Bornstein, eds. Pp. 203–226. Santa Fe: SAR Press.

Feldman, Ilana, and Miriam Ticktin, eds.

　　2010　　Government and Humanity: The Government of Threat and Care. Durham: Duke University Press.

Délégation aux Droits des Femmes et à l'Égalité des Chances entre les Hommes et les Femmes

　　2005　　Compte Rendu no. 7. Assemblée Nationale. www.assemblee-nationale.fr/12/cr-delf/05–06/c0506007.asp#P31_354 (accessed January 5, 2011).

Ferguson, James

　　1994　　The Anti-Politics Machine: "Development," Depoliticization, and Bureaucratic Power in Lesotho. Minneapolis: University of Minnesota Press.

Ferguson, James, and Akhil Gupta

　　2002　　Spatializing States: Governmentality in Africa and India. American Ethnologist 29(4):981–1002.

Ferro, Marc, ed.

　　2003　　Le livre noir du colonialisme. Paris: Robert Laffont.

Foucault, Michel
    1978   The History of Sexuality: An Introduction. Vol. 1. New York: Vintage Books.
Fox, Renée
    1995   Medical Humanitarianism and Human Rights: Reflections on Doctors without Borders and Doctors of the World. Social Science and Medicine 41(12):1607–1616.
Geertz, Clifford
    1963   Agricultural Involution: Social Development and Economic Change in Two Indonesian Towns. Chicago: University of Chicago Press.
Geisser, Vincent
    2003   La nouvelle islamophobie. Paris: La Découverte.
GISTI (Groupe d'Information et de Soutien des Travailleurs Immigrés)
    1994   Entrée et séjour des étrangers: la nouvelle loi Pasqua. Paris: GISTI.
Gordon, David C.
    1966   The Passing of French Algeria. London: Oxford University Press.
Goussault, Bénédicte
    1999   Paroles de sans-papiers. Paris: Les Editions de L'Atelier.
Gozdziak, Elzbieta M. and Micah N. Bump
    2008   Data and Research on Human Trafficking: Bibliography of Research-Based Literature. Washington, D.C.: Institute for the Study of International Migration.
Granjon, B.
    1993   Mission France existe encore. Editorial. Les Nouvelles 32.
Grewal, Inderpal
    1994   The Postcolonial, Ethnic Studies, and the Diaspora. Theme issue, "The Traveling Nation: India and Its Diaspora," Socialist Review 24(4):45–74.
    1998   On the New Global Feminism and the Family of Nations: Dilemmas of Transnational Feminist Practice. In Talking Visions: Multicultural Feminism in a Transnational Age. Ella Shohat, ed. Pp. 501–530. Boston: MIT Press.
    2005   Transnational América: Feminisms, Diasporas, Neoliberalisms. Durham: Duke University Press.
Gubbay, Jon
    1999   The European Union Role in the Formation, Legitimation and Implementation of Migration Policy. In The European Union and Migrant Labour. Gareth Dale and Mike Cole, eds. Pp. 43–66.Oxford: Berg.
Guénif-Souilamas, Nacira, and Eric Macé
    2004   Les féministes et le garçon arabe. Paris: Editions de l'Aube.

Guillemaut, Françoise
    2004   Trafics et migrations de femmes: Une hypocrisie au service des pays riches. Hommes et Migrations 1248 (March–April): 75–87.
Guillot, Philippe
    1994   France, Peacekeeping and Humanitarian Intervention. International Peacekeeping 1(1):30–43.
Gupta, Akhil
    1997   The Song of a Non-aligned World: Transnational Identities and the Reinscription of Space in Late Capitalism. In Culture, Power, Place: Explorations in Critical Anthropology. Akhil Gupta and James Ferguson, eds. Pp. 179–199. Durham: Duke University Press.
Ha'aretz
    2009   Thousands of Palestinians Faking Illness to Flee Gaza Siege. October 12. www.haaretz.com/hasen/spages/1134137.html (accessed August 15, 2010).
Halley, Janet E.
    2006   Split Decisions: How and Why to Take a Break from Feminism. Princeton: Princeton University Press.
    2009   Rape at Rome: Feminist Inventions in the Criminalization of Sex-Related Violence in Positive International Criminal Law, Michigan Journal of International Law 30(1):1–132.
Hamel, Christelle
    2003   "Faire tourner les meufs": Les viols collectifs; Discours des médias et des agresseurs. Gradhiva 33:85–92.
Haraway, Donna J.
    1991   Simians, Cyborgs and Women: The Reinvention of Nature. New York: Routledge.
Hardt, Michael, and Antonio Negri
    2000   Empire. Cambridge, MA: Harvard University Press.
Hargreaves, Alec
    1995   Immigration, "Race" and Ethnicity in Contemporary France. London: Routledge.
Hargreaves, Alec, and Mark McKinney, eds.
    1997   Post-colonial Cultures in France. London: Routledge
Haskell, Thomas
    1985   Capitalism and the Origins of the Humanitarian Sensibility, Part I. The American Historical Review 90(2):339–361.
    1992   Capitalism and the Origins of Humanitarian Sensibility. In The Antislavery Debate: Capitalism and Abolitionism as a Problem in Historical Interpretation. T. Bender, ed. Pp. 107–135. Berkeley: University of California Press.

Hathaway, Jim
    2008   The Human Rights Quagmire of Human Trafficking. Virginia Journal of International Law 49(1):1–59.

Haynes, Dina Francesca
    2009a   Exploitation Nation: The Thin and Grey Legal Lines between Trafficked Persons and Abused Migrant Laborers. Notre Dame Journal of Law, Ethics and Public Policy 33(1):1–71.
    2009b   Good Intentions Are Not Enough: Four Recommendations for Implementing the Trafficking Victim Protection Act. University of St. Thomas Law Journal 6(1):77–95.

Heath, Deborah, Rapp, Rayna, and Karen Sue Taussig
    2007.   Genetic Citizenship. In A Companion to the Anthropology of Politics. David Nugent and Joan Vincent, eds. Pp. 152–167. Malden, MA: Blackwell Publishing.

Herzlich, Claudine
    1995   Professionals, Intellectuals, Visible Practitioners? The Case of "Medical Humanitarianism." Social Science and Medicine 41(2):1617–1619.

Hocquenghem, Guy
    1986   Lettre ouverte à ceux qui sont passés du col Mao au Rotary. Paris: Albin Michel.

Hollifield, James F.
    1994   Immigration and Republicanism in France: The Hidden Consensus. In Controlling Immigration: A Global Perspective. Wayne A Cornelius, Philip L. Martin, and James F. Hollifield, eds. Pp. 143–175. Stanford: Stanford University Press.

Hooper, Charlotte
    2001   Manly States: Masculinities, International Relations and Gender Politics. New York: Columbia University Press.

Incite! Women of Color against Violence.
    2006   Color of Violence: The Incite! Anthology. Cambridge, MA: South End Press.
    2007   The Revolution Will Not Be Funded: Beyond the Non-profit Industrial Complex. Cambridge, MA: South End Press.

Iskander, Natasha
    2007   Informal Work and Protest: Undocumented Immigrant Activism in France, 1996–2000. British Journal of Industrial Relations 45(2):309–334.

Jain, S. Lochlann
    2007   Cancer Butch. Cultural Anthropology 22(4):502–538.

Jeffreys, Sheila
    2006   The Traffic in Women: Human Rights Violation or Migration for Work? *In* Migrant Women and Work. Anuja Agrawal, ed. Pp. 195–217. New Delhi: SAGE.

Jones, Colin
    1989   The Charitable Imperative: Hospitals and Nursing in Ancien Regime and Revolutionary France. London: Routledge.

Julliard, Jacques
    1978   Le tiers monde et la gauche. Nouvel Observateur (Paris). June 5.

Kapur, Ratna
    2002   The Tragedy of Victimization Rhetoric: Resurrecting the "Native" Subject in International/Post-colonial Feminist Legal Politics. Harvard Human Rights Journal 15:1–38.

Keck, Margaret, and Kathryn Sikkink
    1998   Activists beyond Borders: Advocacy Networks in International Politics. Ithaca: Cornell University Press.

Keenan, Thomas
    2004   Mobilizing Shame. South Atlantic Quarterly 103(2–3):435–449.

Kempadoo, Kamala
    2005   Victims and Agents of Crime: The New Crusade against Trafficking. *In* Global Lockdown: Race, Gender and the Prison-Industrial Complex. Julia Sudbury, ed. Pp. 35–56. New York: Routledge.

Kidder, Tracy
    2003   Mountain Beyond Mountains: The Quest of Dr. Paul Farmer, a Man Who Would Cure the World. New York: Random House.

Kirmayer, Lawrence
    2003   Failures of Imagination: The Refugee's Narrative in Psychiatry. Anthropology and Medicine 10(2):167–185.

Kleinman, Arthur
    1997   The Violences of Everyday Life: The Multiple Forms and Dynamics of Social Violence. *In* Violence and Subjectivity. Veena Das, Arthur Kleinman, Mamphela Ramphele, and Pamela Reynolds, eds. Pp. 226–241. Berkeley: University of California Press.

Kleinman, Arthur, Veena Das, and Margaret Lock, eds.
    1997   Social Suffering. Berkeley: University of California Press.

Kleinman, Arthur, and Joan Kleinman
    1996   The Appeal of Experience; the Dismay of Images: Cultural Appropriates of Suffering in Our Times. Daedalus 125(1):1–23.

Kouchner, Bernard
    1986   Charité business. Paris: Le Pré aux Clercs, Belfond.

Laacher, Smaïn
    2002   Après Sangatte: Nouvelles immigrations, nouveaux enjeux. Paris: La Dispute.
La Cimade
    N.d.   Ici et là-bas solidaires. www.cimade.org/la_cimade/cimade/rubriques/5-missions (accessed July 2010).
La Libération
    2000   Des étrangers "comme du bétail" à Roissy. March 24.
    2002   Fermer Sangatte, une autre paire de manches. May 24.
Landesman, Peter
    2002. The Light at the End of the Chunnel. New York Times Magazine, April 14. www.nytimes.com/2002/04/14/magazine/the-light-at-the-end-of-the-chunnel.html (accessed August 14, 2010).
Laqueur, Thomas
    2009   Humanitarianism and Suffering: The Mobilization of Empathy. Richard Ashby Wilson and Richard Brown, eds. Cambridge, UK: Cambridge University Press.
Lazreg, Marnia
    1994.   The Eloquence of Silence: Algerian Women in Question. New York: Routledge.
Lebovics, Hermann
    1992   True France: The Wars over Cultural Identity, 1900–1945. Ithaca: Cornell University Press.
Lecourt, Dominique
    1978   Dissidence ou révolution? Paris: Maspero.
Legoux, Luc
    1995   La crise d'asile politique en France. Cahier 8. Paris: Centre d'Étude sur la Population et le Développement (CEPED).
Le Monde
    2003   Pourquoi des sans-papiers? January 17.
    2007   Nicolas Sarkozy, Cœur de femmes et "les femmes martyrisées dans le monde." May 4. www.lemonde.fr/societe/article/2007/05/04/nicolas-sarkozy-c-ur-de-femmes-et-les-femmes-martyrisees-dans-le-monde_905196_3224.html (accessed August 14 2010).
Le Pape, Marc, and Pierre Salignon, eds.
    2003   Civilians Under Fire: Humanitarian Practices in the Congo Republic 1998–2000. Geneva: Médecins sans Frontières.
Lerougetel, Antoine
    2007   Débat électoral en France: Royal et Sarkozy s'affrontent sur leurs programmes droitiers respectifs. World Socialist website. May 5.

www.wsws.org/francais/News/2007/maio7/050507_debat.shtml
(accessed August 9, 2010).

Les Chinois de France
N.d.   La mutinerie des sans-papiers chinois. www.chinoisdefrance.com
         (accessed June 2010).

Levine, Philippa
2003   Prostitution, Race, and Politics: Policing Venereal Disease in the
         British Empire. London: Routledge.

L'Express
2000   SOS esclavage moderne. March 16.

Liauzu, Claude
2004   Colonisation: Droit d'inventaire. Paris: Armand Colin.

Linhart, Robert
1979   Western "Dissidence" Ideology and the Protection of Bourgeois
         Order. In Power and Opposition in Post-Revolutionary Societies.
         Patrick Camiller, trans. Pp. 249–260. London: Ink Links.

Lochak, Danièle
2001   L'humanitaire perversion de l'état de droit. Sciences Sociales et
         Santé 19(4):35–42.

Lorcin, Patricia
1995   Imperial Identities: Stereotyping, Prejudice, and Race in Colonial
         Algeria. London: I. B. Taurus.

MacFarquhar, Larissa
2009   The Kindest Cut. The New Yorker. July 27. P. 39.

MacKinnon, Catharine
2006   Are Women Human? And Other International Dialogues. Cam-
         bridge, MA: Harvard University Press.

Mahmood, Saba
2001   Feminist Theory, Embodiment, and the Docile Agent: Some Reflec-
         tions on the Egyptian Islamic Revival. Cultural Anthropology
         16(2):202–236.
2005   Politics of Piety: The Islamic Revival and the Feminist Subject.
         Princeton: Princeton University Press.

Malkki, Liisa
1996   Speechless Emisaries: Refugees, Humanitarianism, and Dehistorici-
         zation. Cultural Anthropology 11(3):377–404.
2007   Professionalisme, internationalisme, universalisme. Anthropologie
         et Sociétés 31(2):7–321.

Mamdani, Mahmood
2009   Saviors and Survivors: Darfur, Politics, and the War on Terror. New
         York: Pantheon Books.

Mann, Gregory
  2005   Des tirailleurs sénégalais aux sans-papiers: Universaux et particu-
          larismes. In L'esclavage, la colonisation, et après . . . : France, États-
          Unis, Grande Bretagne. P. Weil and S. Dufois, eds. Pp. 411–436.
          Paris: Presses Universitaires de France.
  2006   Native Sons: West African Veterans and France in the Twentieth
          Century. Durham: Duke University Press.
Masenior, Nicole Franck, and Chris Beyrer
  2007   The US Anti-Prostitution Pledge: First Amendment Challenges and
          Public Health Priorities. PLoS Med 4(7):e207. www.plosmedicine
          .org/article/info%3Adoi%2F10.1371%2Fjournal.pmed.0040207
          (accessed August 9, 2010).
Mbembe, Achille
  2003   Necropolitics. Public Culture 15(1):11–40.
  2007   L'Afrique de Nicolas Sarkozy. Africultures. August 3. www.africul-
          tures.com (accessed August 9, 2010).
McNevin, Anne
  2006   Political Belonging in a Neoliberal Era: The Struggle of the Sans-
          Papiers. Citizenship Studies 10(2):135–151.
Mehta, Uday
  1990   Liberal Strategies of Exclusion. Politics and Society 18(4):427–454.
Merry, Sally
  2006   Human Rights and Gender Violence. Chicago: University of Chi-
          cago Press.
Miller, Alice M.
  2004   Sexuality, Violence against Women and Human Rights: Women
          Make Demands and Ladies Get Protection. Health and Human
          Rights 7(2):17–47.
Moallem, Minoo
  2001   Transnationalism, Feminism, and Fundamentalism. In Women,
          Gender, Religion: A Reader. Elizabeth A. Castelli, ed. Pp. 320–348.
          New York: Palgrave.
Mohanty, Chandra
  1988   Under Western Eyes: Feminist Scholarship and Colonial Discourses.
          Feminist Review 30:61–88.
  2003   Feminism without Borders: Decolonizing Theory, Practicing Soli-
          darity. Durham: Duke University Press.
Morefield, Jeanne
  2009   The League of Nations and Humanitarian Advocacy. Paper pre-
          sented at "Histories of Humanitarianism: A Workshop," Columbia
          University, April 3.

Morse, Jane

2006   Top U.S. Official Cites Progress in Human Trafficking Battle. America.gov. December 13. www.america.gov/st/washfile-english/2006/December/20061212160214ajesromo.4522211.html (accessed August 9, 2010).

Morvant, Cécile

2000   Le médecin face aux violences conjugales: Analyse à partir d'une étude effectuée auprès de médecins généralistes. Thesis, Collège des Médecins Généralistes Enseignants de l'Université Pierre et Marie Curie (Paris 6).

Mouffe, Chantal

2005   On the Political: Thinking in Action. New York: Routledge.

Mouvement des Indigènes de la République

2005   L'appel des indigènes de la république. January. http://indigenes-republique.org/spip.php?page=imprimer&id_article=835 (accessed August 10, 2010).

Moyn, Samuel

2007   On the Genealogy of Morals. The Nation, April 16. www.thenation.com/article/genealogy-morals.

Mucchielli, Laurent

2005   Le scandale des "tournantes": Dérives médiatiques, contre-enquête sociologique. Paris: La Découverte.

Mutua, Makau

2002   Human Rights: A Political and Cultural Critique. Philadelphia: University of Pennsylvania Press.

Ndoye, El Hadji Gorgui Wade

2007   Mamadou Diouf: Pourquoi Sarkozy se donne-t-il le droit de nous tancer et de juger nos pratiques. . . . Sud Quotidien (Dakar).

New York Times

2002   Streetwalking, en Masse, for the Right to Tempt. November 6.

2003   14 Arrested in the Sale of Organs for Transplant. December 8.

2007   In Algeria, Sarkozy Denounces Colonialism. December 4.

Nguyen, Vinh-Kim

2005   Anti-retroviral Globalism, Biopolitics and Therapeutic Citizenship. In Global Assemblages: Technology, Politics and Ethics as Anthropological Problems. Aihwa Ong and Stephen J. Collier, eds. Pp. 124–144. Oxford: Blackwell Publishing.

NoBorder Network

2005   Sans Papiers Occupation in Paris—No Quotas: Legalisation! www.noborder.org/news_index.php (accessed July 26, 2010).

Noiriel, Gérard
  1996   The French Melting Pot: Immigration, Citizenship, and National
             Identity. Geoffroy de Laforcade, trans. Minneapolis: University of
             Minnesota Press.
Notes from Nowhere, ed.
  2003   We are Everywhere: The Irresistible Rise of Global Anticapitalism.
             London: Verso.
O'Brien, Paul
  2004   Politicized Humanitarianism: A Response to Nicolas de Torrente.
             Harvard Human Rights Journal 17:31–39.
O'Dy, Sylvie
  2001   Esclaves en France. Paris: Albin Michel.
Ong, Aihwa
  1999   Flexible Citizenship: The Cultural Logics of Transnationality. Dur-
             ham: Duke University Press.
  2003   Buddha Is Hiding: Refugees, Citizenship, the New America. Berke-
             ley: University of California Press.
Pandolfi, Mariella
  2008   Laboratory of Intervention: The Humanitarian Governance of the
             Postcommunist Balkan Territories. In Postcolonial Disorders. Mary-
             Jo DelVecchio Good, Sandra Teresa Hyde, Sarah Pinto, and Byron J.
             Good, eds. Pp. 157–186. Berkeley: University of California Press.
Parreñas, Rhacel Salazar
  2001   Servants of Globalization: Women, Migration and Domestic Work.
             Stanford: Stanford University Press.
Péan, Pierre
  2009   Le monde selon K. Paris: Fayard.
Pendse, Sandeep
  1995   Toil, Sweat and the City. In Bombay: Metaphor for Modern India.
             S. Patel and A. Thorner, eds. Pp. 3–25. Bombay: Oxford University
             Press.
Petryna, Adriana
  2002   Life Exposed: Biological Citizens after Chernobyl. Princeton:
             Princeton University Press.
Practical History
  1998   Do You Remember the First Time? Resistance to the 1991 Gulf Mas-
             sacre. February. www.oocities.com/capitolhill/senate/7672/gulf
             .html (accessed December 22, 2010).
Procacci, Giovanna
  1989   Sociology and Its Poor. Politics and Society 17(2):163–187.

Rabinow, Paul

   1995   French Modern: Norms and Forms of the Social Environment. Chi-
           cago: University of Chicago Press.

   1996   Essays on the Anthropology of Reason. Princeton: Princeton Uni-
           versity Press.

   2002   Midst Anthropology's Problems. Cultural Anthropology
           17(2):135–149.

Rajfire (Réseau pour l'Autonomie des Femmes Immigrées et Réfugiées)

   2007   Je suis homosexuelle, quels sont mes droits? October. http://rajfire
           .free.fr/spip.php?article144 (accessed July 21, 2010).

Rancière, Jacques

   1995   On the Shores of Politics. Liz Heron, trans. London: Verso.

   2004   Who Is the Subject of the Rights of Man? South Atlantic Quarterly
           103(2–3):297–310.

   2010   Dissensus: On Politics and Aesthetics. Steven Corcoran, trans. Lon-
           don: Continuum International Publishing Group.

Razack, Sherene

   1995   Domestic Violence as Gender Persecution: Policing the Borders of
           Nation, Race and Gender. Canadian Journal of Women and the Law
           8(1):45–88.

   2003   A Violent Culture or Culturalized Violence? Feminist Narratives of
           Sexual Violence against South Asian Women. Studies in Practical
           Philosophy 3(1):81–104.

Redfield, Peter

   2005   Doctors, Borders and Life in Crisis. Cultural Anthropology
           20(3):328–361.

   2006   A Less Modest Witness. American Ethnologist 33(1):3–26.

   2008   Vital Mobility and the Humanitarian Kit. In Biosecurity Interven-
           tions. Stephen J. Collier and Andrew Lakoff, eds. Pp. 147–171.
           New York: Columbia University Press and Social Science Research
           Council.

   2010   The Verge of Crisis: Doctors Without Borders in Uganda. In States
           of Emergency: Anthropology of Humanitarian Intervention. Didier
           Fassin and Mariella Pandolfi, eds. Pp.173–195. Cambridge, MA:
           Zone Books.

   2011   The Impossible Problem of Neutrality. In Forces of Compassion:
           Humanitarianism between Ethics and Politics. Erica Bornstein and
           Peter Redfield, eds. Pp. 53–70. Santa Fe: SAR Press.

Rich, Adrienne

   1986   Blood, Bread, and Poetry: Selected Prose 1979–1985. New York:
           W. W. Norton and Company.

Richmond, Anthony H.
  1995   Global Apartheid: Refugees, Racism and the New World Order.
            Oxford: Oxford University Press.
Rieff, David
  2002   A Bed for the Night: Humanitarianism in Crisis. New York: Simon
            and Schuster.
Robins, Steven
  2009   Humanitarian Aid beyond "Bare Survival": Social Movement
            Responses to Xenophobic Violence in South Africa. American Eth-
            nologist 36(4):637–650.
Rocard, Michel
  1996   La part de la France. Le Monde, August 24.
Rodier, Claire
  1997   L'Europe et les exclus de la libre circulation. *In* Les lois
            d'inhospitalité: La société française à l'épreuve des sans-papiers.
            Didier Fassin, Alain Morice, and Catherine Quiminal, eds. Pp. 219–
            233. Paris: La Découverte.
  2003   Les camps en France. http://pajol.eu.org/article36.html.
Rose, Nikolas
  2001   The Politics of Life Itself. Theory, Culture and Society 18(6):1–30.
  2007   The Politics of Life Itself: Biomedicine, Power and Subjectivity in
            the Twenty-First Century. Princeton: Princeton University Press.
Rose, Nikolas, and Carlos Novas
  2005   Biological Citizenship. *In* Global Assemblages: technology, Politics,
            and Ethics as Anthropological Problems. Aihwa Ong and Stephen J.
            Collier, eds. Pp. 439–463. Oxford: Blackwell Publishing.
Rosello, Mireille
  1997   North African Women and the Ideology of Modernization: From
            Bidonvilles to Cités de Transit and HLM. *In* Post-colonial Cultures
            in France. Alec Hargreaves and Mark McKinney, eds. Pp. 240–254.
            London: Routledge.
Ross, Kristin
  2002   May '68 and Its Afterlives. Chicago: University of Chicago Press.
Rytkonen, Helle
  2002   Europe and Its "Almost-European" Other: A Textual Analysis of
            Legal and Cultural Practices of Othering in Contemporary Europe.
            Stanford: Stanford University Press.
S. (fille de Smaïl et Dahbia)
  2004   Femmes, féminismes et immigration (première partie). *In* Les
            mots sont importants. http://lmsi.net/Femmes-feminismes-et-
            immigration (accessed January 5, 2011).

Samers, Michael

2003   Invisible Capitalism: Political Economy and the Regulation of
        Undocumented Immigration in France. Economy and Society
        32(4):555–583.

Sanchez, Lisa E.

1997   Boundaries of Legitimacy: Sex, Violence, Citizenship, and Com-
        munity in a Local Sexual Economy. Law and Social Inquiry
        22(3):543–580.

Sarkozy, Nicolas

2007   Discours sur l'Afrique. Quotidien Le Soleil (Dakar), July 26. www
        .lesoleil.sn/article.php3?id_article=27234 (accessed August 15, 2010).

Sartre, Jean-Paul

1987   Preface to SPK: Turn Illness into a Weapon [1972]. In SPK: Turn
        Illness into a Weapon, for Agitation by the Socialist Patients'
        Collective at the University of Heidelberg. Pp. 1–4. Heidelberg:
        KRRIM—self-publisher for illness.

Sassen, Saskia

1996   Losing Control? Sovereignty in an Age of Globalization. New York:
        Columbia University Press.

2006   Territory, Authority, Rights: From Medieval to Global Assemblages.
        Princeton: Princeton University Press.

Scarry, Elaine

1985   The Body in Pain: The Making and Unmaking of the World. New
        York: Oxford University Press.

Scheper-Hughes, Nancy

2000   The Global Traffic in Human Organs. Current Anthropology
        41(2):191–224.

2002   Commodity Fetishism in Organs Trafficking. In Commodifying
        Bodies. Nancy Scheper-Hughes and Loïc J. D. Wacquant, eds. Pp.
        31–62. London: Sage Publications.

2006   Consuming Difference: Post-human Ethics, Global (in) Justice, and
        the Transplant Trade in Organs. In A Death Retold: Jessica Santillan,
        the Bungled Transplant, and Pardoxes of Medical Citizenship.
        K. Wailoo, J. Livingston, and P. Guarnaccia, eds. Pp. 205–234. Cha-
        pel Hill: University of North Carolina Press.

Scheper-Hughes, Nancy, and Loïc J. D. Wacquant

2002   Commodifying Bodies. London: Sage Publications.

Schmitt, Carl

1985   Political Theology: Four Chapters on the Concept of Sovereignty.
        G. Schwab, trans. Boston, MA: MIT Press.

Scott, Joan
    2005   Symptomatic Politics: The Banning of Islamic Head Scarves
             in French Public Schools. French Politics, Culture and Society
             23(3):106–127.
Scullion, Rosemary
    1995   Vicious Circles: Immigration and National Identity in Twentieth
             Century France. In Theme issue, "France's Identity Crises," Sub-
             Stance (76–77):30–48.
Shepard, Todd
    2006   The Invention of Decolonization: The Algerian War and the Remak-
             ing of France. Ithaca: Cornell University Press.
Silverman, Maxim
    1992   Deconstructing the Nation: Immigration, Racism and Citizenship in
             Modern France. London: Routledge.
Silverstein, Paul
    2004   Algeria in France: Transpolitics, Race and Nation. Bloomington:
             Indiana University Press.
Siméant, Johanna
    1993   La violence d'un répertoire: Les sans-papiers en grève de la faim.
             Culture et Conflits 9(10):315–338.
    1998   La cause des sans-papiers. Paris: Presses de Sciences Po.
Simon, Jonathan
    1998   Refugees in a Carceral Age: The Rebirth of Immigration Prisons in
             the United States. Public Culture 10(3):577–607.
Slaughter, Joseph R.
    2007   Human Rights, Inc.: The World Novel, Narrative Form, and Inter-
             national Law. New York: Fordham University Press.
Smillie, Ian
    1995   The Alms Bazaar: Altruism Under Fire—Non-profit Organizations
             and International Development. London: IT Publications.
Smith, Andrea
    2005   Conquest: Sexual Violence and American Indian Genocide. Cam-
             bridge, MA: South End Press.
    2006   Heteropatriarchy and the Three Pillars of White Supremacy:
             Rethinking Women of Color Organizing. In Color of Violence: The
             Incite! Anthology. Pp. 66–73. Cambridge, MA: South End Press.
Sondorp, Egbert
    2005   Français et Anglo-Saxons: Une approche éthique différente? In Cri-
             tique de la raison humanitaire. Karl Blanchet and Boris Martin, eds.
             Paris: Le Cavalier Bleu.

Spivak, Gayatri Chakravorty
    1988   Can the Subaltern Speak? *In* Marxism and the Interpretation of Cul-
             ture. C. Nelson and L. Grossberg, eds. Pp. 271–313. Urbana: Univer-
             sity of Illinois Press.
Stoler, Ann Laura
    1989   Making Empire Respectable: The Politics of Race and Sexual
             Morality in 20th Century Colonial Cultures. American Ethnologist
             16(4):634–660
    1995   Race and the Education of Desire: Foucault's "History of Sexuality"
             and the Colonial Order of Things. Durham: Duke University
             Press.
    1997   Sexual Affronts and Racial Frontiers: European Identities
             and the Cultural Politics of Exclusion in Colonial Southeast
             Asia. *In* Tensions of Empire. Frederick Cooper and Ann
             Laura Stoler, eds. Pp. 198–237. Berkeley: University of California
             Press.
    2001   Colonial Aphasia and the Place of Race in France: The Politics of
             Comparison. Keynote address at the conference "1951–2001: Trans-
             atlantic Perspectives on the Colonial Situation," New York Univer-
             sity, April 27–28.
    2008   Imperial Debris: Reflections on Ruins and Ruination. Cultural
             Anthropology 23(2):191–219.
    2010   Beyond Sex: Bodily Exposures of the Colonial and Postcolonial
             Present. *In Genre et postcolonialismes: Dialogues transcontinentaux.*
             Anne Berger and Eleni Varikas, eds. Pp. 191–220. Paris: Editions des
             Archives Contemporaines.
    2011   Colonial Aphasia: Race and Disabled Histories in France. Public
             Culture 23(1):121–156.
Stora, Benjamin
    1999   Le transfert d'une mémoire: De l'Algérie française au racisme anti-
             arabe. Paris: La Découverte.
Sunder Rajan, Kaushik
    2005   Subjects of Speculation: Emergent Life Sciences and Market Log-
             ics in the United States and India. American Anthropologist
             107(1):19–30.
    2006   Biocapital: The Constitution of Postgenomic Life. Durham: Duke
             University Press.
Tabet, Marie-Christine
    2003   De nouveaux centres de rétention pour les étrangers en situation
             irrégulière. Le Figaro. May 22.

Taithe, Bertrand
　　2004　　Reinventing (French) Universalism: Religion, Humanitarianism
　　　　　　and the "French Doctors." Modern and Contemporary France
　　　　　　12(2):147–158.
　　2006　　"Cold Calculation in the Faces of Horror?": Pity, Compassion and
　　　　　　the Making of Humanitarian Protocols. In Medicine, Emotion and
　　　　　　Disease, 1700–1950. Fay Bound Alberti, ed. Pp. 79–99. New York:
　　　　　　Palgrave Macmillan.

Teitel, Ruti
　　2004　　For Humanity. Journal of Human Rights 3(2):225–237.

Terrio, Susan J.
　　2009　　Judging Mohammed: Juvenile Delinquency, Immigration, and
　　　　　　Exclusion at the Paris Palace of Justice. Stanford: Stanford Univer-
　　　　　　sity Press.

Terry, Fiona
　　2002　　Condemned to Repeat?: The Paradox of Humanitarian Action.
　　　　　　Ithaca: Cornell University Press.

Tévanian, Pierre
　　2004　　Une loi antilaïque, antiféministe et antisociale. Le Monde
　　　　　　Diplomatique. February. www.monde-diplomatique.fr/2004/02/
　　　　　　TEVANIAN/10890 (accessed August 9, 2010).
　　2005　　Le voile médiatique, un faux débat: "L'affaire du foulard
　　　　　　islamique." Paris: Raisons d'Agir Editions.
　　2007　　Ni putes, ni soumises ou la logique du bouc émissaire: Aux sources
　　　　　　du Fadela-Sarkozysme. In Les mots sont importants. http://lmsi
　　　　　　.net/Ni-putes-ni-soumises-ou-la-logique (accessed December 22,
　　　　　　2010).

Thompson, E. P.
　　1971　　The Moral Economy of the English Crowd in the Eighteenth Cen-
　　　　　　tury. Past and Present 50(1):76–136.

Ticktin, Miriam
　　2005　　Policing and Humanitarianism in France: Immigration and the
　　　　　　Turn to Law as State of Exception. Interventions 7(3):347–368.
　　2006　　Where Ethics and Politics Meet: The Violence of Humanitarianism
　　　　　　in France. American Ethnologist 33(1):33–49.
　　2008　　Sexual Violence as the Language of Border Control: Where French
　　　　　　Feminist and Anti-immigrant Rhetoric Meet. Signs 33(4):863–889.

Ticktin, Miriam, Paola Bacchetta, and Ruth Marshall
　　2008　　A Transnational Conversation on French Colonialism, Immigration,
　　　　　　Violence and Sovereignty. Theme issue, "Borders on Belonging:

Gender and Immigration," The Scholar and Feminist Online 6(3). www.barnard.edu/sfonline/immigration/conversation_01.htm (accessed August 9, 2010).

Time magazine
2010   What Happens If We Leave Afghanistan. August 9. www.time. com/time/covers/0,16641,1101100809,00.html (accessed August 15, 2010).

Tissot, Sylvie
2007   L'état et les quartiers: Genèse d'une catégorie de l'action publique. Paris: Seuil.
2008   "French Suburbs": A New Problem or a New Approach to Social Exclusion? Working Paper Séries 160, Center for European Studies, Harvard University.

Traub, James
2008   A Statesman without Borders. New York Times Magazine, February 3.

Tuhiwai Smith, Linda
1999   Decolonizing Methodologies: Research and Indigenous Peoples. London: Zed Books.

Vallaeys, Anne
2004   Médecins sans Frontières, la biographie. Paris: Fayard.

Vance, Carole
2001   Innocence and Experience: Narratives of Trafficking in the World of Human Rights. Paper presented at the American Ethnological Society Meetings, Montreal, May.

van der Veer, Peter
2006   Pim Fortuyn, Theo van Gogh, and the Politics of Tolerance in the Netherlands. Public Culture 18(1):111–124.

Vernier, Johanne
2005   La loi pour la sécurité intérieure: Punir les victimes du proxénetisme pour mieux les protéger? In La Prostitution à Paris. M.-E. Handman and J. Mossuz-Lavau, eds. Pp. 121–52. Paris: Editions de la Martinière.

Viner, Katharine
2002   Feminism as Imperialism. The Guardian (London). September 21. www.guardian.co.uk/world/2002/sep/21/gender.usa (accessed August 10, 2010).

Visweswaran, Kamala
1994   Fictions of Feminist Ethnography. Minneapolis: University of Minnesota Press.

Volpp, Leti

    2006   Disappearing Acts: On Gendered Violence, Pathological Cultures and Civil Society. Publications of the Modern Language Association of America 121(5):1632–38.

Waldby, Catherine

    2000   The Visible Human Project: Informatic Bodies and Posthuman Medicine. London: Routledge.

Walkowitz, Judith

    1980   The Politics of Prostitution. Signs 6(1):123–135.

Warren, Kay

    2010   The Illusiveness of Counting "Victims" and the Concreteness of Ranking Countries: The Practice of Combating Human Trafficking from Colombia to Japan. *In* Sex, Drugs, and Body Counts. Peter Andreas and Kelly M. Greenhill, eds. Pp. 110–126. Ithaca: Cornell University Press.

Weil, Patrick

    1991   La France et ses étrangers: L'aventure d'une politique de l'immigration de 1938 à nos jours. Paris: Gallimard.

Weissman, Fabrice, and Médecins sans Frontières, eds.

    2004   In the Shadow of "Just Wars": Violence, Politics, and Humanitarian Action. Ithaca: Cornell University Press.

Wihtol de Wenden, Catherine

    1995   Ethnic Minority Mobilisation against Racism in France. *In* Racism, Ethnicity and Politics in Contemporary Europe. Alec Hargreaves and Jeremy Leaman, eds. Cheltenham, UK: Edward Elgar Publishing.

Wijers, M., and L. Lap-Chew

    1997   Trafficking in Women, Forced Labour and Slavery-Like Practices in Marriage, Domestic Labour and Prostitution. Utrecht: The Global Alliance against Trafficking in Women (GAATW).

Wilson, Richard, ed.

    1997   Human Rights, Culture and Context: Anthropological Perspectives. London: Pluto Press.

    2005   Human Rights in the War on Terror. Vol. 1. Cambridge, UK: Cambridge University Press.

Wilson, Richard A., and Richard D. Brown, eds.

    2009   Humanitarianism and Suffering: The Mobilization of Empathy. Cambridge, UK: Cambridge University Press.

Woodhull, Winifred

    1991   Unveiling Algeria. Genders 10:112–131.

Yuval-Davis, N.
    1997   Gender and Nation. London: Sage Publications.
Žižek, Slavoj
    2004   From Politics to Biopolitics . . . and Back. South Atlantic Quarterly
            103(2–3):501–521.

Index

Abbé Pierre, 80, 180, 216
abolitionism, 170, 175–79, 244n8, 244n10, 246n21
Abramson, Kara, 177
Abu-Lughod, Lila, 23, 145, 151
Access to Essential Medicines Campaign, 85
Act Up Paris, 192, 195
Afghanistan, 23, 151, 222
Agamben, Giorgio, 14, 15
Agier, Michel, 8, 229n16, 246n19, 248n12
Ahmad (interviewee), 42–43
Aicha (Senegalese woman interviewee), 198–99, 214
AIDS. *See* HIV/AIDS
Akayesu decision (International Criminal Tribunal for Rwanda), 229n15
Algerians: applicants requesting papers for illness, 120t, 121; bilateral treaties, 139–40; detention of, 37; family code, 241n16; forced marriages in, 145–46; French personal status laws, 139–40; independence struggle, 147, 149; out-migration for labor, 47; polygamy, 241–42n16; regulation of the private realm in, 148–49; as

territorial asylum applicants, 146; visas for, 57–58; women, 144–45, 148–49, 150, 231n4, 241–42n16
Ali, Ayaan Hirsi, 155, 156–57, 243n33
Allen, Tim, 70, 76, 235–36n8
Allwood, Gill, 184
Althusserianism, 73
Dr. Amara (interviewee), 13, 102
AME (L' Aide Médicale de l'État [health care coverage]), 125–26, 171, 239n21
Amina (interviewee), 195–96
Amnesty France, 131
Amnesty International, 73, 131, 162
ANAFE (national association for border assistance to foreigners), 37–38, 39–40, 232n14, 232n15, 232–33n17
Annette (nurse interviewee), 116, 124, 125
anti-immigration policies: antitrafficking measures, 181–82, 183, 245n15; center-right-wing government, 7; cultural Otherness in, 137–38, 149, 153–54, 213, 225; Direction Centrale contre l'Immigration et pour la Lutte contre l'Emploi des Clandestins, 55, 234n35; labor code

Text:	10/14 Palatino
Display:	Univers Condensed Light and Bauer Bodoni
Compositor:	BookComp, Inc.
Indexer:	Nancy Zibman
Printer and binder:	IBT Global